VOCATION AND DESIRE

VOCATION AND DESIRE

George Eliot's Heroines

DOROTHEA BARRETT

Routledge
London and New York

First published 1989
by Routledge
11 New Fetter Lane, London EC4P 4EE
29 West 35th Street, New York, NY 10001

Printed and bound in Great Britain by
Biddles Ltd, Guildford and King's Lynn

British Library Cataloguing in Publication Data
Barrett, Dorothea, *1955–*
Vocation and desire: George Eliot's heroines
1. Fiction in English. Eliot, George – Critical studies
I. Title
823'.8

ISBN 0-415-00979-0

Library of Congress Cataloging in Publication Data
Barrett, Dorothea, 1955–
Vocation and desire : George Eliot's heroines / Dorothea Barrett.
p.   cm.
Bibliography: p.
Includes index.
1. Eliot, George, 1819–1880——Characters——Heroines.   2. Heroines in
literature.   3. Women in literature.   4. Feminism and literature——
Great Britain——History——19th century.   I. Title.
PR4692.H47B37   1989
823'.8——dc19   88-32168

For Edgar and Sheila Barrett

CONTENTS

PREFACE

Biographical and psychoanalytic approaches to literature have been rightly criticized for their tendency to be reductionist in their treatments of texts, relying on simple binary correspondences, and stressing the personal at the expense of the historical. The psychoanalytic in particular is prone to an essentialist view of authors and authorship. Both are in danger of posing as 'apolitical' yet being inherently reactionary in that their methods deny the centrality of the political dimensions of history, class, race, and gender to the analysis of texts. The present work nevertheless relies to some extent on biographical and psychoanalytic methods.

While reading the body of George Eliot criticism, I was struck by the disparity between the prevailing opinion of the political content of her work and my own reaction to the novels. Critics of all political colours were in basic agreement that George Eliot was a reactionary, both as to class and gender politics. This consensus was not clear in her contemporary reviews but coalesced over the course of the ensuing century of George Eliot criticism (1880–1980). In the last few years the consensus has been significantly eroded, but radical reinterpretations of George Eliot's work are still impeded by the absence of a sound theoretical basis for such reinterpretation. A major obstacle has been the apparent conservatism of Marian Lewes herself. Critics have allowed the woman of the letters and essays, of Sunday salons at the Priory, to dictate their interpretations of her fiction, yet the fiction itself, especially its mimetic content, is often very clear in its opposition to and contradiction of that staid and sibylline figure, the later Marian Lewes. In order to understand this self-dividedness, recourse to the biography and the application of psychoanalytic methods to the relation between her life and her work were essential. These methods, however, have been applied in a manner similar to Harold Bloom's treatment of influence, in the belief that the dangers of reductionism, of settling for binary correspondences, can be avoided if the critic sees the relation between biography, psyche, and text as a problematic relation. The source materials (life, anxieties, personal pain) are not simply mirrored, just as the literary influences that Bloom discusses are not mirrored in the texts: rather, they are transmuted, and in a sense destroyed, in the process of textual production.

Mary Jacobus has suggested that the tendency of feminist critics to emphasize the psycho-sexual when analysing female writers is simplistic and unwittingly sexist (Jacobus 1981:520). In the case of George Eliot, however, conservative interpretations have traditionally stressed the intellectual in her work, seeing her as a passive receptacle of male intellectual influences, seeing her, in fact, as an honorary man. It was only through stressing her femininity and the psycho-sexual that it was possible to uncover her radicalism.

What has emerged from this approach to George Eliot is a picture of an embattled woman with a remarkable will to power. The rebelliousness and iconoclasm of her work is closely related to its erotic content, an element that was effectively ignored in the century between her contemporary reviews and Gillian Beer's recent book *George Eliot*. Desire of all kinds, sexual desire, vocational desire, the desire for freedom, the desire for a new order, is submerged, but only just beneath the surface of her texts.

Beyond the use of biography and psychoanalysis, it was essential to employ close reading in order to substantiate what might otherwise have seemed rather extravagant claims. This, once again, is a somewhat unpopular critical approach, especially among left-wing critics. Bakhtin's comment that close textual analysis of the novel is like transcribing an orchestral piece onto the piano keyboard is a valid one – certainly the danger of close reading is that it may produce a slanted and selective view of a structurally and linguistically integrated novel – but the antipathy of most left-wing critics to close reading and internal analysis is not rooted in this fear of selectivity (after all, any analysis is selective and in that sense distortive of the text). It is rooted, rather, in the antipathy between socialism and art: left-wing critics frequently feel themselves at odds with the text and the author. This is epitomized in Terry Eagleton's book *Against the Grain*. There is an element of masochism in this willingness to abandon canonical writers to the *status quo*; it leaves the left-wing critic with a pleasingly tragic sense of lonely virtue. A far more constructive and positive undertaking is the attempt to reclaim the canonical writers, to point out the radicalism that has been obscured by generations of conservative interpretation. This alternative approach to left-wing criticism has been elucidated by Kiernan Ryan, in his essay 'Toward a socialist criticism: reclaiming the canon'.

There is another feminist dimension to the issue of internal, biographical, and psychoanalytic approaches to the text versus external, historical, and theoretical approaches. Anyone who describes her political or intellectual position as socialist–feminist is haunted by the suspicion that the description is on some level oxymoronic. On the one hand, nothing could seem more natural and intellectually consistent than a position in which one analyses and criticizes oppression in all its forms (class, race, gender). On the other hand the intense masculinity of the socialist tradition, in its association with manual labour and thus physical strength and thus the male body, seems to exclude the female and the feminine by constituting itself, in its literature and iconography, as virile labour force as opposed to effeminite ruling class. One need only look at the images of women in socialist–realist painting and sculpture to realize that woman must be seen as virile in order to be comfortably accommodated in the socialist vision. In socialist literary criticism this translates itself as a muscular preference for the political over the personal, which is not only conducive to an explicitly radical rather than an implicitly reactionary reading but is also a choice for the public sphere over the private, the intellect over the emotions, the world of men over the world of women.

It will be remarked that the present work is far more concerned with feminist than with socialist issues. That is certainly the case, primarily because the radical in George Eliot is most apparent in areas more accessible to feminist than to socialist analysis: the heroines, the vocational, the erotic. However, the foundation of conservative interpretations of George Eliot, the belief that throughout the canon she advocates 'sublime resignation', has profoundly negative implications for both socialism and feminism. The central effort of this book is to undermine that foundation.

ACKNOWLEDGEMENTS

I would like to thank Gillian Beer, Tony Tanner, David Carroll, Michael Wolff, Iain Wright, Lee Edwards, Heather Glen, and the Governing Body of Clare Hall, Cambridge, for all their help and support.

THE MAKING AND REMAKING OF GEORGE ELIOT

Thirteen years before she began to write fiction, Marian Evans wrote to her friend Sara Hennell,

> Those who can write, let them do it as boldly as they like, and let no one hesitate at the proper season to make a full *con*fession (far better than a *pro*fession).[1]

Yet the bulk of George Eliot criticism has praised or damned her for doing the opposite of what she recommends here: for professing much and confessing little. Most critics during the century following her death in 1880 saw her as sibylline: intellectual, sexless, and essentially conservative. Right-wing critics embraced her, and left-wing critics disparaged her, on these grounds. It is only in the last fifteen years that this sibylline image has really been brought into question. The commentaries of Marghanita Laski, Ruby Redinger, Sandra Gilbert and Susan Gubar, Gillian Beer, Dierdre David, and Jennifer Uglow have all, in their various ways, modified the traditional view of the woman and the author, of Marian Lewes and George Eliot. This opening chapter will explore the origins and elaboration of the sibyl image, in an effort to establish that the undue emphasis placed on this image is profoundly misleading, while the second chapter will offer an alternative emphasis; the chapters that follow will reassess the novels of George Eliot, seeking to establish that they are indeed *con*fessions, dialectical, turbulent, polyphonic, and open-ended in their structures, quite the opposite, in fact, of the controlled and didactic masterpieces that the sibyl image has encouraged readers to expect.

When George Eliot came into existence, in 1857, Marian Lewes was known primarily as the woman who lived with George Henry Lewes and yet was not his wife. This image of Marian Lewes as image-breaker and rebel was very present to her contemporary reviewers after the incognito of her *nom de plume* dissolved in 1859, and she was justifiably anxious that it would affect the reception of her work. In July 1859, William Hepworth Dixon, writing in the *Athenaeum*, called *Adam Bede*:

> such [a tale] as a clever woman with an observant eye and and unschooled moral nature might have written . . . a rather strong-minded lady, blessed with an abundance of showy sentiment, a profusion of pious words, but kept for sale rather than use.
>
> (Haight 1968: 290)

However, it was not just the circumstances of her personal life that alarmed reviewers. The fiction itself was perceived by many as dangerously erotic and iconoclastic. An anonymous reviewer of *The Mill on the Floss* in April 1860, writing for *Saturday Review*, is clearly disturbed by the sexual content of her work, although he is careful to dissociate himself from allusions to her personal reputation:

> But there is a kind of love-making which seems to posess a strange fascination for the modern female novelist. Currer Bell and George Eliot, and we may add George Sand, all like to dwell on love as a strange overmastering force which, through the senses, captivates and enthrals the soul. They linger on the description of the physical sensations that accompany the meeting of hearts in love. Curiously, too, they all like to describe these sensations as they conceive them to exist in men. We are bound to say that their conceptions are true and adequate. But we are not sure that it is quite consistent with feminine delicacy to lay so much stress on the bodily feelings of the other sex. No one could be less open to the charge of thinking lightly of purity than George Eliot. . . . But she lets her fancy run on things which are not wrong, but are better omitted from the scope of female meditation.
>
> (Carroll 1971: 118)

Swinburne, writing in 1877, is thoroughly incensed by her sexual and psychological realism:

> that a woman of Maggie Tulliver's kind can be moved to any sense but that of bitter disgust and sickening disdain by a

2

thing – I will not write, a man – of Stephen Guest's [sic]; if we
are to accept as truth and fact, however astonishing and
revolting, so shameful an avowal, so vile a revelation as this; in
that ugly and lamentable case, our only remark, as our only
comfort, must be that now at least the last word of realism has
surely been spoken, the last abyss of cynicism has surely been
sounded and laid bare.

(Carroll 1971: 32–3)

And Ruskin, writing in 1881, is disturbed not only by the sexual
content of her work but by its social content. He senses in George Eliot
the threat of trade, industry, reform, and the mob:

And it is very necessary that we should distinguish this
essentially Cockney literature, – developed only in the London
suburbs, and feeding the demands of the rows of similar brick
houses, which branch in devouring cancer round every manufac-
turing town, – from the really romantic literature of France.
Georges Sand is often immoral; but she is always beautiful. . . .
But in the English Cockney school, which consummates itself in
George Eliot, the personages are picked up from behind the
counter and out of the gutter; and the landscape, by excursion
train to Gravesend, with return ticket for the City-road.

(Carroll 1971; 167)

These disturbances are obscured for the modern critic because our
image of George Eliot has been refracted through the lenses of inter-
vening criticism. For most of her lifetime her image was far from that
of the heavy-footed sibyl into which it gradually metamorphosed, and
for that reason, her reviewers were better able than their successors to
appreciate or deplore the rebelliousness and eroticism of her fiction.

Marian Lewes herself was responsible for the initial misrepresenta-
tion, and to some extent the actual modification, of her character, and
she is therefore also responsible in part for the resultant misinterpretation of her work. Eliza Lynn Linton called George Eliot 'a made
woman'(Linton 1899: 97), and although the early stages in the process
of remaking herself have been elucidated by Ruby Redinger
(1976: 167–224), and the later stages more recently by Dierdre David
(1987: 161–176), the question 'why did she find it necessary to remake
herself?' has not been adequately answered. Redinger, in order
to retain sympathy for Marian Lewes, sees the 'emergent self' as

positive; David, in facing the fact that it was not entirely positive, loses sympathy for Marian Lewes. If the novels are, as I shall try to establish, more radical than this sibylline image would lead us to expect, it is essential to come to a thorough, sympathetic, and yet at the same time critical understanding of Marian Lewes's 'made' self and the extent to which that self enters into and effects her work.

In an early letter, Marian Evans wrote: 'I feel that my besetting sin is the one of all others most destroying, as it is the fruitful parent of them all, Ambition, a desire insatiable for the esteem of my fellow creatures' (Letters I: 19). Until the height of her writing career, this desire remained unsatisfied. There is strong evidence that as a child and a young woman her love and esteem for her father and her brother were inadequately returned. Although she formed strong friendships throughout her life, her letters, especially the early letters, are riddled with feelings of inadequacy and self-hatred. Her years as John Chapman's editor for *The Westminster Review* (1851–3), though fulfilling in that they afforded scope for her talents, did not satisfy her desire for esteem; Chapman reaped the credit for her work, and two unrequited loves, for Chapman himself and for Herbert Spencer, fed her despondency. After her elopement with George Henry Lewes in 1854, she faced disapprobation on a grand scale: Lewes was invited to dinner without her; few women would call on her; her brother broke off communication with her. And yet,

> In the 1870s her drawing room was crowded with what Lord Acton called the most remarkable society in London. 'Poets and philosophers united to honour her,' he wrote; 'the aristocracy of letters gathered round the gentle lady, who was justly esteemed the most illustrious figure that has arisen in literature since Goethe died.' Two of Queen Victoria's daughters, eager to meet her, contrived to have the Leweses invited to dinner parties with them.
>
> (Haight 1985: 285)

Already, by the 1870s, the image of Marian Lewes had metamorphosed from the 'strong-minded woman' of 1854 to sibyl and moral guide. This had been achieved, to a large extent, by the effect of her fiction in its character of passionate *apologia pro vita sua*, but that only served to undermine disapprobation. Such heroines as Maggie of *The Mill on the Floss* and Dorothea of *Middlemarch*, by showing that a woman who is disapproved by the society in which she lives may nevertheless be morally superior to that society, vicariously vindicated their author. Thus far, the change of image was legitimate and from a feminist point of view, positive.

There was, however, a further evolution of George Eliot's image from this middle point of the respected but nevertheless disturbing and challenging female artist, literary sister of George Sand, to the 'severe moralist' of later appraisals. This was undoubtedly fostered by the way she presented herself, and the way Lewes presented her, at the Sunday salons. He was in the habit of calling her 'Madonna'; accounts of Sunday visits to the Priory reveal a deliberate seriousness of tone and democracy of attention that must have been a strain for both of them. They evince, in fact, a concerted effort on the part of both George Henry and Marian Lewes to manufacture and disseminate an image of George Eliot that would be powerful, morally authoritative, and spotless enough to erase the prior image of Marian Lewes. This can only be understood in the context of the severe disapprobation she had suffered all her life, for being plain, for being passionate, for being intellectual, and above all for being unmarried. The initial creation of the sibyl image was the means by which an embattled woman, whose character and circumstances threatened the dominant ideology, gained peace, power, and acceptance in Victorian England.

The appearance, in 1871, of Alexander Main's book, *Wise, Witty, and Tender Sayings in Prose and Verse from the Works of George Eliot* contributed to the growing impression of the sibylline didacticism of George Eliot. That Marian Lewes approved this fulsome vivisection of her works is evidence of the extremity and persistence of the need for approbation, even to the point of worship, to which she confessed in the letter quoted above, and which she criticized in her characterizations of Maggie and Dorothea.

In the enormous contemporary success of her work and in the almost religious devotion of various young admirers both male and female, she presumably found satisfaction of that desire, but the very measures that secured admiration at the height of her career were also instrumental in her posthumous decline. A generation later, Virginia Woolf recalls,

> She became one of the butts for youth to laugh at, the
> convenient symbol of a group of serious people who were all
> guilty of the same idolatry and could be dismissed with the same

scorn. . . . Asked to describe an afternoon at the Priory, the story-teller always intimated that the memory of those serious Sunday afternoons had come to tickle his sense of humour.

(Woolf 1919: 657–8)

Her last book, *The Impressions of Theophrastus Such*, published in 1879, added to the sibylline image. The Theophrastan form was an unfortunate choice. Any non-fictional form would have facilitated the domination of what I will later refer to as the conscious conservative in George Eliot, but the Theophrastan is particularly conducive to, and has a long heritage of, wisdom handed down from on high. The placement of *Theophrastus Such* at the end of the George Eliot canon unfortunately gives it the authority of a last word; had she survived to complete another novel, her popularity might not have proceeded with such momentum on its downward spiral.

In 1885, John Walter Cross published *George Eliot's Life as Related in her Letters and Journals*, which opens with the following claim:

With the materials in my hands I have endeavoured to form an *autobiography* (if the term may be permitted) of George Eliot. The life has been allowed to write itself in extracts from her letters and journals. Free from the obtrusion of any mind but her own.

Yet he seems to see no self-contradiction in the ingenuous admission of his bowdlerism on the following page: 'Each letter has been pruned of everything that seemed to me irrelevant to my purpose – of everything that I thought my wife would have wished to be omitted' (Cross 1885: I: 5–6). Even so, the choice of 'my wife' here (a phrase not repeated for more than one hundred pages of ensuing text) evinces a need to announce by what right he can tell what she would have wished to be omitted. Although Marian Lewes may well have appreciated his editing, this sanitizing of her life and letters certainly contributed to the distortion of her image, and thereby almost as certainly to the decline in her literary reputation. Marghanita Laski, in her acerbic biography, *George Eliot and her World*, claims that the Cross biography was

disastrous for George Eliot, for in attempting to conceal not merely possible scandal but the smallest flaw, he presented only a whited sepulchre; and it is impossible to feel confident that all the whitewash has yet been removed. The hagiolatrous biography was more than contemporaries could stomach, and

George Eliot's literary reputation, till then almost supreme, almost immediately slumped.

(Laski 1973: 117)

Although her point about the removal of whitewash is a crucial one, Laski, in locating Cross as the sole source of whitewash, is over-simplifying the case. By the time the Cross biography was published in 1885, major damage had already been done by F. W. H. Myers and Charles Bray. Perhaps the most frequently quoted description of George Eliot is Myers's account, written in 1881, of his conversation with her in Trinity Fellows' Garden:

> she, stirred somewhat beyond her wont, and taking as her text the three words which have been used so often as the inspiring trumpet-calls of men, – *God, Immortality, Duty*, – pronounced, with terrible earnestness, how inconceivable was the *first*, how unbelievable the *second*, and yet how peremptory and absolute the *third*. Never, perhaps, have sterner accents affirmed the sovereignty of impersonal and uncompromising Law. I listened, and night fell; her grave, majestic countenance turned toward me like a sibyl's in the gloom; it was as though she withdrew from my grasp, one by one, the two scrolls of promise, and left me the third scroll only, awful with inevitable fates. And when we stood at length and parted, amid that columnar circuit of the forest-trees, beneath the last twilight of starless skies, I seemed to be gazing, like Titus at Jerusalem, on vacant seats and empty halls, – on a sanctuary with no Presence to hallow it, and Heaven left lonely of a God.

(Haight 1968: 464)

This account offers no new information: the ideas can be found in the novels themselves, simply explained, and free from the melo-dramatic morbidity with which Myers's purple prose invests them. The passage suggests associations with every major establishment institution: 'text', 'pronounced', and 'scrolls' suggest the ecclesiasti-cal; 'trumpet-calls' the military; 'sovereignty' the governmental; and 'Law' the judicial. This authoritarian atmosphere prepares us for the causal relationship implied in 'I listened, and night fell' which in turn prefigures the utterly apocalyptic suggestion of 'last twilight of starless skies'.

This passage is quoted in most book-length treatments of George

Eliot, and in many shorter commentaries. Its effect is most insidious when its language seeps into the prose of other writers, and in doing so, it takes on the appearance of a universally acknowledged truth. G. M. Young, in his *Victorian England: Portrait of an Age*, introduces George Eliot as follows:

> Thus it came about that the pagan ethic which, when faith in God and Immortality had gone, carried into the next, the agnostic, age the evangelical faith in duty and renunciation, was a woman's ethic. George Eliot's rank in literature has, perhaps, not yet been determined: in the history of ideas her place is fixed. She is the moralist of the Victorian revolution.
>
> (Young 1936: 4)

In 1884, Charles Bray published his *Phases of Opinion and Experience during a Long Life*. In it he gives his often quoted description of George Eliot based on his memories of her and a phrenological study:

> She was of a most affectionate disposition, always requiring some one to lean upon, preferring what has hitherto been considered the stronger sex, to the other and more impressionable. She was not fitted to stand alone.
>
> (Bray 1884: 75)

Fragments of this evaluation have been absorbed, often without attribution, into almost every major document of George Eliot scholarship. They seem to have insinuated their way into other evaluations even before the publication of *Phases of Opinion*, presumably being circulated by word of mouth among people who were interested in and thinking of writing about George Eliot. Charles Kegan Paul, writing in 1883, had clearly heard and inwardly digested, with somewhat chaotic stylistic results: 'Mrs Lewes's intensely feminine nature had found the strong man on whom to lean in the daily business of life, for which she was physically and intellectually unfitted' (Paul 1883: 153).

Mathilde Blind, in her biography of George Eliot published in 1884, uses a phrenological term from the same Bray account in her initial description of Marian Lewes's character, 'One of the leading traits of her nature was its adhesiveness' (Blind 1884: 37), and uses the adjective 'clinging' to describe her four times during the next one hundred pages. She accounts for Marian Lewes's marriage to Cross with language that is familiar from both Cross and Bray: 'But George Eliot's was a nature that needed some one especially to love.'

These, however, are only traces which might have dwindled and died out, had not the suggestion of weakness in George Eliot intimated by Bray's language, language that employs a metaphor of physical paralysis, been disseminated throughout George Eliot scholarship by Gordon Haight. In the course of his many volumes on George Eliot, Haight uses Bray's words as a kind of refrain. In *George Eliot: A Biography*, which is read by most serious students of George Eliot, they appear nine times.[2] On each occasion, Bray's words are used to excuse Marian Evans's sexual attractions to François D'Albert, John Chapman, Herbert Spencer, G. H. Lewes, and John Walter Cross, respectively.

The debt that George Eliot scholarship owes to Haight is incalculable. Nevertheless it must be said that at times his chivalrous protectiveness toward her does more harm than good. Had the author under discussion been male, this catholicity of sexual interests over the course of a lifetime would have been interpreted as a sign of independence rather than of abject need and would not have required excuse, would, rather, have been seen as admirable. One might, for that reason, have expected the dissemination of Bray's language to stop at the door of feminist criticism, but unfortunately this is not the case. Gilbert and Gubar have used it as freely as any non-feminist critic, and to more consciously destructive ends:

> Certainly the saddest sign of her inability to stand
> alone – whether or not it is true that the single word *Crisis* in her
> diary refers to her discovery five and a half months after Lewes's
> death of his infidelity – is Eliot's precipitous marriage to a man
> young enough to be her son and troubled enough to need a
> replacement for the recent death of his mother.
>
> (Gilbert and Gubar 1979: 467)

Both Myers's image of the sibyl in the gloom and Bray's metaphor of physical paralysis echo throughout the critical heritage, explaining away George Eliot's power, staunching the discomfiture felt by a male intelligentsia that found itself dominated by a female intellectual and the fear of impending anarchy which inevitably accompanied female sexual licence. Inquiry into the credentials of these two evaluations produces little other than this consciously or unconsciously political motive to justify their ubiquity.

Myers's description of the Fellows' Garden, 'that *columnar* circuit of the forest-trees' (my emphasis), illuminates the choice of the sibyl metaphor. The conversation he describes took place in what might reasonably be described as a nursery of male ruling-class power. Marian Evans Lewes, female and of lower middle-class origins, had intruded upon the ground traditionally reserved for products of that nursery by becoming the leading novelist of her day. Myers's metaphor tries to reconcile actual antagonists: George Eliot and the Fellows' Garden. In a Hellenic context, a woman's voice can be heard in the seat of learning, and the reality of class structures that would have excluded Marian Evans even if she had been male is comfortably obscured in the mists of mythology. The Hellenic metaphor allows the Cambridge man to appropriate George Eliot rather than to admit how thoroughly out of place she was in the Fellows' Garden and how, by becoming the leading novelist of her day, she had in fact appropriated what had traditionally belonged to the Fellows.

Bray's remarks originated in a phrenological appraisal of Marian Evans's character, and none of the critics who have absorbed his language would have been likely to have espoused his phrenology. Furthermore, Bray's appraisal follows an attempt to claim himself as the origin of all George Eliot's ideas, and this puts into question his disinterestedness: if we believe that she, more than others, was emotionally dependent, we are more likely to believe that she was also intellectually dependent. This is supported by his choice of 'the other and more impressionable [sex]' to describe women: Bray is supporting his earlier claim that Marian Evans received the impress of his ideas (Bray 1884: 73-4).

Beyond this, it seems very questionable that anyone is 'fitted to stand alone.' Bray himself married at 25, and few of the critics who adopted this phrase were alone until middle age, as was Marian Evans. She not only stood alone but she stood against: in 1842 she opposed her father's authority on the issue of church attendance; in 1854, through her elopement with Lewes, she violated conventions about love and marriage; her erudition and her life-long scholarship contradicted assumptions about woman's sphere; and finally, by marrying John Walter Cross, a man twenty years her junior, she offended against still more conventions about what a woman may and may not do, this time alienating people who had supported her though her earlier battles. [3]

George Willis Cooke's *George Eliot: A Critical Study*, published in 1883, is not often mentioned by later critics and biographers. It is probably safe, therefore, to assume that his effect on the critical heritage has been slight. Nevertheless, he was the first of a series of com-mentators, the effect of whose work, like that of Cross's *Life*, was to sanitize George Eliot, to rid her of her less respectable elements, but who, unlike Cross, did so by reducing her work to its intellectual content alone. Cooke begins his account with a characteristic reduc-tion: 'George Eliot came after Comte, Mill and Spencer. Her books are to be read in the light of their speculations, and she embodied in literary forms what they uttered as science or philosophy' (Cooke 1883: 2). The tone of his entire narrative is similarly dry, and when he gets to the less conventional areas of George Eliot's life, he is hard pressed to render simultaneously the truth as he understood it and an image in keeping with this dryasdust imitator of great men.

The prioritization of the intellectual at the expense of the passional in George Eliot has not only been the means by which conservative criticism has appropriated her but also has been the reason why non-conservative commentators, from liberal humanists to Marxist radi-cals, have abandoned her. Henry James gives this reason for his detraction in 1885: 'We feel in her, always, that she proceeds from the abstract to the concrete; that her figures and situations are evolved, as the phrase is, from her moral consciousness, and are only indirectly the products of observations' (Carroll 1971: 498). In an earlier review, James had already implicitly focused on the intellectual while making a more explicit charge of conservatism:

> her inclination to compromise with the old tradition . . . which
> exacts that a serious story of manners shall close with the
> factitious happiness of a fairy tale. I know few things more
> irritating in a literary way than each of her final chapters, – for
> even in *The Mill on the Floss* there is a fatal 'Conclusion'. Both as
> an artist and a thinker, in other words, our author is an
> optimist; and although a conservative is not necessarily an
> optimist, I think an optimist is pretty likely to be a conservative.
>
> (Haight 1966: 54)

The same basic view of George Eliot's work is espoused by Terry Eagleton and Colin MacCabe, who consider her a reactionary writer and seem content to hand her over to the conservative tradition (Eagleton 1983: 33; MacCabe 1978: 15). The similar way in which feminist critics have abandoned her to the patriarchal tradition will be discussed in the concluding chapter.

The examples I have given here are key examples but are certainly

11

not unusual. They suffice to indicate the broad outlines of a critical trend which saturated thought about George Eliot so throughly by the 1920s and 1930s as to elicit the following comments from Lord David Cecil:

> Our task is pretty well over now. On the floor round us in motley heaps, here a big one there a small, lie the works of Dickens and Thackeray and Trollope and Mrs Gaskell and the Brontes; re-read and re-considered. Only eight volumes still remain upright on the shelves – the novels of George Eliot. And there is no doubt one shrinks from tackling them as one has not shrunk from the others. Their very names – *Silas Marner, Felix Holt, Adam Bede* – are forbidding; there is something at once solemn and prosaic about them, heavy and humdrum, they are more like the names in a graveyard than the titles of enthralling works of fancy. Nor, if one turns from them to their author's portrait, does one feel more encouraged. That osseous lengthy countenance, those dark, lank bands of hair, that serious conscientious gaze, seem to sum up and concentrate in a single figure all the dowdiness, ponderousness and earnestness which we find most alien in the Victorian age.
>
> Yet, as a matter of fact, George Eliot's books are nearer to us than any of those we have yet examined. It is one of her principal claims to fame that she is the first modern novelist.
>
> (Cecil 1934: 283)

Here Cecil describes a fissure within his own critical perception: the former paragraph constitutes the fullest and most vivid description of the sibyl image and the antipathy it generated; the latter indicates Cecil's awareness that the novels are far from what that image leads one to expect. The former paragraph is the result of what Laski calls 'the whitewash'; the latter is an early and tentative effort at removing the whitewash. The removal of whitewash began in earnest with F. R. Leavis and Joan Bennett in 1948. The body of George Eliot criticism written since 1948 is too copious and complex to deal with here, but in the following chapters I take issue with various more recent critics, and often the point of difference originates in their unquestioned absorption of the sibyl image. Reading with preconceived idea that her work is conservative and didactic, one inevitably selects and prior-itizes elements that support that preconception. If, however, one is conscious that these are in fact preconceptions, and as such should remain open to question, the suppressed readings rise to the surface in alarming abundance. What is most striking about George Eliot is her inclusiveness: she is both passionate and prudish, radical and conservative, capable of an almost superhuman extension of sympathies and of the most corrosive disdain. All these conflicting elements struggle together in her fiction, and the result is not a series of elaborate moral fables but rather a protean vision of the dialectical engagement of human realities and possibilities.

RECONSTRUCTING GEORGE ELIOT

A few lines after his phrenological description, Charles Bray wrote of Marian Evans, 'She saw all sides, and there are always many, clearly and without prejudice'(Bray 1884: 75). What an enormous difference it would have made to George Eliot's image if this latter comment had been quoted as often as, and in place of, 'She was not fitted to stand alone.' It is certainly truer to the George Eliot of the novels, although still misleading as to its nuances. Seeing all sides clearly and without prejudice suggests a dispassionate, even-handed neutrality, whereas George Eliot saw each side with the passion of a partisan. One feels that, when writing from Dorothea's viewpoint, she is genuinely resentful of Casaubon; when writing from Casaubon's, genuinely fearful of Dorothea. The antagonism of equally valid claims in *The Mill on the Floss* is argued from both sides with equal force, as is the antagonism between Savonarola and Romola.

This ability to enter into both sides of a conflict not only intellectually but also emotionally lies behind a series of fascinating reflexive characterizations in George Eliot's fiction. These are far from the 'day-dream self-indulgences' that Leavis has taught us to see in the self-portraitive elements of the heroines, and they reveal a very different implied author.

Henry James, in his review of the Cross biography, made the following observation:

> She enumerates diligently all the pictures and statues she sees,
> and the way she does so is proof of her active, earnest intellectual
> habits; but it is rarely apparent that they have, as the phrase is,
> said much to her, or that what they have said is one of their
> deeper secrets. She is capable of writing, after coming out of the

great chapel of San Lorenzo, in Florence, that 'the world-famous statues of Michael Angelo on the tombs . . . remained to us as affected and exaggerated in the original as in copies and casts'. The sentence startles one, on the part of the author of *Romola*, and that Mr Cross should have printed it is a commendable proof of his impartiality.

(Carroll 1971: 499)

The implied charge is undeniably true, but when looked at in the context of Cross's precious accounts of George Eliot's attachment to *A Linnet's Life* and her fondness for housework it takes on a maiden-auntish aspect that is completely absent from it when considered in a quite different context, that is beside the characterization of Casaubon in *Middlemarch*, whose constant references to other people's opinions of works of art and whose own desiccated lack of feeling for them form one of several startlingly insightful critical self-portraits in the George Eliot canon.

Gordon S. Haight, in his *George Eliot: A Biography*, remarks that when asked about the source of Casaubon, George Eliot pointed to her own heart (Haight 1968: 450). Haight interprets this as a reference to the overconscientious research she did for *Romola*. Here again, Haight desires to protect George Eliot, in this case from the unpleasant implications of her own confession. Surely the first available interpretation of pointing to her heart is that she herself is the source of Casaubon, and not merely in one instance of misguided scholarship but in a fundamental and personal sense. In the characterization of Casaubon, George Eliot acknowledges and thereby in a sense cancels out the Casaubonish elements of her own personality. That is to say, she might be insensitive enough to see galleries of the finest art and remain unmoved, but she is aware of her own insensitivity and regrets it deeply.

Similarly, in the characterizations of Maggie and Dorothea she criticizes her own love of worship; in Savonarola she criticizes her own tendency towards what Nietzsche calls 'slave-mentality'; and in Mrs Transome she criticizes her own self-hating egoism, of which all these critical self-portraits are but a symptom. In this we receive the first intimation of the self-dividedness, the personal and fictional polyphony of George Eliot.

These self-portraits are intensely disturbing because they bespeak a capacity for anger and bitterness (here directed at herself) that is

completely inimical to the benign and calmly wise image of the sibyl.
However, once we have admitted anger and bitterness into our picture
of George Eliot, other previously perplexing elements yield quite
easily to analysis. For example, several critics have noted that
Maggie's elopement with Lucy's lover in *The Mill on the Floss* is
foreshadowed by her childhood revenge of pushing Lucy in the mud.
None of these critics has followed the interpretative implications of the
parallel, because of an *idée fixe* that George Eliot and her heroines are
too nice, too sincere and earnest, to avenge themselves on an innocent
in that way. But actually the novels are riddled with tales of love and
murder, as Alexander Welsh has remarked (Welsh 1984: 282–3),
often involving a woman with a knife wanting to stab her lover or
husband: Tina in 'Mr Gilfil's love story'; Laure in *Middlemarch*;
Gwendolen in *Daniel Deronda*. In both her male and her female characters, the sexual is closely related to the violent: Janet Dempster is
beaten by her husband; Hetty kills the child that is evidence of her
sexual knowledge; Lydgate is in danger of strangling Rosamond.

The only escape from the murderous feelings excited by passion is
through the absorption of one's entire being in one's work. This is why
the need registered in George Eliot's novels is for vocation, not merely
occupation, for a task engrossing enough to preclude obsession with
the self and the pain to which the self is constantly subjected. The
reflexivity of 'Armgart', which Gillian Beer has discussed at length
(Beer 1986: 211–13), illuminates George Eliot's view of the relation
between vocation, love, and murder:

> She often wonders what her life had been
> Without that voice for channel to her soul.
> She says, it must have leaped through all her limbs –
> Made her a Maenad – made her snatch a brand
> And fire some forest, that her rage might mount
> In crashing roaring flames through half a land,
> Leaving her still and patient for a while.
> 'Poor wretch!' she says, of any murderess –
> 'The world was cruel, and she could not sing:
> I carry my revenges in my throat;
> I love in singing and am loved again.'[1]

In *The Gay Science*, E. S. Dallas quotes *Felix Holt*: 'that higher consciousness which is known to bring higher pains' (Dallas
1866: II: 123–4). Dallas deduces from this that the lower conscious-

ness is the only one capable of pleasure. This might explain why, as several critics have noted, all seductions and murders in George Eliot's fiction take place in a haze of semi-consciousness. They are seen as equal and related pleasures, both for the perpetrator (the seducer, the murderer) and for the victim (because if pleasure is in inverse proportion to consciousness, the extinction of one's own consciousness coincides with the ultimate pleasure, as indicated in the use of the verb to die to suggest orgasm in poetry and song). The association of love and death in this way anticipates what Freud was to approach at the end of his career: the notion that Eros and Thanatos are perhaps identical.[2]

This evidence suggests that there is a great deal of anger where right-wing critics have usually seen 'sublime resignation ', and left-wing critics have seen a hierarchy of discourses controlled by a sort of English nanny figure. It implies not an earnest, painfully serious, sibylline author but a rather bitter, cynical, self-obsessed personality, a personality clearly recognizable from the essays and letters, and memorable in the occasional anomaly in Mathilde Blind's biography, where the information given seems to clash with the pervasive impression of sweet dependent womanhood:

> In criticizing [the portrait of George Eliot by Samuel Lawrence] a keen observer of human nature remarked that it conveyed no indication of the infinite depth of her observant eye, nor of that cold, subtle, and unconscious cruelty of expression which might be occasionally detected there.
>
> (Blind 1884: 207–8)

Another instance is Blind's comment on *The Impressions of Theophrastus Such*: 'Its cutting irony and incisive ridicule are no longer tempered by the humourous laugh, but have, the corrosive quality of some acrid chemical substance' (Blind 1884: 213).

It is by way of the treatment of vocation and desire in George Eliot's potrayal of her heroines that this other aspect of her personality becomes most apparent, and it is in the interpretation of these issues that a sensitivity to that other George Eliot becomes essential. The two terms of my title, vocation and desire, are intended to embrace, between them, all human need. They are therefore meant in their widest possible senses, and they form a dichotomy that is implicit in all George Eliot's work. The need she describes is for a vocation rather than for an occupation or for a means of gaining financial independence, although these two latter needs are often encompassed by the former. George Eliot dramatically portrays what even Karl Marx, the father of modern materialism, allows, that what we seek in work is more than sustenance:

> an animal only produces what it immediately needs for itself or its young. It produces one-sidedly, while man produces universally. It produces only under the dominion of immediate physical need, while man produces even when he is free from physical need, and only truly produces in freedom therefrom.
>
> (Baxandall and Morowski 1974: 51)

In his book, *George Eliot and the Novel of Vocation* (1978), Alan Mintz has explored the issue of vocation in *Middlemarch*, tracing the historical roots of the notion of vocation, establishing their relation to Marian Evans's early religious enthusiasm, and touching upon the reflexivity of the theme of vocation. Mintz's study centres on *Middlemarch* and, in large part, on the vocational problems of male characters. Although *Middlemarch* is perhaps the most explicit of George Eliot's novels in its dealings with vocation, her fascination with the subject is clear in and central to most of her novels; and although the issue is most often and most explicitly dealt with in male characters, George Eliot's centre of interest lay in the negative space of female vocation – a space that could only be defined by the surrounding positive forms of men's vocations or vocational troubles and the ever-present if invisible form of George Eliot's own vocation. Behind the androgynous fiction 'George Eliot' was a woman whose vocation was to explore again and again the question, how can women satisfy their need for vocation? The George Eliot canon simultaneously answers this question and leaves it unanswered: the novels answer it by being themselves the evidence of a woman's vocational success; nevertheless, by taking as their subject-matter this negative space of woman's vocation, they themselves in a sense constitute a negative space, a preparation for work as yet undefined and unaccomplished. We must look first to Jane Austen's portraits of the empty lives of women, then to Charlotte Brontë's portraits of life as a governess and a spinster-teacher to prepare ourselves for the turbulent painful leitmotiv of the absence of vocational possibility for women in the works of George Eliot.

Kathleen Blake has taken issue with Mintz over his claim that *Middlemarch* is a novel of vocation, as distinct from a novel that revolves around love stories. Blake claims that the central concern of

Middlemarch is the intertwining of and the friction between the two. She also notes that Elizabeth Barrett Browning and Marian Lewes, the two women writers who perhaps came closest to reconciling the two elements in their own lives, are also the most obsessed with their irreconcilability (Blake 1983: 34, 198). Feminist critics have deplored George Eliot for not allowing her heroines the freedoms that she herself attained. Yet, if Blake's point is tenable, George Eliot's preoccupation with problems no longer her own bespeaks a firm solidarity with other women for whom the reconciliation of vocation and desire continue to be problematic.

In the discussions of desire that follow, the word 'sexual' is also intended in its broadest sense, the sense in which Freud used it (Freud I: 344–5), to encompass all relationships that are determined by sex: with parents, with offspring, with siblings, with spouses, and with lovers, so that the term 'sexual need' when used in reference to a woman's marriage applies not only to the carnal intimacy of husband and wife but also to the satisfactions of child-bearing and nurturing.

This broader definition of the word 'sexual' is useful in approaching George Eliot's choice of parental metaphors to describe sexual love: these metaphors can be understood as an extension rather than a denial of the realm of the sexual. The parent–child metaphors are only part of a cluster of apparently inappropriate metaphors which have led critics to the conclusion that, through them, George Eliot is in some way denying the sexual. This, again, is in keeping with a rather prudish and conciliatory George Eliot, one who avoids the disturbing and the problematic. Foremost of these metaphors are the child images she uses to describe adults, especially when they are in sexual or potentially sexual situations. F. R. Leavis, Barbara Hardy, and W. J. Harvey have discussed George Eliot's use of child imagery to describe adult characters. Hardy comes to the following conclusion:

> Will and Dorothea are in places reduced, as Dr Leavis says, by
> the pathetic image which George Eliot uses for several of her
> love-scenes, and this kind of reducion to childish sweetness and
> innocence is often a weakness in her treatment of sex.
>
> (Hardy 1959: 210)

Certainly the use of child imagery creates problems, not only in the desexualization of sexual situations but also in the diminution of heroines whom she has gone to some trouble to represent in monumental proportions. For example, when Dorothea is alone, pained and angry at what she perceives as Will's betrayal (*Middlemarch*, chapter 80), George Eliot monumentalizes her by using the phrase 'her grand woman's frame', but when she has accepted Will as the best option available to her, she is described as childlike. Similarly, when we first see Gwendolen, she is defiant in the gambling casino, and the description of her gains scope from mythic associations: she is a naiad, a sylph, a Lamia. When she confesses to Daniel, she too is childlike.

W. J. Harvey has examined George Eliot's use of the words 'childish' and 'childlike' and has found it to be unsatisfactory, a rejection of adulthood. Harvey asks, 'Is there not some evasion here, some regression on George Eliot's part from the problems of adult life?' (Hardy 1970: 176) and in this he essentially agrees with Barbara Hardy. Harvey finds that, in George Eliot's prose, the two words do not remain in their distinct areas of meaning. The OED defines 'childish' as 'like a child, unsuitable for a grown person', whereas 'childlike' is defined as 'having the good qualities of a child, simple and innocent'. However, in chapter 1 of *Middlemarch*, for example, we are told that Dorothea, 'retained very childlike ideas about marriage', whereas in chapter 81 'Dorothea looked almost childish with the neglected trace of a silent tear'. To be precisely appropriate, these adjectives, it seems, should be reversed.

George Eliot espoused the Wordworthian admiration for the innocence of the child. In her first published essay, she wrote: 'true wisdom, which implies a moral as well as an intellectual result, consists in a return to that purity and simplicity which characterize early youth, when its intuitions have not been perverted' (Pinney 1963: 20). However, it is not necessarily the case, and *The Mill on the Floss* renders it difficult to argue the case, that George Eliot considers childhood a pre-sexual or non-sexual time. The difference between Maggie and Tom's embraces and conflicts in childhood and those in adulthood is primarily that in childhood they are honest and unselfconscious, whereas in adulthood they have learned to falsify their emotions:

> We learn to restrain ourselves as we get older. We keep apart when we have quarrelled, express ourselves in well-bred phrases, and in this we preserve a dignified alienation, showing much firmness on the one side, and swallowing much grief on the other.
>
> (*The Mill on the Floss* I: 54)

It is in this sense, and not in the simpler Christian sense of sexual innocence, that George Eliot intends us to understand 'childlike'. When she characterizes her heroines as childlike, she is highlighting their unselfconsciousness and the honesty of their motives rather than trying to desexualize them. The characterization of Maggie sufficiently proves this point: George Eliot goes to great trouble to establish how intensely passionate and sexually attractive Maggie is, and yet she is nevertheless characterized in adulthood as childlike.

The other unfortunate result of the use of child imagery to describe adult women stems from the traditional association of women and children in patriarchal discourse. George Eliot can hardly have been oblivious of this association which was so palpably irritating to feminist writers with whose work George Eliot was intimately acquainted. Margaret Fuller, in *Woman in the Nineteenth Century*, which Marian Evans reviewed for the *Westminster Review*, makes repeated references to it:

> knowing that there exists in the minds of men a tone of feeling toward women as toward slaves, such as is expressed in the common phrase, 'Tell that to women and children.'

> while we hear from men . . . the frequent remark, 'You cannot reason with a woman' – when from those of delicacy, nobleness, and poetic culture, falls the contemptuous phrase, 'women and children' – can we feel that Man will always do justice to the interests of Woman?

> (Fuller 1844: 33, 36)

Barbara Bodichon described the same phenomenon in English law:

> For who else among us, entitled by law to hold property to a certain amount, is nevertheless deprived of the vote which the British Constitution looks upon as the safeguard of property? The answer will be – Minors, idiots, lunatics, and criminals. These, and these only, are classed politically along with women.
> (Bodichon 1867: 10)

In the choice of child imagery to describe her heroines, as in her use of the idea of submission, George Eliot deliberately chooses an ambiguous term or metaphor in order to sustain the profound ambiguity of all choices in her novels. For example, in *Daniel Deronda* Gwendolen moves from being childish to being childlike, and that movement is seen as positive, but the last scene between Gwendolen and Daniel, in which we see her as childlike, is a stage beyond which she must progress if she is to survive. For the first time in her life she is honest and unselfconscious – she has the virtues of the child – but she is also weakly dependent upon Daniel; she must learn to be self-sustaining, and we leave her pledging to do just that.

The tendency amongst modern critics, when reconsidering the sexual in George Eliot's work, to attribute to it a naïve or at best maternal cast has been detrimental to the appreciation of both her aesthetic worth and her radical content. For example, in the love-affairs between Maggie and Stephen, in *The Mill on the Floss*, and Dorothea and Will, in *Middlemarch*, misapprehension of George Eliot's insistence on a purely erotic need in women – a need quite distinct from the need for companionship or 'womanly duties' – has been critically disastrous. Many critics, among them Virginia Woolf, have declared George Eliot incapable of creating fit mates for her heroines:

> but both [Philip Wakem and Stephen Guest], in their weakness and coarseness, illustratrate not so much George Eliot's inability to draw the portrait of a man, as the uncertainty, the infirmity, and the fumbling which shook her hand when she had to conceive a fit mate for a heroine.
>
> (Woolf 1919: 658)

George Eliot never intended to create fit mates. Her much more artistically challenging and radical subject-matter is what happens to a woman who meets with no fit mate and for whom the finding of a fit mate (even if possible) would in no way constitute an adequate ending or response to her potentialities.

Marian Lewes would probably have approved of a discussion focusing on vocation and desire, but she may well have objected to the emphasis the following chapters will place upon the heroines. She clearly wanted to get beyond gender, to attain a position from which she could speculate, through fiction, about human existence in general. If one gender was to be prioritized, it was, in her mind, the masculine, presumably because men have more power to change the world. In a letter to John Blackwood (1867), she wrote of 'people who care about every one of my books and continue to read them – especially young men, who are just the class I care most to influence' (IV: 397).

Edith Simox, in her 'Autobiography of a shirt-maker', writes that Marian Lewes claimed to have a personal preference for men:

> Then she said – perhaps it would shock me – she had never all her life cared much for women – it must seem monstrous to me.

I said I had always known it. She went on to say, what I also
knew, that she cared for the womanly ideal, sympathised with
women and liked for them to come to her in their troubles, but
while feeling near to them in one way, she felt far off in another;
the friendship and intimacy of men was more to her.

(Haight 1968: 535)

Marian Evans Lewes's many close friendships with women – most
notably with Maria Lewis, Sara Hennell, and Barbara Bodichon –
would seem to contradict her stated preference for men. However,
she had little in common with most women of her day, and the
sharpest disapprobation about her union with Lewes had come
from those whose sense of self-worth rested entirely on their
unquestioned virtue. Regardless of what Marian Lewes felt about
women, George Eliot's clear bias towards her own sex saturates the
canon: books named for male characters are focused on female protagonists; and these female protagonists are subjected to a more rigor-
ous examination of the moral nuances of their behaviour and feeling
than are their male equivalents. This last point was raised by R. H.
Hutton, writing in 1876:

It is quite true, we suppose, that many of the women of this
great novelist will be the delights of English literature as long as
the language endures. . . . She is always in earnest about her
women, and she makes the reader earnest too. . . . There is the
Puritan intensity of feeling, the Miltonic weight of thought, in all
George Eliot's drawings of women. If they are superficial in
character and feeling, the superficiality is insisted on as a sort of
crime. If they are not superficial, the depth is brought out with
an energy that is sometimes almost painful. . . . Thus her world
of women, at all events, is a world of larger stature than the
average world we know; indeed, she can hardly sketch the shad-
ows and phantoms by which so much of the real world is
peopled, without impatience and scorn. She cannot laugh at the
world – of women at least – as other writers equally great
can. . . . With men, it is true, George Eliot can deal more
lightly. . . . Our author probably indulges more neutrality of
feeling in relation to men than she does in relation to women.
She does not regard them as beings whose duty it is to be very
much in earnest, and who are almost contemptible or wicked if
they are otherwise. . . . There is something of the large and

23

grave statuesque style in all George Eliot's studies of women. She cannot bear to treat them with indifference. If they are not what she approves, she makes it painfully, emphatically evident. If they are, she dwells upon their earnestness and aspirations with an almost Puritanic moral intensity, which shows how eagerly she muses on her ideal of women's life.

(Holmstrom and Lerner 1966: 170–1)

Modern feminist critics have often criticized George Eliot for being too hard on women, for being, in fact, biased toward men, but R. H. Hutton seems much closer to the mark when he suggests that her comparative gentleness to male characters may well be the gentleness of condescension.

Much of the tension in her novels derives from the disjunction between the idea of the relative scope of men and women and the reality in any given case. Dempster, in 'Janet's repentance' goes home to beat his wife, on the assumption that his wife is his inferior and is therefore beatable:

Yet a few seconds, and the figure of a tall woman, holding aslant a heavy-plated drawing-room candlestick, appeared at the turning of the passage that led to the broader entrance.

She had on a light dress which sat loosely about her figure, but did not disguise its liberal, graceful outline. A heavy mass of straight jet-black hair had escaped from its fastening, and hung over her shoulders. Her grandly-cut features, pale with the natural paleness of a brunette, had premature lines about them, telling that the years had been lengthened by sorrow, and the delicately-curved nostril, which seemed made to quiver with the proud consciousness of power and beauty, must have quivered to the heart-piercing griefs which had given that worn look to the corners of the mouth. Her wide open black eyes had a strangely fixed, sightless gaze, as she paused at the turning, and stood silent before her husband.

(Scenes of Clerical Life, II: 102–3)

The words that suggest a literal largeness – 'tall', 'liberal', 'heavy', 'power' – unite with equine suggestion in the description of her nostril to produce an image of unusual scope and impressiveness. This is compounded by a subtle but sustained allusion to classical Greek statuary: the description of her dress is reminiscent of drapery;

24

'grandly-cut' is a sculpting metaphor; paleness and fixed sightless eyes also suggest sculpture. Janet is the first of George Eliot's monumental women: Maggie, Romola, Mrs Transome, Dorothea, and Gwendolen are all described with the same scope.

Peter Garrett has remarked on what he calls a spatial metaphor in *Middlemarch*:

> [the spatial metaphor] is also present in the suggested
> metaphorical overtones of the contrast between Dorothea's
> 'voice of deep-souled womanhood', whose depth suggests
> perhaps the space for reverberation in her 'grand woman's
> frame' (LXXX, 576), juxtaposed, in the same paragraph, with
> Rosamond's 'silvery neutral' voice (LVIII, 433), whose high
> fluting tones seem to be extruded through her graceful long neck.
>
> (Garrett 1969: 30)

Hugh Witemeyer, in his *George Eliot and the Visual Arts*, comments in detail on George Eliot's fondness for the monumental:

> She was particularly fond of heroic and monumental images of
> women, such as the cockle-woman she once saw at Swansea: 'the
> grandest woman I ever saw – six foot high, carrying herself like
> a Greek Warrior, and treading the earth with unconscious
> majesty' (*Letters*, II, 251). This taste for massive, Amazonian
> figures also manifests itself in Eliot's admiration of several pieces
> of contemporary sculpture: August Kiss's *Mounted Amazon
> Attacked by a Tiger* (*Essays*, p. 126) and Ludwig Schwanthaler's
> *Bavaria* (Cross, II, 21–2). Given her predilection for grand,
> statuesque female forms, she naturally visualized her own
> heroines as imposing creatures. Dorothea, for example,
> resembles the reclining Ariadne in the Vatican Museum, and the
> similarity is of amplitude as well as attitude.
>
> (Witemeyer 1979: 86)

George Eliot monumentalizes her heroines by the simple use of largeness in her descriptions – Dorothea's beautiful hands, for example, are large – and by the imbrication of classical, biblical, saintly, queenly, and androgynous images. Dorothea is compared to St Theresa of Avila, Don Quixote, Santa Clara, Cleopatra, Ariadne, and the Madonna. Romola is compared to Antigone, Ariadne, Gostanza from Boccaccio's *Decameron*, and the Madonna. Gwendolen is compared to Saint Cecilia, Lamia, Hermione, Diana the huntress, and Rosalind in *As You Like It*. All three are compared to classical sculpture. The effect of this imbrication is to qualify and modify specific images. The passivity of the Virgin Mary is completlely eclipsed by the power and activity of the classical female deities while the frivolity and amorality that the Victorians associated with the classical deities is similarly eclipsed by the spirituality of the female saints. The androgynous imagery – the description of women by comparing them to men or to the masculine – contributes to monumentality by suggesting physical largeness and strength but also by suggesting that this heroine is not limited by her gender. Here George Eliot moves out of the realm of physical metaphor and suggests greater scope in qualities of mind, such as intellectuality, strength of will, or bravery, in which greatness is traditionally supposed to be restricted to men. But most importantly, androgynous imagery helps in the representation of heroines as fully human agents, in the evaluation of whom gender is not nearly as central as humanity.

Tree metaphors are also used to monumentalize the heroines. Maggie is compared to a hamadryad and, we are told, 'she seems to have a sort of kinship with the grand Scotch firs' (*The Mill on the Floss*, II: 49); Mrs Transome is compared to the thorn bushes in Dante's under world; Romola is 'as tall as the cypressses' (*Romola*, II: 406). All the heroines are tall, with the single exception of Dinah, whose monumentality is achieved by more complex means

> Dinah walked rather quickly, and in advance of her
> companions. . . . While she was near Seth's tall figure she
> looked short, but when she had mounted the cart, and was away
> from all comparison, she seemed above the middle height of
> woman, though in reality she did not exceed it – an effect which
> was due to the slimness of her figure.
>
> (*Adam Bede* I: 28–9)

Most of George Eliot's heroines walk quickly as an indicator of their energy and lack of self-consciousness, and one gets the feeling that they are all metaphorically in advance of their companions, but, unlike the other heroines, Dinah is tall only when seen away from men and at her work. Her slenderness intimates the energy and selflessness of her work and is also symbolic in that it makes her seem taller, more monumental. When Dinah is considering marriage she sees it in terms of taking for herself as opposed to her work which is giving to others. This ability to give to others, to starve one's own needs in catering for the needs of others, is what monumentalizes Dinah: paradoxically, her monumentality is the result of her emaciation. In the epilogue, Dinah is seen beside Seth and Adam, and she has become plump.

Peter Garrett implies that the spatial metaphor illuminates the comparative moral greatness of the women it is used to describe. It is certainly true that only the heroines, and not the other female characters that George Eliot repeatedly uses in counterpoint to her heroines, are represented monumentally. Dinah, Maggie, Romola, Dorothea, and Gwendolen are all described in terms likely to inspire awe rather than sensuality or protectiveness in men. Each has some sort of greatness about her, which is absent in the counterpoint characters, Hetty, Lucy, Tessa, Rosamond, and Mirah. The relationship between Mrs Transome and Esther is not one of straightforward counterpoint, but in this novel too monumental imagery is reserved for one female character only, for Mrs Transome, and for this and other reasons it is arguable that she is the heroine of *Felix Holt*. The monumentality of Mrs Transome and Gwendolen makes it clear that the scope of George Eliot's heroines does not necessarily correspond with moral greatness: both women are morally inferior to their counterpoint characters (Esther and Mirah). George Eliot, in painting her monumental heroines, is moving away from the Victorian model of virtue in women to her own more complex and challenging concept of greatness in women.

Having created monumental heroines whose very scope forbids the reader to pigeon-hole them in the less than human categories to which female characters have traditionally been relegated, George Eliot goes on to give them unashamedly womanly plots. The heroines' lives pose a two-fold problem: marriage and motherhood are inadequate outlets for their intellect and ardour, yet they are the only available vocations; but having invested their hopes in marriage, they find no adequate partner. A woman of conventional values, whether she be a Dorothea or a Rosamond, has been taught to seek a husband who is at least her intellectual equal and ideally her superior, whereas a man of similarly conventional values, Lydgate for example, has been taught to be content, or even delighted, with a wife who is his intellectual inferior. The problem with Rosamond is not her stupidity but her vanity and selfishness. Had Lydgate found a loving considerate helpmate of Rosamond's intellectual limitations, he might well have been perfectly happy. The George Eliot heroine finds herself ambitious without vocational possibility and passionate without an adequate object of love.

In their discussions of vocation and desire in women, George Eliot's narrators come to no definite conclusions. Their occasional certainties are questioned or refuted within the text by clashes of meaning and conflicts of mimetic and diegetic presentation. The heroines' plots pose sequences of questions, interleafed with sequences of tentative answers, some of which linger in qualified and still problematic forms, some of which are extinguished as the plots unfold.

A variety of difficult and fascinating questions concerning gender, character, and status surround George Eliot and her narratorial avatars. The subject deserves a book to itself, and its treatment here is necessarily partial and allusive. In the following chapters, 'George Eliot' indicates the implied author behind the works, while 'Marian Evans' and 'Marian Lewes' indicate the woman of the biography. The distinction between Marian Evans and Marian Lewes has its own complications: the former is the 'unmade woman', the younger, more transparent personality of the early letters and essays; the latter is complicated by the emergence of George Eliot and by her own efforts, both in fiction and in person, to remake and re-present herself. What is known to or characteristic of George Eliot is not necessarily known to or characteristic of Marian Lewes. Beyond this, the question of the gender(s) of the narrators is open to endless debate, and the feminine pronoun is used here for all but the contrivedly masculine narrators of *Scenes of Clerical Life, Adam Bede*, and 'The lifted veil', partly because one must choose a pronoun and partly in opposition to the critics who avoid it, one suspects, because they consider George Eliot's narrators too rational to be female. Gilbert and Gubar have most nearly resolved the problem when they claim: 'Doing in a woman's way a traditionally male task of knowing, combining "a man's mind and a woman's heart", Eliot makes such gender-based categories irrelevant . . . this narrator becomes an authentic "we" ' (Gilbert and Gubar 1979: 523).

The revised view of George Eliot that this chapter has been suggesting necessarily entails and is dependent upon, a revised view of her narrators. In *Problems of Life and Mind*, G H. Lewes gives a definition of a 'real' which could as easily serve as a description of George Eliot's novels: 'Every Real is the complex of so many relations, a conjunction of so many sensations, that to know one Real thoroughly could only be possible through an intuition embracing the universe' (Lewes 1874–9: I: 342–3). If this were a description of George Eliot's novels, the crucial question would be, is each of George Eliot's narrators possessed of 'an intuition embracing the universe'? Is each narrative like a Rubik's cube, the confusion and complexity of which is ultimately resolvable into a tidy and symmetrical solution? Or is the pleasure of George Eliot's texts a Barthesian pleasure taken in the proliferation of complexity, a pleasure sustained and heightened by the constant and ultimte deferral of a solution? Do George Eliot's novels function as Proust believed that all novels must, by asking more and more questions, being able to answer none?

After Bakhtin and Barthes it is no longer possible naïvely to declare that this or that sentence sums up a given author's 'message'. It is possible, however, to criticize an author for attempting such monologism, and Colin MacCabe has dismissed George Eliot on these grounds (MacCabe 1978: 15). David Lodge has taken issue with MacCabe in a fascinating close reading of the long paragraph in chapter 1 of *Middlemarch* which begins 'She was open, ardent, and not in the least self-admiring' (Kettle 1981: 219–38). Lodge establishes that the 'text outside the area of inverted commas' is not fully controlled by the narrator, as MacCabe suggests, but is in fact polyphonic. He does this with the deftness of a card dealer, sorting the various phrases into two piles: those voiced by the narrator and those voiced by Dorothea herself. However, this contains problems, and on close consideration Lodge's analysis can be seen as inadvertently strengthening MacCabe's point. Dorothea's voice might be heard outside inverted commas, but only such fragments of her discourse as can be used for the narrator's own ends. MacCabe might well reply that in that case the narrator is even more insidious, and even more thoroughly in control of the hierarchy of discourses than he had previously supposed, in that she has such complete control over Dorothea's discourse that she can use Dorothea's own language against her; the jokes at Dorothea's expense are achieved by the skilful manipulation of Dorothea's own language, which is trapped in the diegesis like a fly in amber.

The narrator of *Middlemarch* is a far less secure and constant presence than that suggested in the analyses of either MacCabe or Lodge. The figure MacCabe is reacting to – the 'wise women' narrator – certainly exists, but she is neither as ubiquitous nor as powerful as MacCabe assumes. At the points where the wise woman seems to be out of control or absent we glimpse an implied author who is very different from that earnest, authoritative, and sometimes irritatingly arch persona. Irritation with the narrator is rooted in the conviction that she is in complete control: once we detect cracks in what was the apparently smooth surface of her narrative, she becomes more interesting and less easily defined. An example can be found in the first half of the paragraph under discussion, which Lodge describes as frankly diegetic:

> She was open, ardent, and not in the least self-admiring; indeed, it was pretty to see how her imagination adorned her sister Celia with attractions altogether superior to her own, and if any gentleman appeared to come to the Grange from some other purpose than that of seeing Mr Brooke, she concluded that he must be in love with Celia: Sir James Chettam, for example, whom she constantly considered from Celia's point of view, inwardly debating whether it would be good for Celia to accept him. That he should be regarded as a suitor for herself would have seemed to her a ridiculous irrelevance. (I: 12)

There is a conflict of meaning between the first sentence and the last of this excerpt. That phrase 'not in the least self-admiring' seems to claim too much, and this impression is compounded when we find that in the case of Sir James's romantic aspirations becoming apparent to Dorothea, she would find it not a source of sympathetic pain, regret, and perhaps embarrassment, as one might expect from a woman who was 'not in the least self- admiring' but 'a ridiculous irrelevance'. The implication is that in that case Dorothea would be incensed, her pride offended, that Sir James, a mere 'amiable baronet', should thus aspire.

The impression, given by the opening clause, of claiming too much is not just a matter of diction but also of grammar and punctuation. The simple declaration of a triad of attributes, followed by a semicolon gives the statement an assertiveness which in retrospect and with the benefit of the last-quoted sentence seems to be a case of the narrator doth protest too much. Once we accept this, the smooth surface breaks up, the archness vanishes: complacent security and omniscience are replaced by an anxious rushing back and forth between extremes which anticipates the more explicit case of 'Was she beautiful or not beautiful?' in the opening of *Daniel Deronda*.

This is not only true of the narrator of *Middlemarch* but of all the narrators of George Eliot's major novels. Another instance is to be found in *The Mill on the Floss*. Several critics have remarked on the disjunction between the portrayal of the pains of childhood in the first

Book, 'Boy and girl', and the saccharine sentimentality of the closing lines of the penultimate chapter:

> The boat reappeared – but brother and sister had gone down in an embrace never to be parted: living through again in one supreme moment the days when they had clasped their little hands in love, and roamed the daisied fields together.
>
> (*The Mill on the Floss*, II: 400)

It is just possible that this is an instance of forgetting. George Eliot is not immune to forgetting; she changed the ending of *Middlemarch* because readers had justifiably objected to the claim that society had smiled upon the union of Dorothea and Casaubon. Nevertheless, it is arguable that in this image of daisied fields, George Eliot is fully conscious of her narrator's forgetfulness and is using it for pathos. Chapter 4 will discuss the relationship between the narrator of *The Mill on the Floss* and Maggie. This narrator too is chameleon-like, she shifts and changes, and her attitude to Maggie, like the *Middlemarch* narrator's attitude to Dorothea, is in flux. At times she is almost identical to Maggie and seems to function as Maggie's more powerful *alter ego*. In a letter, Marian Lewes wrote that childhood is only a happy time in retrospect. The implication is that our lives are so unfulfilling that we have to create a mythical fulfilment in the past, that the individual fallen human does what fallen humanity as a whole has done in Christian and other mythologies: creates a mythical beginning in which they were not fallen. The poignancy of this is exploited by George Eliot as she allows her narrator conspicuously to forget what is too painful to remember: that we never were fulfilled, nor are we likely to be so.

My final example is from *Felix Holt*. On the surface, it would appear that the narrator's attitude to Mrs Transome is one of concerned and sympathetic disapprobation, mixed with admiration for a character who, despite the unloving and even squalid aspects of her life, nevertheless retains a certain greatness. This much can be contained within a fairly predictable and conservative analysis of *Felix Holt* in which Mrs Transome's story yields a definable improving message. But the undermining of that potential analysis is latent in the idea of greatness. There is some indication that, like the tragic heroines of Sophocles, Mrs Transome's greatness not only survives the tainting elements of her life but is in fact derived from them: her greatness lies in her survival of suffering. This too can be contained within a slightly more complex but nevertheless conservative and coherent critical framework. The cracks begin to appear when we notice the reflexive elements in the characterization of Mrs Transome. These are several, and they will be discussed in detail in chapter 6, but for the purposes of this argument one example is of particular interest.

At the time she wrote *Felix Holt*, as for most of her career, George Eliot was in poor health, and her letters of the time are full of references to sickness and to medicines. It is interesting and probably not coincidental, then, that Mrs Transome is described as constantly fiddling with medicines: in chapter 1 (I: 34) we find her 'insisting on medicines for infirm cottagers', and we learn that she 'liked to change a labourer's medicine fetched from the doctor, and substitute a prescription of her own' (I: 43); in chapter 45 we are told that 'Mrs Transome was dressed just as usual, took her seat as usual, trifled with her drugs and had her embroidery before her as usual' (II: 287–8).

Once we have detected the reflexivity of the characterization of Mrs Transome, the narrator's attitude to her must be revaluated or at least put into a new perspective, but just as the implications of that reflexivity are becoming clear a second parallel comes to light: that between Mrs Transome and Mrs Holt, who is also associated with medicines. Both have troublesome sons who shame them by becoming Radicals; Mrs Transome's grandson, Harry, bites both of them; Mrs Transome lives in dread of anyone inquiring into her character, whereas Mrs Holt is always inviting people to inquire into hers. They are an image of tragedy and 'a tragedian whose part is in abeyance to an ill-timed introduction of the humorous' (II: 260). In this, again, we can see George Eliot's remarkable self-knowledge and her ability to lose herself in her narrative maze. Just as one decides that Mrs Transome is a critical self-portrait, and further suspect that there is something self-indulgent in giving one's own faults such minute and deadly serious scrutiny, up pops Mrs Holt, the tragic heroine is ridiculed, and the implied author vanishes from one's grasp.

In each of these examples, as in others that will come to light in the following chapters, the narrator emerges as genuinely self-divided and polyphonic, the 'wise woman' being just one aspect of a fluctuating presence in whom, as in Maggie Tulliver, 'a fierce collision is imminent'. The divisions between the radical and the conservative, the passional and the intellectual, the unconsciously betrayed and the consciously contrived in George Eliot's work are not static but dynamic. Their constant struggle, their lack of ultimate resolution, is itself a victory for the radical, passional, and unconscious in that it refuses the kind of hierarchy that MacCabe describes. The terms 'subconscious subversive' and 'conscious conservative', therefore, will not be employed to distinguish what Marian Lewes was and was not conscious of but rather to distinguish between what is openly acknowledged and what – either because it was subconscious or for reasons of self-protection – lies just beneath the surface of the text.

3

HETTY AND DINAH: THE BATTLE FOR PREDOMINANCE IN *ADAM BEDE*

The characterizations of Hetty Sorrel and Dinah Morris form the first full exploration of a dichotomy that is worked and reworked throughout the George Eliot canon. The first instance of this dichotomy, as Barbara Hardy has noted (Hardy 1959: 80–1), is the article entitled 'A little fable with a great moral', one of Marian Evans's earliest publications (Pinney 1963: 21–2). It describes the lives of two hamadryads, one of whom uses the lake as a mirror to examine her own beauty, while the other uses it as a mirror in which to explore the vastness of the heavens. The vain hamadryad sees herself growing old and ugly and dies in misery, while the soulful hamadryad grows old in peace, oblivious of her beauty and the loss of it. This simple tale provides the paradigm for all the major pairs of contrasting women in George Eliot's work: Hetty and Dinah, Tessa and Romola, Rosamond and Dorothea all correspond directly to the vain/soulful paradigm; Maggie and Lucy, Gwendolen and Mirah are rather more complex variations on it.

At first, this may seem to be another example of the harlot/madonna contrast which has pervaded western literature since the advent of Christianity. Here, however, the oppositions are not static but dynamic: George Eliot describes a struggle of opposites, each of which is ambivalently perceived, through which she discusses basic questions about how women should live, questions to which she has no preconceived answers, and which receive tentative, highly qualified, and increasingly sophisticated answers as the canon develops and the characterizations of these contrasting women become more and more complex.

Adam Bede is of particular critical interest in that its unresolved structural and aesthetic problems allow the critic a rare glimpse of the armatures beneath George Eliot's creative process. The reason for these problems in the novel seem to lie in George Eliot's own unresolved and highly problematic relation to the dichotomy as manifested in her own life and personality. Marian Lewes was both the female preacher and the fallen woman, both the soulful intellectual who pursued a vocation as moral leader and the woman with sexual needs who received the disapprobation of her community for gratifying them.

Seen in this light, the madonna/harlot dichotomy is clearly an inadequate critical tool for approaching George Eliot's contrasting heroines because it suggests a clear-cut division of good and evil – a division too simple and dismissive for a writer who must, however reluctantly, have identified with both the madonna and the harlot figures. For instance, at first glance the desire for a vocation seems to be an attribute of George Eliot's soulful madonna-like heroines, and sexual desire seems inextricably intertwined with the desire for gratified vanity and material wealth characteristic of her vain harlot-like characters. Yet the distinction between vocational and sexual desires is often blurred in George Eliot's work, as indeed it must be when discussing women, for whom marriage has been the only readily available vocational option.

In her own life, the emergence of her vocation coincided with the beginning of her long love affair with George Henry Lewes. Biographers have discussed Lewes's role as midwife in the birth of George Eliot the fiction writer: he encouraged her, helped overcome her reticence, and acted as her agent. These are services that a friend might have rendered, and the emergence of George Eliot at that particular moment might therefore be seen as a result of the catalystic effect of Lewes as friend rather than as lover, but certain passages from her letters encourage speculation about the relation between the termination of her long celibacy and the freeing of her creative powers. In 1855, she wrote to John Chapman: 'The day seems too short for our happiness and we both of us feel that we have begun life afresh – with new ambitions and new powers' (Letters VIII: 134), and in 1857, the year in which she began her career, she wrote the following to her friend, Mary Cash: 'I am very happy – happy in the highest blessing life can give us, the perfect love and sympathy of a nature that stimulates my own to healthful activity' (Letters II: 343).

This suggests a link between sexual and vocational energies quite at variance with both the Marxian view that the desire to work is a separate instinct (Bottomore 1963: 127) and the Freudian view that work is the sublimtion of thwarted sexual energies (Freud I: 136). It suggests that sexual fulfilment is connected with our relation to work, but that, far from lulling the individual into contented non-productivity, it releases productive energies hitherto benumbed by repression and its resultant unhappiness.

This notion is implicit in George Eliot's frequent intertwining of sexual and vocational desires by means of metaphor and juxtaposition, in the coexistence of sexual and vocational frustration in such heroines as Maggie and Dorothea, and above all, in the ideal set forth repeatedly in the novels, of love and duty flowing in one stream. However, in the cases of both Dinah and Dorothea, marriage supplants vocation, or the desire for vocation, without becoming a vocation in itself.

The reader is not encouraged to feel, at the end of *Adam Bede*, that marriage and motherhood have adequately replaced preaching as a vocation for Dinah. The final image of Dinah in the epilogue is diminished, eclipsed, in discouraging contrast to our first view of her in 'The preaching'. Nor do we feel at the end of *Middlemarch* that Dorothea has found fulfilment in marriage. For Dinah and Dorothea marriage is the extinction of vocational possibility, not the awakening of it, as it was for their author.

Possibly George Eliot recognized how exceptional her relationship with Lewes was and therefore left that rare combination out of her fictional explorations. The only approaches to it in the novels are marginal, like the relationship between Maggie and Philip Wakem and the marriage of Fred Vincy and Mary Garth: Philip and Maggie's early meetings in the Red Deeps reveal the possibility of a relationship of mutual learning and symbiotic growth between man and woman; similarly, Mary and Fred both write books after their marriage, having helped themselves and each other to realize their hidden potential. The more central sexual relationships, Dinah and Adam, Maggie and Stephen, Romola and Tito, Dorothea and Casaubon, Dorothea and Will, Gwendolen and Grandcourt, and even Gwendolen and Daniel, all involve an eclipse and diminution of the woman. In this, George Eliot is not simply describing the conventional subjection of women, because, as Marian Lewes's marriage indicates, the conjunction of vocational and sexual fulfilment can be attained despite that subjection. Her more disturbing suggestion is that most women, because of poor education, paucity of options, and the weaknesses of character produced by those disadvantages, would still be unable to choose an appropriate mate and to find a fulfilling vocation, even if such options presented themselves.

Dinah is an example of both these problems. Although George Eliot uses the historical fact of the exclusion of women from the Methodist ministry as the cause of Dinah's retirement, it is clear that marriage to Adam was likely to conflict with Dinah's work in any case. The 'original' for Dinah, Marian Lewes's aunt, Elizabeth Evans, did not set the example of submitting. In a letter of 1859, Marian Lewes told Sara Hennell that her aunt had '*left the society when women were no longer allowed to preach*, and joined the New Wesleyans' (Letters III: 175; Marian Lewes's emphasis). This is used at the end of the novel as the unrealized possibility that Seth has suggested and Dinah has rejected. Adam does not believe that women should be allowed to preach:

> 'What! are *ye* a-turnin' roun', Adam? I thought ye war dead
> again th' women preachin', a while agoo?'
> 'Nay, I'm not turnin' noway'
>
> (I: 8)

This dialogue is from the opening chapter, and Adam does develop and change as the action unfolds, but his attitude to women changes very little. The narrator tells us of a conversation with Adam in his old age, after a lifetime with Dinah, in which he is still capable of saying that someone is 'as ignorant as a woman' (I: 273). This, from the pen of a female intellectual, can hardly be inadvertency. Adam's uncompromising nature and attitude to women are unlikely to leave Dinah much scope for the development of her own aspirations. Seth, on the other hand, would have helped and supported her in her work, but Dinah does not fall in love with Seth. The main difference between Adam and Seth is the uncompromising strength that inevitably eclipses Dinah. In Dinah's choice of that strength over Seth's flexible mildness, George Eliot suggests that women in some measure desire that which entails their own subjection, that is to say that the attractions of the 'strong arm' to which George Eliot so frequently refers in her work are but the flip side of subjection. The strong arm is both an object of sexual desire and an instrument of oppression. The choice of the strong arm is reworked in *The Mill on the Floss* in Maggie's choice of Stephen over Philip. Whereas in *Adam Bede* the difference between Adam and Seth is strength of character rather than physical strength, in *The Mill on the Floss* Philip's short stature, effeminacy, and deformity are used both as literal impediments to the possibility of Maggie feeling for him sexually and as symbolic of her inability to be sexually attracted to the sort of man who would allow her to develop her own potential.

The second problem, that of finding a fulfilling vocation, is particularly complex in Dinah's case. How seriously are we to take Dinah's vocation? On the one hand it is clearly a way for George Eliot to discuss her own vocation, and as such, must be taken very seriously indeed. Through Dinah's preaching, George Eliot explores the power of language ('the Word was given to me abundantly' (I: 49)) and the problems of a woman taking on a pastoral role:

> The stranger had ceased to doubt, as he had done at the first
> glance, that she could fix the attention of her rough hearers, but
> still he wondered whether she could have that power of rousing
> their more violent emotions, which must surely be a necessary
> seal of her vocation.

(I: 37)

This is reminiscent of Lewes's doubts about George Eliot's abilities in fiction writing, which she recorded in her journal in 1857: 'There still remained the question whether I could command any pathos, and that was to be decided by the mode in which I treated Milly's death' (Letters II: 408).

Marian Lewes clearly saw herself as a sort of secular cleric, a teacher and moral guide, so her treatment of Dinah's vocation may well be, in part, a serious meditation on her own vocation. On the other hand, Dinah is a Methodist preacher created by an agnostic author.[1] This not only encourages us to interpret Dinah's ministrations in a secular light but also casts real doubt on the value of at least some of her work. This divided attitude creates a fascinating dialectic in 'The preaching', similar to the dialectic in 'The workshop' and in the first chapter of *Middlemarch*. In all three chapters, an apparently exemplary character is viewed with an odd mixture of admiration and irony from two conflicting perspectives contained within one apparently consistent narrative. In 'The workshop', we are clearly meant to see Adam as a cut above the other workmen. However, the humour with which George Eliot paints Wiry Ben reveals a love of the comic completely absent from Adam's character, and this contrast between the character and his narrator stresses the impression that Adam, though admirable, is also a humourless prig. In chapter 7 the similar ambivalence in our introduction to Dorothea will be discussed at length.

In all three cases, detractions are gentle but significant. They provide a tension within the narrative and demand reader participation in the formation of judgements. The affectionate description of the sins of Sandy Jim and especially of Chad's Bess casts Dinah's passionate pleading in an equivocal light:

> The gentle tones, the loving persuasion, did not touch her, but when the more severe appeals came she began to be frightened. Poor Bessy had always been considered a naughty girl; she was conscious of it; if it was necessary to be very good, it was clear she must be in a bad way. She couldn't find her places at church as Sally Rann could, she had often been tittering when she 'curcheyed' to Mr Irwine, and these religious deficiencies were accompanied by a corresponding slackness in the minor morals, for Bessy belonged unquestionably to that unsoaped, lazy class of feminine characters with whom you may venture to eat 'an apple, an egg, or a nut'.
>
> (I: 37)

Is this diegesis, or is it another case, like the *Middlemarch* example discussed in chapter 2 (pp. 29–30), of a character's discourse being caught and framed within the narrator's discourse? Clearly this is the way that Bess herself feels about her sins, but is it also the way the narrator feels about them? Is it possible for a narrator who fully endorses Dinah's view of the gravity of such sins to adopt the terms 'naughty' and 'minor morals' when hinting at sexual availability ('an apple, an egg, or a nut, you may eat though dressed by a slut' *Oxford Dictionary of Proverbs*: 17)?[2] We are made to feel that Dinah is trying to deny the villagers the few harmless pleasures available to them.

W. J. Harvey has noted that Chad's Bess is a foreshadowing of Hetty (Haight 1966: 300). This connection encourages the reader to hark back to 'The preaching', with all its narratorial ambivalence, when reading that second and more important instance of Dinah's preaching, 'In the prison'. But the narrator assures us that Dinah will not have a lasting effect: 'the village mind does not easily take fire, and a little smoldering vague anxiety, that might easily die out again, was the utmost effect Dinah's preaching had wrought in them at present' (I: 38). Dinah's work, then, is portrayed as potentially detrimental but actually ineffectual. And there are strong indications that her passion for ministry is in fact sublimated sexual energy. Her portrait of Christ is intensely personal and physical:

> 'Ah! wouldn't you love such a man if you saw him – if he was here in this village? what a kind heart he must have!'
>
> (I: 35)

> 'See!' she exclaimed, turning to the left, with her eyes fixed on a point above the heads of the people – 'see where our blessed Lord stands and weeps, and stretches out his arms towards you.'
>
> (I: 40)

The idea of the confusion of religious and sexual feeling has already been touched on in the context of Seth's love for Dinah:

> Love of this sort is hardly distinguishable from religious feeling. What deep and worthy love is so? whether of woman or child, or art or music. Our caresses, our tender words, our still rapture under the influence of autumn sunsets, or pillared vistas, or calm majestic statues, or Beethoven symphonies, all bring with them the consciousness that they are mere waves and ripples in an infathomable ocean of love and beauty; our emotion in its keenest moment passes from expression into silence, our love at its highest flood rushes beyond its object, and loses itself in the sense of divine mystery.
>
> (I: 51)

In light of this, Dinah's religious meditations in her bed- chamber take on a broader secular and sexual significance. During the day that culminates in 'The two bed-chambers', Dinah has met Adam for the first time:

> Dinah, for the first time in her life, felt a painful self-consciousness; there was something in the dark penetrating glance of this strong man so different from the mildness and timidity of his brother Seth. A faint blush came, which deepened as she wondered at it.
>
> (I: 173)

William Myers has pointed out that Dinah's concern over Hetty's future travails can be seen as sadistic fantasies about her rival in Adam's love (Myers 1984: 148). Certainly Adam has been on her mind all day, as is evident in her conversations with the Poysers.

When Dinah returns from the Bedes', Mr and Mrs Poyser each enquire about Lisbeth; on both occasions, Dinah's response moves quickly from the subject of Lisbeth to that of Adam (I: 214, 218). Adam is, therefore, ⁻conceivably the actual though consciously unrecognized object of her religious meditations:

> She closed her eyes, that she might feel more intensely the presence of a Love and Sympathy deeper and more tender than was breathed from the earth and sky. That was often Dinah's mode of praying in solitude. Simply to close her eyes, and to feel herself enclosed by the Divine Presence; then gradually her fears, her yearning anxieties for others, melted away like ice-crystals in a warm ocean.

> (I: 235)

The succession of verbs in this passage describes the systole and diastole of female sexual response: closed, feel, breathed, close, feel, enclosed, melted. Read in conjunction with a letter from Marian Evans to Maria Lewis in 1840 it suggests that George Eliot was drawing on her own youthful religiosity as a case study of this very issue of the sublimation of sexual passion into religious zeal:

> I feel that a sight of one being whom I have not beheld except passingly since the interview I last described to you would *probably* upset *all*; but as it is, the image now seldom arises in consequence of entire occupation and, I trust in some degree, desire and prayer to be free from rebelling against Him whose I am by right, whose I would be by adoption. I endeavoured to pray for the beloved object to whom I have alluded, I must still a little while say *beloved*, last night and felt soothingly melted in thinking that if mine be really prayers my acquaintance with him has probably caused the *first* to be offered up specially in his behalf.

> (Letters I: 46–7. Marian Evans's emphasis)

If Dinah's religion that is her vocation, is in large part a sublimation of sexual feeling, there should be no sense of loss, but on the contrary a sense of completion and realization in her marriage to Adam. However, certain small details prevent us from feeling this, just as we are prevented from feeling satisfied with Dorothea's lot in the finale of *Middlemarch*. Dinah's children are named Adam and Lisbeth, a reconstitution of the original Bede family which seems to deny and exclude Dinah herself; Seth says that Dinah has taken over Lisbeth's role of watching for Adam, a chilling thought when we remember the nature and lot of Lisbeth; but perhaps most disturbing is the discussion of the Conference decision to stop women from preaching. Adam argues Dinah's motives on her behalf, which is in itself disquieting, but then those motives sound far more like Adam's own reasoning than Dinah's. Dinah did not contest the Conference decision because ' "Most o' the women do more harm nor good with their preaching – they've not got Dinah's gift nor her sperrit; and she's seen that, and she thought it right to set th' example o' submitting" ' (II: 378).

George Eliot's heroines often set the example of submitting: Romola drops to her knees before Savonarola; Esther submits to Felix; Dorothea submits to wifedom and motherhood; Gwendolen submits to Daniel. Submissiveness is a positivist virtue, that is to say a Christian virtue rationalized into secular application by positivist philosophy. Marian Lewes clearly intends to recommend it, but the texts themselves subvert her intention, which is hardly surprising in the work of a woman who seldom submitted and was remarkably self-assertive and defiant. The descriptions of the heroines in a state of independence and non-submission are monumental; the language describing them in a state of submission is a language of diminution. In the early part of the novel, Dinah is monumentalized by images of incorporeality. She is an angel, a ghost, a risen Christ.[3] For this reason, the two references in the epilogue to Dinah's plumpness surprise and disturb the reader. They seem inappropriate, almost humiliating, rather like the portrait of the matronly Natasha at the end of *War and Peace*. The mode of description makes one feel that some essential individualizing and elevating quality has been lost and that she who formerly seemed unique has now joined the undifferentiated herd of mothers. It is a description of motherhood quite unlike the description of Mrs Ramsay in *To the Lighthouse*, for example, who is monumentalized by motherhood.

Dinah's story, then, ends on an unresolved and unsatisfying note. The only heroine in any of the George Eliot novels who has a definite vocation chooses a marriage which is bound to conflict with her work, relinquishes her work without apparent pain, and subsides into the role of helpmate and mother. The feeling of 'subsiding' is imparted by the narrator's choice of detail in the epilogue and is in complete contradiction to the strain of evidence suggesting that the desire for sexual fulfilment was at the root of Dinah's preaching all along, evidence which should, to be consistent, lead to a more affirmative description of Dinah's wifedom and motherhood. The only interpetation that makes sense of this equivocal ending is that which sees vocation and sexual fulfilment as mutually affecting but essentially separate needs which, in the case of women, because of various internal and external impediments (women's sexual preference for the 'strong arm'; cultural attitudes which perpetuate the subjection of women) can rarely be simultaneously fulfilled. Nevertheless, the intimate connection between these needs renders the complete satisfaction of one impossible if the other is denied and frustrated. The celibate with a vocation will work less well, the lover without a vocation will love less completely, than will the individual who finds fulfilment in both hemispheres of her life.

This discussion, so far, has focused on Dinah as if she were the centre, the heroine of the novel. The novel's structure, beginning and ending with Dinah and Adam, suggests that this is the emphasis George Eliot intended. However, critics generally agree that Hetty, not Dinah, is at the centre of *Adam Bede*. This is not a recent critical prioritization. An anonymous Victorian reviewer referred to Hetty as 'the central figure', and Henry James saw her as George Eliot's most successful young woman.[4] Françoise Basch's remarks on the writing of *Adam Bede* offer a possible partial explanation of this conflict between authorial intention and finished text:

> The novel was originally supposed to end with Hetty's execution
> . . . and it was at the instigation of G. H. Lewes that the author
> decided to marry [Dinah] off to Adam. Dinah dominates the last
> section as a result of a change grafted on as an afterthought.
>
> (Basch 1974: 252)

Gillian Beer points out that the landscape described at the beginning of 'The preaching' takes the form of Hetty's body, while the presence of sorrel foreshadows Hetty (Beer 1986: 61–2). In addition, I would say that since the description serves to place Dinah and her preaching in context, the fact that the landscape *is* Hetty, that Hetty metaphorically contains Dinah, gives Hetty enormous importance and arguable ascendancy over Dinah from the beginning of the novel.

Hetty, it seems to me, became a kind of Frankenstein's monster for George Eliot. Created for a specific and limited purpose, Hetty breaks her confines and threatens to take over the novel. The narrator's lack of sympathy for Hetty defeats its apparent purpose – it wins readers to Hetty perhaps more than a gentler treatment would have done. Hetty

is a thoroughly subversive figure: at odds with her community, disliked by her narrator, and ultimately evicted from the novel of which
she threatened to become the unquestionable centre, her strength and
stature are a victory of what can be seen as the subconscious subversive in George Eliot, whereas Dinah is a product of the conscious
conservative moralist in her author. This formulation, like any formulation about George Eliot's art, is crude and oversimplified: the narration of Hetty's story is dominated by the conscious moralist, and it is
only the failure of the narrator to alienate us from Hetty that enables
us to see Hetty's power as a product of the subconscious subversive.
Similarly, the equivocal ending of Dinah's story, and the diminishing
imagery of Dinah after her submission is clearly the work of the subconscious subversive, questioning and undermining what is otherwise
a successful creation of the conservative moralist: a character who
typifies and advocates selflessness and submission, the traditional
virtues of women. That is to say, what George Eliot tells us elevates
Dinah and condemns Hetty, but what she shows us tends to question
Dinah and vindicate Hetty.

To return to the beginning of the novel, Hetty, like Dinah and
Adam, is introduced to us in the context of her work. The titles of the
three chapters which introduce Adam, Dinah, and Hetty are (respectively) 'The workshop', 'The preaching', and 'The dairy'. All three
characters are introduced by their occupations, are seen as central
objects in their places of work.

> The dairy was certainly worth looking at: it was a scene to sicken
> for with a sort of calenture in hot and dusty streets – such
> coolness, such purity, such fresh fragrance of new-pressed
> cheese, of firm butter, of wooden vessels perpetually bathed
> in pure water; such soft colouring of red earthenware and
> creamy surfaces, brown wood and polished tin, grey limestone
> and rich orange-red rust on the iron weights and hooks and
> hinges.
>
> (I: 120)

The colours of the dairy are Hetty's colours (red, creamy, brown);
its attributes are Hetty's attributes, as Arthur perceives them
(coolness, purity, fragrance, firmness). The description of the dairy
and the process of butter-making is seen by the reader and the narrator, intimately engaged, watching them through Arthur's eyes. All
three observers, reader, narrator, and Arthur, are sufficiently

removed from what is probably the monotony and aggravation of butter-making to see it in a romantic light, but enjoying the sensuousness of butter-making does not necessarily require the perspective of the non-butter-maker. Mrs Poyser obviously feels the same way, although it is important to remember that the relation of the dairy-owner to butter-making must be more satisfying than that of the dairy-worker. We are told that Hetty is a good butter-maker, yet her experience of her work is not ours or Mrs Poyser's. She sees it as something that coarsens her hands. (Marian Evans had experience in butter-making when she lived with her father, and she also noticed its effect on her hands (Blind 1884: 20).) If Hetty did see butter-making as the narrator and Mrs Poyser see it, if she had any attachment to or felt the value of her life at the beginning of the novel, she probably would never have got into trouble, but that does not illegitimize her view of butter-making. Hetty's indifference to her work is used, together with her indifference to children, animals, and the Poyser home, to discredit her. But there is actually no reason for the dairy-worker to love the dairy as the dairy-owner does, for Totty's baby-sitter to love her as her mother does, or for a penniless relation tolerated in the home as an act of charity and source of cheap labour to love that home in the way a daughter of the family would.

The case built up against Hetty seems particularly weak when we see it, as we are encouraged to do, in contrast to Dinah. There is something either unconvincing or unhealthy about Dinah's indiscriminate and forced loving. Her love for Snowfield is like her loving treatment of Lisbeth. In both cases the object of love is distinctly unlovable, and the decision to love is just that – a decision, not a spontaneous emotional reaction. Again, Marian Lewes clearly intends to recommend this, and Lisbeth's abrasiveness is probably developed to underline the moral necessity of loving despite the unlovableness or perhaps in proportion to the unlovableness of the love object. On the surface, this seems selfless to the point of masochism but beneath it lurks the egoism of the martyr. In a letter of 1842 to Maria Lewis, Marian Evans wrote,

> The martyr at the stake seeks its gratification as much as the court sycophant, the difference lying in the comparative dignity and beauty of the two egos. People absurdly talk of self-denial – why there is none in Virtue to a being of moral

excellence – the greatest torture to such a soul would be to
run counter to the dictates of conscience, to wallow in the slough
of meanness, deception, revenge or sensuality.

(Letters I: 127)

The implication of this is that everyone is motivated by self-
interest, but some people, by accident of congenital disposition or
early training, find it in their own interest to act in a way that serves
the purposes of altruism.[5] It follows that the simplicity of Hetty's
egoism is an accident of nature or other circumstances beyond her
control. She acts simply and honestly from her true motives, and to a
modern reader, she provides a welcome relief from the artificiality of
Dinah's forced selflessness.

This is not a matter of reading against the grain: Dinah's concealed
egoism is briefly but repeatedly exposed to us in a sleight of hand
technique that will become familiar as the George Eliot canon unfolds.
I have already touched on this aspect of 'The preaching' and 'The two
bed-chambers'; it is also present at the beginning of the chapter
entitled 'A vocation'. Dinah remarks of Irwine, 'What a well-
favoured countenance! Oh that the good seed might fall on that soil,
for it would surely flourish' (I: 128). Is this not rather vain and condescending? We know that Irwine is a good man. It does not matter
that he is a vicar of the Church of England; George Eliot shows us
repeatedly in her fiction that goodness can be found under cover of any
belief, as can egoism. That Dinah assumes that Irwine has need of 'the
good seed' simply because he is not of her sect shows a narrowness and
vanity in her that was never present in her author.

Rather than a simple opposition of Dinah the madonna versus
Hetty the harlot, we have in *Adam Bede* an opposition of oppositions, a
dialectic in which each term is itself a dialectic. Dinah and Hetty are
opposites, but within Dinah is the prior opposition we glimpsed in
'The preaching'. Is Dinah an admirable woman with a vocation who
works selflessly and with positive results for the community? Or is she
a repressed egoist who unconsciously disguises her egoism as altruism,
her sexuality and vanity as religous vocation, and her desire for ascendancy over Hetty, both in the affections of the man, Adam Bede, and
the battle for centrality in the novel, *Adam Bede*, as a sincere and
disinterested desire to help? Similarly, is Hetty a vain and heartless
opportunist who meets with condign punishment, or a blameless 18
year-old girl who is crucified for the sins of others, not least of women

like Dinah who falsify their own, and by extension their gender's, true motives and desires?

Marian Lewes claimed the first in each pair of alternatives. In a letter of 1858 to John Blackwood she worte 'I am especially pleased that you appear to feel with me about my pet characters – Adam and Dinah' (Letters VIII: 201), and in her journal she wrote:

> Dinah's ultimate relation to Adam was suggested by George, when I had read to him the first part of the first volume: he was so delighted with the presentation of Dinah and so convinced that the readers' interest would centre in her, that he wanted her to be the principal figure at the last. I accepted the idea at once, and from the end of the third chapter worked with it constantly in view.
>
> (Letters II: 503)

Nevertheless, the strength of *Adam Bede* lies in the uneasy coexistence of these oppositions, the submerged insistence of the latter readings. The possibility that the subversive is subconscious not only in the sense of being below the acknowledged consciousness of the text but also literally subconscious in Marian Lewes herself is supported by her account, in a letter, of the writing of 'The journey in despair': 'The opening of the third volume – Hetty's journey – was, I think written more rapidly than the rest of the book, and was left without the slightest alteration of the first draught' (Letters II: 504). George Eliot, as novelist and great moralist of her time, managed to supersede Marian Lewes, the single woman who lived openly with a married man, in the consciousness of Victorian England, and perhaps this is not irrelevant to an examination of the novel with which she succeeded in accomplishing that difficult task.

Book One of *Adam Bede* introduces us to Dinah, then to Hetty, and develops the two women in contrast to each other, but by the beginning of Book Two Dinah has returned to Snowfield, and she does not reappear in the novel until Book Five. In Dinah's absence, Hetty's story engrosses the reader so completely that Dinah is more or less forgotten. This is partly because Dinah leaves us with no unanswered questions of sufficient interest to preoccupy us in her absence, but mostly because Hetty's predicament raises her to a level of universality and suffering on which her limitations become irrelevant. Hetty is transfigured by her suffering. The animal imagery used to diminish her in Book One has a different effect during her 'journey in despair':

her animal nature, which before made her seem petty and trivial in contrast with Dinah's spirituality, now becomes awesome in its own right, so that when Hetty kisses her own arms with joy to be alive, her vitality gives her a dignity and significance beside which Dinah's Methodist enthusiasm seems pale and deformed. One of the most sympathetic animal images of Hetty is one that will only become apparent on a second reading. When we are first introduced to Arthur, he reveals his opinion of *Lyrical Ballads* (produced by Wordsworth and Coleridge the year before that in which the action of the beginning of the novel is set). Arthur dislikes Wordsworth's contributions (a bad sign) but is uncomprehendingly impressed by *The Ancient Mariner* (I: 94). On a second reading, Arthur's lack of understanding of the poem has a tragic irony: in the story that follows he will play mariner to Hetty's albatross. U. C. Knoepflmacher has suggested that the child is the albatross, the innocent killed by lack of thought and feeling in both Arthur and Hetty (Knoepflmacher 1968: 95). However, the fact that Arthur is alone in this first reference to *The Ancient Mariner* and the fact that Hetty, as I shall establish, becomes the Christ figure of the latter half of the novel, suggests that the image is being used in both ways.

Hetty is nature beside Dinah's civilization, Eros beside Dinah's Logos, and the movement of the novel up to the end of the 'journey in despair' – a movement which I maintain was beyond George Eliot's control – is from a worship of language, civilization, law and order, and spirituality, to a worship of desire, nature, anarchy, and physicality.[6]

At this point, the point at which George Eliot is losing control of the values in her own novel, the artistry begins to crumble. It crumbles because the artist is involved in a desperate effort to recapture and reassert the values she consciously set out to support. The organic movement of the novel away from Dinah and toward Hetty is deliberately thwarted by a series of plot convolutions which remove the problem of Hetty without solving it. If we feel too much for Hetty at the end of the 'journey in despair', the infanticide is calculated to dispel that sympathy, yet Hetty's confession in the prison is not the confession of a crime but the account of a state of semi-consciousness in which what little reason Hetty ever had has deserted her.

In the courtroom, Adam has a moment of hope: the fact that Hetty took the baby from Sarah Stone's house proves that she had, at that point, no intention of murder. In Adam's mind, this hope is dispelled by the testimony of John Olding, but John Olding's testimony merely establishes Hetty's actions: she is none the less innocent of the intention to murder her child. Adam's despair when he hears Olding's testimony implies that he sees no distinction between action and intention, yet George Eliot, we know, was deeply interested, as was Dostoyevsky, in this distinction.[7] In 'Mr Gilfil's love story', in the story of Laure in *Middlemarch*, and Gwendolen's story in *Daniel Deronda*, George Eliot examines, with a clarity that anticipates Freud, the extent to which the intention is equal to the act. This calls to mind Ivan's courtroom speech in *The Brothers Karamazov*, in which he asks, 'Who has not wished to kill his father?' (a question which is heavily underlined in Freud's copy). Whereas Tina, Laure, and Gwendolen are guilty of the intention to murder but arguably innocent of the act, Hetty, on the contrary, is guilty of the act but innocent of the intention. Adam's failure to see this distinction enables him more readily to dismiss Hetty as evil and get on with his life.

Hetty's innocence of intention also calls into question the efficacy of Dinah's ministrations in the prison cell. If she has not acted with malicious intention, Hetty has no sin to confess. Certainly, from a secular point of view, we are supposed to see Dinah's human presence in the cell as good, regardless of how she spends her time there. Yet the question nags at us: why is an agnostic author apparently trying to win our admiration for her heroine, Dinah, by making her battle with an already war-torn 18-year-old girl on the eve of her execution? The answer, I think, has already been given. What Hetty must repent of is not the murder of her child but the usurpation of Dinah's place in the novel. Dinah's battle with Hetty is a battle for repossession of that novel. Through it, the conscious conservative in George Eliot seeks to re-establish the supremacy of language, culture, law and order, spirituality, values which have been undermined by Hetty in Dinah's absence. It is perhaps no accident that when Dinah first enters the cell she refers to herself in the third person, saying, 'Hetty . . . Dinah is come to you' (II: 240), when we remember that the name 'Dinah' means 'judgement'. This is why the narrator forces from Hetty such unconvincing statements as, 'I wouldn't mind if they'd let me live' (II: 243). Hetty does mind, and she did mind before she was arrested and faced with the prospect of execution. How else can we explain her auditory hallucination of the child crying after the time of its death? Or her return to the place where she abandoned the child because she could not bear the sound of crying – which is the cause of her arrest?

How, then, can we construe, 'I wouldn't mind if they'd let me live' other than as a sign of collapse of meaning? The prison scene is an inflated and more significant version of 'The preaching', in which the sinners whom Dinah is calling to repentance are not truly sinners. We feel rather that Hetty has been sinned against, and will be sinned against more grievously after the verdict. We feel that she has been and will continue to be tortured simply for being human, female, and simple-minded.

Hetty's suffering is the source of her strength in the novel. As in Dostoyevsky's novels, the character who has sinned and suffered for those sins is elevated by suffering to a point where the non-sinner seems pale and dwarfish by comparison. Dinah, in contrast does not suffer personally in this novel. Her closest approach is vicarious involvement with the sufferings of others. Adam's suffering is unconvincing, despite the narrator's efforts to awaken our interest in it, partly because he recovers so quickly and marries Dinah, and partly because it is insignificant next to Hetty's suffering. Arthur exasperates us at the end of the novel, not necessarily because we feel he is to blame but because he is equally at fault – yet he suffers nothing in comparison. In fact, suffering dissociates itself from the concepts of blame and punishment during Hetty's travails. In the 'journey in despair', Hetty is simply a living being in pain, and as such demands our sympathy: the extent to which she is blameworthy becomes irrelevant.

Myers attacks this elevation of suffering by applying Nietzsche's slave-mentality argument from *The Genealogy of Morals* (Myers 1984: chapter 7). On the narratorial level of formulation, judgement, and editorial comment, George Eliot is certainly open to this charge: throughout the canon, until she creates Gwendolen Harleth, George Eliot focuses on selflessness, submission, renunciation, and meekness, although it is important to remember that these attributes are the hard-won achievements of heroines by nature anything but meek. Nietzsche's argument focuses on the slave-mentality of the Jews, but it has certainly been inherited by Christians, and recently by the extreme political left. ('The meek shall inherit the earth' has obvious secular applications). Myers does not take account of the political spectrum possible within the confines of slave-mentality and attacks George Eliot for her conservatism, on the assumption that slave-mentality is inherently conservative. In fact, slave-mentality can embrace various political colours, just as master-mentality can lead to ancient Athens or Nazi Germany. The glorification of Hetty's suffering can either be seen as a morbid worship of suffering for its own sake, conservative in that it reaffirms the slave-mentality values by which the ruling class buys off the less fortunate with myths of a posthumous redistribution of wealth, or it can be seen as a radical demand for change by highlighting the suffering of women and labourers at the hands of men and landowners.

Hetty becomes, as Myers points out, a Christ figure, an icon of extreme suffering with which readers can identify all their own lesser sufferings (Myers 1984: 36). John Goode has argued that 'Hetty is a deceptive appearance behind which is the reality of Dinah' (Hardy 1970: 32). Myers's argument that Hetty replaces Dinah as Christ figure can be used to support the opposite view: that Dinah is the deceptive appearance behind which we find the reality of Hetty. I would append to Myers's evidence the fact that the image of Dinah as 'a lovely corpse' (I: 238) is transferred to Hetty during her journey. When Hetty finds that Arthur is no longer at Windsor, she faints, and is described as a 'beautiful corpse' (II: 132). This is the moment at which Hetty takes over as Christ figure, and her suffering provides such a rich background for the image (Christ's significance, after all, lies in his suffering) that it seems, for the first time, to have found its true place.

Because of this, her transportation from the centre of the novel disappoint the reader. It is a strain to turn our attention to Dinah and Adam. The fact that they have neither sinned nor suffered to any appreciable extent makes it more difficult than ever to empathize with them.

Several critics have noted similarities between Hetty's story in *Adam Bede, Tess of the D'Urbervilles*, and *The Scarlet Letter*. The most significant difference between these stories is that the male novelists found it easier to sympathize with the fallen woman than did the female novelist whose personal experience might lead one to expect a deeper sympathy. However, that would be a naïve expectation. George Eliot had much to lose by openly sympathizing with female sexual delinquency; Hardy and Hawthorne, as men and novelists whose private lives had remained within the pale of conventional respectability, had comparatively little to lose.

4

DEMONISM, FEMINISM, AND INCEST IN
THE MILL ON THE FLOSS

The three elements of my title have been discussed separately by Nina
Auerbach, Elizabeth Ermarth, and David Smith (Auerbach 1975;
Ermarth 1974; Smith 1965). These three analyses yield radically different visions of the novel and especially of the heroine, Maggie
Tulliver. Auerbach discusses the demonic images around Maggie,
but evades interpreting them by declaring at the outset that this is a
'perspectiveless novel'. Therefore the article leaves us with the
impression that Maggie is evil or at least manipulative. Ermarth sees
Maggie as a woman crippled by her environment, the result of the
debilitating effects of oppression and poor education on the female
mind. Smith sees Maggie as an example of abnormal psychology. It is
my contention that these three elements work together in the novel,
and that the vision they yield is neither internally contradictory nor
essentially negative, as the findings of these critics would suggest.

The novel opens with the narrative character, not simply a voice in
this case, in an act of reconstructing the past which anticipates, and
strongly influenced, Proust. Unlike George Eliot's earlier narrators,
this voice is feminine. The absence of the intrusive and artificial assertions of maleness in the narrator, such as are frequently found in the
earlier work, unites with a new impressionistic sensibility in the narrator of 'Outside Dorlcote Mill' to give the reader the impression that
the narrator is female. This is reinforced by such narratorial comments as 'I am afraid to think how long it is since fan-shaped caps were
worn' (I: 8), in which both the attention to fashion and the coyness
about age seem calculated to suggest a female narrator. She is also
clearly remembering her own past: 'I remember those large dipping
willows . . . I remember the stone bridge' (I: 4). The reader tends,
therefore, to identify the narrator with Maggie, which introduces, in

the opening chapter, the largest problem of the novel as a whole: Maggie's death. If this is an autobiographical fiction, the very fact of narration falsifies Maggie's death at the end. Maggie's story is clearly not Marian Evans's history, but it has so many elements in common, so many close parallels, that the ending seems like a fantasy of suicide in the author. This problem can be resolved with the help of Barbara Hardy's idea of 'possibilities' in George Eliot's fiction (Hardy 1958: 135–6). In Maggie's life, George Eliot explores an unrealized possibility of her own life. Maggie is the other possible Marian Evans who never left her home, never broke the ties most sacred to her, never discovered the George Eliot in herself. The only end that George Eliot can see for such a life is frustration, a deathlike life, or death itself come early.

This reading of George Eliot's relation to Maggie opposes Leavis's contention that in Maggie 'there is an element of self-idealization' (Leavis 1948: 56). The central difference between Maggie and her author is not beauty, purity of intention, or any of the minor variations that seem to be accounted for by Leavis's rather condescending analysis: it is a fundamental difference of life decision. George Eliot, as the woman who decided differently and thereby gained the fulfilment of her life both in terms of work and love, must necessarily be critical of Maggie. Her relation to Maggie is extremely ambivalent. Far from being a self-indulgent weakness, as Leavis would have us believe, it provides the central tension of the work.

Incest is related to retentiveness in that it is one manifestation of the desire to retain or conserve original attachments. Freud's essay 'Character and anal eroticism, (Freud VII: 205–15) is strongly suggestive of these connections, and examines the relation between demonism and anal retentiveness; Michael Steig has discussed the issue of anal retentiveness in *The Mill on the Floss* (Steig 1971). Maggie's incestuous love for Tom, seen in this light, is connected with the wider conservatism of George Eliot's thought, the cultural, aesthetic, and political retentiveness that pervades her work. The connection is made explicit when Maggie tells Philip that she loves Tom because it was holding his hand that she first saw the Floss (II: 61). The incestuous implication of this is clear given the sexual symbolism of the river in the novel, but the idea of valuing this sexual connection *because it was the first* relates her feelings for Tom to the highly emotional passages describing the narrator's preference for the landscape of her childhood, and to George Eliot's interest in life-long loves (Fred and Mary in *Middlemarch* and Gilfil's love for Tina in *Scenes of Clerical Life*). The underlying assumption is that we are inextricably interwoven with the people and places of our childhood, that these people and places moulded our aesthetic and moral tastes, and that we are therefore unable to judge things on objective moral or aesthetic grounds. This primitive bias means that for each individual new elements are *a priori* bad because they are discontinuous with his life and personality, whereas old elements are *a priori* good because they are of one fabric with his life and personality. Applied to culture, George Eliot's retentiveness informs her cherishing treatment of 'Old Christmas' in *The Mill on the Floss*, 'Old leisure' in *Adam Bede*, and the old way of travelling on a coach in the introduction to *Felix Holt*. Applied to aesthetics, it yields her diatribe against the corruption of the English language by non-native speakers in *The Impressions of Theophrastus Such* (283–4). Applied to politics, it yields her fear of the trade union man and the rabble in *Felix Holt*.

The formless yearning that Maggie feels, like Dorothea's yearning in *Middlemarch*, can be understood in light of this Freudian and Proustian obsession with the past. Various critics have seen this yearning as something impossible to fulfil. No epic life, no perfect marriage, no great achievement or vocation will satisfy it. At the height of her career, Marian Lewes is reported to have said, 'I am so tired of being set on a pedestal and expected to vent wisdom' (Haight 1968: 256), evincing a lingering dissatisfaction, even though she had become the leading novelist of her day and had spent twenty-five years in what seems a near perfect union with G. H. Lewes. This is the peculiar problem of the individual who has fulfilled her early aspirations and can therefore no longer explain her dissatisfaction in terms of frustrated possibility. Dissatisfaction becomes depoliticized: social and economic restraints having been overcome, the source of dissatisfaction can no longer be located in a potentially changeable political context and is therefore attributed to the human condition itself, that is to say, the yearning for something more than the present offers moves from the realm of the possible to that of the utterly hopeless.

This explains why George Eliot rarely shows her heroines making sincere energetic attempts to actualize their yearning for something better: in Maggie and Dorothea it remains a formless longing, never really acted upon; in Dinah the attempt to follow a vocation is reliquished with little pain; in Gwendolen it is ridiculed. The only women in the works of George Eliot who attempt anything as ambitious as George Eliot's own work, Armgart and Alcharisi, are seen as embittered, hardened, and unfulfilled. Yet Daiches is, I think, wrong when we suggests that the central values of *Middlemarch* lie with Mary Garth, who has no ridiculous epic aspirations (Daiches 1963: 57). No matter how insatiable Maggie's yearning nor how groundless Dorothea's pretentions, the yearning itself is seen as a positive value, just as, in *Adam Bede*, as William Myers has remarked, Dinah and Adam are valued above other characters because of the intensity of their yearning for God and Hetty respectively, two love objects whose existence, as the lover conceives it, is illusory (Myers 1984: 30).

If the yearning that distinguishes George Eliot's protagonists can find no gratifying consummation in the future, we get the distinct impression that the narrator has succeeded in assuaging her own yearning by the very process not of proceeding forward but of reflecting back. The retrospective passages in the novels (chapter 1 of *The Mill on the Floss*, the introduction to *Felix Holt*) have a sensual rocking quality, a quality of complete satiation and catharsis. The satisfaction that can only be achieved by reunion with the past is symbolized, in *The Mill on the Floss*, by quasi-incestuous union with the brother, just as Proust, in his effort to recapture the past, begins by recounting his childhood yearning for his mother.

At this point in the analysis, a socialist critic begins to lose heart, to feel that George Eliot is irremediably lost to a conservative world view. And yet, at the time she wrote *The Mill on the Floss*, she had completely severed herself from her own past. Estranged from her brother Isaac because of her own life decisions, her parents and recently her sister having died, she had changed her name, class, location, profession, and belief-system. It is from the presence of this other side of George Eliot in her characterization of Maggie that *The Mill on the Floss* gains its tension and complexity.

Elizabeth Ermarth's feminist analysis sees Maggie as a failure, partly because Ermarth cannot accept George Eliot's respect for renunciation and submission. From a feminist perspective, the two concepts seem suspiciously like giving in. But, as Gillian Beer has pointed out, renunciation in George Eliot is linked with independence, and is perhaps the only independence possible to women in Maggie's situation (Beer 1986: 84).

The entire novel can be seen as a sustained and ultimately successful battle against various kinds of metaphorical rape, a series of assertions of self against invasion and coercion. From childhood, Maggie is surrounded by male violence, not only the psychological violence of Tom's abuse but the reminder of physical violence implicit in dead moles and speared worms (I: 41, 55). When we see the novel as a tale of resistance against male coercion, it becomes apparent that Maggie does not fail as a feminist: she achieves a hard-won, though admittedly fruitless, victory.

In childhood, Maggie is an obstinate, clumsy, irritating cry-baby, but her obstinacy is a form of self-defence. Tom tries to bully Maggie into submission by judging and punishing her. The reader may conclude that obstinacy is a form of stupidity in Maggie, a view reinforced by constant suggestions that Maggie looks like an idiot, is possessed by demons, resembles various forms of animal life. However, if Maggie submitted to be modified by Tom she would lose his attention. Tom is an egoist. The only thing that inspires him to take an interest in others is the prospect of punishing. Usually, Tom strides off, Maggie follows. It is only when she does something wrong that he turns to her, looks at her, advances toward her. It is only when they make up after these fights that he volunteers physical signs of affection. In childhood she has discovered that the assertion of self, the refusal to be modified by outside influences, has resulted in the attainment of her desire – Tom's attention. This means of gratifying her desire resurfaces in her elopement with Stephen.

There is a series of sexually suggestive scenes between Tom and Maggie in childhood. The sharing of the cake in chapter 5, and the sharing of the jam puff in chapter 6, both graphically foretell the kind of sexual sensibility Tom is likely to have in adulthood. The most overt of these is the sword-exercise scene (Book Two, chapter 5), which is a microcosm of Tom and Maggie's entire relationship. Tom, savagely costumed and painted, flourishes his sword at Maggie who crouches fearfully on the bed. In this case, Maggie's demons come to her rescue. 'You'll hurt yourself, you'll chop your head off!' says Maggie, and Tom promptly does injure himself with the sword. Looking forward, as the sword-exercise scene encourages us to do on a second reading, to Maggie's argument with Stephen in Mudport, Maggie again holds her own against a strong masculine threat of invasion, this time with no demonic assistance but by her own strength of will. Strength of all sorts, of intellect, character, or sexual desire in women is described by George Eliot as demonic because it was seen as demonic by the society in which she lived.

Both Charlotte Brontë, in *Villette* (1853), and Elizabeth Barrett Browning, in *Aurora Leigh* (1857), had used demonic imagery to describe female power, and these texts, both of which impressed Marian Lewes deeply, are possible sources of the demonic in Maggie Tulliver. Demon imagery in George Eliot is not restricted to *The Mill on the Floss*; it pervades *Daniel Deronda* and George Eliot's letters.[1] Lucy's comment on Maggie's learning, that it 'always seemed to [her] witchcraft before – part of [Maggie's] general uncanniness' (II: 187), is autobiographical. Marian Evans was deeply disturbed, as a young woman, by the fact that other woman thought her 'uncanny' (Haight 1968: 535). The choice of demonic imagery to describe the alienation of being thought uncanny associates the various strengths that Marian Evans perceived in herself with madness. The association of demonic possession and madness is implicit in the choice of the drowning witch picture from Defoe's *The Political History of the Devil* (I: 21) and is suggested again and again throughout the novel: Tom tells Maggie that she looks 'like the idiot we throw our nutshells to at school' (I: 95); he tells her that tossing her head makes her 'look as if [she] were crazy' (I: 225); Uncle Pullet compares Maggie to the 'Nutbrown Maid', adding, 'I think she was crazy like' (II: 181); and Stephen tells her, 'you rave' (II: 334).

Being exceptional, and therefore socially unacceptable, is enough to drive one mad. The fear of madness and the pain of alienation produce violent eruptions in Maggie from time to time. These are directed toward Tom because Tom is both the person Maggie loves most and the person who most severely criticizes her, attempting to force her into the mould of traditional womanhood.

The second book, 'School time', is a drawn-out metaphorical castration of Tom, as punishment for forcing his world view on Maggie. At the beginning of Book Two, George Eliot seems to have relented a little toward Tom. She seems to be extending her sympathies, trying to understand Tom's equivalent centre of self, so that it comes as a shock when we realize that the purpose is, on the contrary, vindictive. Maggie is unable to punish Tom because nothing that Maggie could do would hurt him. Tom has all the power in the relationship between them because he loves less. In the power hierarchy of the novel, Maggie can punish Lucy, Tom can punish Maggie, but who can punish Tom? Who better than Maggie's more powerful *alter ego*, the narrator?

During his first term at Stelling's Tom, we are told, becomes more like a girl than he has ever been. He is humiliated; he is made to tend to a child; he is told that he lacks the equipment necessary to be a man. The equipment, in this case, is Latin, and Tom is having trouble with epicene nouns, nouns taking either gender.[2] Under the pressure of suffering, Tom misses Maggie and comes to need her more than she needs him. The moment when Tom longs for Maggie is comparable to the moment in *Adam Bede* when Hetty, during her 'journey in despair', finally longs for the home she used to hold cheap. George Eliot uses certain characters as Maggie uses the fetish in her attic, banging nails into their heads until they finally submit to feel what she thinks they ought to feel, and in this tendency to judge and punish, she resembles Tom more than Maggie.

The second coercive threat that Maggie encounters comes from Philip. Maggie's reluctance to pledge herself to Philip must be obvious to one of his morbid sensitivity. Philip begins his petition aware of the facts: 'Then you would never have the heart to reject [a lover] yourself – should you, Maggie?' (II: 103). He protests against her misgivings, demands assent to declarations of her love that he has put into words, requests signs of affection not freely volunteered by Maggie. The form of coercion explored here is that in which the man persists in pressing his suit on the woman, because his pleasure consists in possessing the woman rather than in knowing that he is desired by her. It is epitomized at the end of Book Five, chapter 4, as written in the original manuscript version:

> 'I am waiting for something else – I wonder whether it will come.'
> Maggie smiled, with glistening tears, and then stooped her tall head to kiss the low pale face that was full of pleading timid love – like a woman's.
> She had a moment of real happiness then – a moment of belief that if there were sacrifice in this love – it was all the richer and more satisfying.
>
> (1979: 43)

The strong sense here that Philip is exploiting Maggie's sympathy is an unusual variation on the theme of male aggression. His insistence succeeds not by means of masculine force but by the manipulation of Maggie's sympathy for his feminine vulnerability. The need to fight off this rarified form of masculine insistence contributes to the motivation of her elopement with Stephen.

In the scene following Maggie's pledge to Philip, when Tom mercilessly abuses Philip, Maggie is uncharacteristically quiet and passive. In a letter to Blackwood, Bulwer-Lytton pointed this out as a defect in the novel. Marian Lewes, having read this letter, said in her reply to Blackwood that Bulwer-Lytton's criticism was reasonable and that she would now alter the scene if she had the opportunity (Carroll 1971: 121). This is a clear example of the gap between authorial intention and the unconscious fecundity of the text. There are two reasons for Maggie's silence. The first, as several critics have noted, is that she wants to be severed from Philip, having become more involved than she ever intended, but her sympathy makes it impossible for her to do this herself. Tom's intervention can only postpone the problem, as Maggie later realizes; in the meantime she uses Tom's brutality in an effort to achieve an end she wants but is not brutal enough to achieve herself. The chapter ends as follows:

> And yet – how was it that she was now and then conscious of a certain dim background of relief in the forced separation from Philip? Surely it was only because the sense of deliverance from concealment was welcome at any cost?
>
> (1979: 451)

The concluding question mark leaves the issue open, and the reader recalls the end of the previous chapter .

The second reason for Maggie's passivity again underlines the primacy of Tom in her affections. While yelling abuse at Philip, Tom, for the first time in the novel, says complimentary things about Maggie. He calls her 'a handsome girl', 'a fine girl', says that she is 'what's too good for [Philip] – what [he'd] never get by fair means'. Having loved Tom passionately for years without any clear sign of reciprocal esteem, Maggie is hardly likely to interrupt this speech.

However, when Tom has served his purpose in disengaging her from the involvement into which her sympathy has led her, Maggie is free to attack him. The timing of this unprecedented combativeness on Maggie's part is not accidental. The evidence of Tom's love for her has put her on an equal footing with him for the first time. Because she now briefly sees herself as the beloved of Tom, she suddenly has the self-confidence to confront Tom where before she could only whimper and apologize.

Maggie's third battle is against Stephen's insistence at Mudport. She has told Philip that she would be able to reject a lover 'if he were very conceited' (II: 103). Stephen's 'diamond ring, attar of roses, and air of *nonchalant* leisure at twelve o'clock in the day' (I: 149) certainly indicate conceit in the common sense of the word, but Maggie, in her conversation with Philip in the Red Deeps, qualifies and elaborates her notion of conceit: ' "I think perhaps I could [reject a lover] if he were very conceited; and yet, if he got extremely humiliated afterwards, I should relent" '(II: 103).A little later, she goes on: ' "I've never any pity for conceited people, because I think they carry their comfort about with them" ' (II: 104). Maggie's notion of conceit is one that embraces the concepts of emotional security, social acceptance, and the absence of intense need. She is able to leave Stephen not because he is conceited in the usual sense of the word but because he can live without her. He wants her but does not need her, as Philip does. This susceptibility to need has been with Maggie since childhood:

> Maggie, moreover, had rather a tenderness for deformed things;
> she preferred the wry-necked lambs, because it seemed to her
> that the lambs which were quite strong and well made wouldn't
> mind so much about being petted; and she was especially fond of
> petting objects that would think it very delightful to be petted by
> her. She loved Tom very dearly, but she often wished that he
> *cared* more about her loving him.
>
> (I: 276–7)

She identifies with the vulnerable and neglected because she herself has been vulnerable and neglected and has therefore such a poor opinion of herself that she thinks her love can only be reciprocated by one as inadequate as she believes herself to be.

Stephen is top dog at St Ogg's: handsome, charming, wealthy, sought-after, he is, to use the phrase applied to Mrs Tulliver, the flower of his sex for beauty and amiability. His admiration for Maggie flatters and surprises her. It reflects the image of a self she longs to be – the image of a beloved rather than a lover, and beloved not by virtue of the lover's inadequacy in the eyes of St Ogg's but by virtue of her own excellence. This is linked to her desire for wealth and ease and her hitherto repressed sexual need.

The descriptions of Stephen's sexual attractiveness are developed side by side with descriptions of his spiritual inadequacy as a mate for Maggie. Both lines of description are sharpened by their contrast to the descriptions of Philip, the only other suitor on Maggie's horizon.

From Philip's first appearance at Stelling's, George Eliot is relentless, and occasionally rather brutal, in her insistence on his effeminacy and deformity. Philip's body is described as being perched 'like an amorphous bundle on the high stool' (I: 268). When Maggie kisses him, the insistence on the difference between her stature and his goes so far as to strain the semantic integrity of the sentence: 'Maggie smiled . . . then stooped her tall head to kiss the low pale face that was full of pleading, timid love – like a woman's.'[3] Three words here indicate this contrast in stature: stooped, tall, low. Generally speaking, 'to stoop' is an intransitive verb; 'tall' would seem an inapplicable adjective for heads not painted by El Greco; and 'low face', though not so obtrusive as the other two, also strains our sense of appropriate qualification. The choice of a dash rather than a comma before the final phrase emphasizes its importance over the more sympathetic description of the intensity of Philip's love which precedes it. A similar strain occurs earlier and achieves the same effect: 'She put out her hand and looked down on the lower deformed figure before her.' The awkwardness of these descriptions is very unusual in George Eliot's prose. It is possibly deliberate in that it reflects the awkwardness and inappropriateness of Maggie and Philip's union, or it might be the inadvertent product of strain in George Eliot's urgency to foreground that inappropriateness. In either case, the message is clear: no matter how intellectually and spiritually appropriate Philip might be for Maggie, Maggie also has sexual needs that cannot be fulfilled by Philip. The cloven tree (II: 197 and Book Six, chapter 5) is an unmistakable symbol of this important objection to their union.

Stephen is described as follows:

It was very charming to be taken care of in that kind graceful manner by some one taller and stronger than oneself. Maggie had never felt just in the same way before.

(II: 180)

There is something strangely winning to most women in that offer of the firm arm: the help is not wanted physically at the moment, but the sense of help – the presence of strength that is outside them and yet theirs – meets a continual want of the imagination.

(II: 220)

And then, to have the footstool placed carefully by a too self-confident personage – not *any* self-confident personage, but

61

one in particular who suddenly looks humble and anxious,
and lingers, bending still, to ask if there is not some draught
in that position between the window and the fireplace, and if
he may not be allowed to move the work-table for her – these
things will summon a little of the too ready, traitorous
tenderness into a woman's eyes, compelled as she is in her girlish
time to learn her life-lessons in a very trivial language. And to
Maggie such things had not been everyday incidents, but were
a new element in her life, and found her keen appetite for
homage quite fresh.

(II: 237)

These passages vividly suggest the overpowering effect of a sexually
vibrant presence, and this impression is in no way vitiated by the fact
that Stephen's behaviour is morally culpable and evinces a weak,
shallow, vain personality. The two are entirely separate issues. If the
reference to 'the violin, faithful to rotten boroughs' (II: 157) refers to
Stephen, and it certainly fits his politics, 'a reforming violoncello' is
not, of course, Lucy but Maggie. This is another example of what
Peter Garrett calls the spatial metaphor in George Eliot's fiction. The
relative scope of violin and violoncello makes clear George Eliot's
awareness of the relative scope of her characters and the deliberate
way in which she has developed their incompatibility in every area but
the sexual.

The descriptions, however, are not altogether sexual in content.
They dwell, as Patricia Spacks has pointed out, not only on sexual
temptation but also on the temptation to passivity (Spacks 1976: 43),
and on the desire for homage, worship, tending, which will reappear
in the queen/royalist imagery of Dorothea's relationship with Will in
Middlemarch, and which was seen in Maggie's attitude to the gypsies
(I: 169) and to Philip (II: 92). These two last influences are clearly
weaknesses, but George Eliot seems to see them as having been knitted
into female sexual feeling. George Eliot's ambivalence, her simultaneous celebration of sexual feeling and exasperation that it should
find its object in one so spiritually inadequate, is encapsulated in the
narratorial irony overlaying Lucy's remark to Stephen, 'You do the
"heavy beasts" to perfection' (II: 157), expressing both his philistinism and his sexual vitality.

Stephen is measured by the standard of Tom and found wanting.
He condemns himself in his languid remark,

'They think of doing something for young Tulliver: he saved
them from a considerable loss by riding home in some
marvellous way, like Turpin, to bring them news about the
stoppage of a bank, or something of that sort. But I was rather
drowsy at the time.'

(II: 155)

Here Stephen's moral sense is dwarfed by Tom's, just as earlier, in the
confrontation between Philip and Tom, the physical inadequacy of
Philip is highlighted by contrast: 'Her imagination, always rushing
extravagantly beyond an immediate impression, saw her tall, strong
brother grasping the feeble Philip bodily'(II: 121).

The shallowness and arrogance of Stephen's personality does not,
as some critics have maintained, abate under the influence of his love
for Maggie. To the end of the novel he remains a shallow egoist. It is in
this light that the idea of treachery can be best understood. We are told
that Stephen's attentions 'summon a little of the too ready, traitorous
tenderness into a woman's eyes'(II: 237–8), and later that Maggie was
'allowing a moment's happiness that was treachery to Lucy, to
Philip – to her own better soul'(II: 275). As William Myers has
pointed out, Maggie does not leave Stephen for the sake of others –
she does it for herself (Myers 1984: 186–7). Myers sees this as
perverse, and relates it to Nietzsche's analysis of altruism for the sake
of the altruist in *The Genealogy of Morals*. Myers works on the assumption that staying with and marrying Stephen is the most desirable
course for Maggie at Mudport, and that her return to St Ogg's is a
sacrifice yielding no satisfaction except the perverse masochistic satisfaction of martyrdom. This is a faulty assumption. The constant
undermining of Stephen's moral and intellectual fitness forces us to
see Maggie's conflict not merely as a trite re-enactment of the traditional Christian temptation theme, desire versus rectitude, but as a far
more complex issue of desire divided against itself. The third item of
that list of treacheries, 'to Lucy, to Philip – to her better soul' is
ambiguous. The punctuation encourages us to think that 'her better
soul' is a rephrasing of the two preceding items, and that the treachery
to her better soul is simply a matter of failing to keep to her own
standards of moral action with respect to her old ties: Lucy and Philip.
But it can also be read as an entirely separate and third treachery, in
which case the use of the dash encourages us to give this third treachery priority over the other two. This reading illuminates Maggie's

decision at Mudport, and is supported by the irrefutability of Stephen's arguments with regard to Lucy and Philip. The idea that a woman can come to love a man who is utterly unworthy of her is explored again and again in the novels of George Eliot. It is expressed most explicitly in *Felix Holt*, when Esther contemplates marrying Harold: 'and there was the vague consciousness that the love of this not unfascinating man who hovered about her gave an air of moral mediocrity to all her prospects'(*Felix Holt*, II: 251).

Neil Roberts has discussed the conflicting critical opinions of Joan Bennett and Bernard Paris on Maggie's renunciation of Stephen. Bennett maintains that when they first discovered their love, Maggie and Stephen should have admitted their problem to Lucy and Philip. Paris maintains that this approach, which he admits would cause least pain to least people, is not in accordance with George Eliot's moral system of self-suppression on behalf of others. Roberts sees the problem as one of George Eliot's didacticism: she is forcing her characters to exemplify her moral code. But all three of these critics underestimate the complexity of Maggie's character, and their mistake is rooted in the earnest altruistic impression of George Eliot yielded by the sibyl image. Bennett, in suggesting this alternative ending, is writing another novel about a far less interesting character; Paris is assuming that the novel is a satisfying moral fable; Roberts also assumes that the novel is a moral fable but does not find it satisfying (Roberts 1975: 95–6).

The general critical aversion to Stephen, like the aversion to Will Ladislaw in *Middlemarch*, stems in part from a romantic unwillingness on the part of critics to accept the idea that a woman's sexual need will seek an object of love even when no worthy object is available to her. Philip, who as he develops away from peevishness and bitter egoism toward sympathy and understanding, becomes the most reliable voice in the novel, says in his letter to Maggie, 'I have felt the vibration of chords in your nature that I have continually felt the want of in his' (II: 370). Philip's letter is so generally clear-sighted in its understanding of Maggie that we should pay attention to his evaluation of Stephen, and the contrast between this letter and the egoistic outpouring of Stephen's letter reinforces Philip's evaluation.

Maggie elopes with Stephen for many reasons, all jostling uneasily below the surface of consciousness: Lucy and Philip have gradually removed the impediments to Maggie's union with Philip, impediments on which she was relying; and Stephen, especially in contrast to Philip, exerts a strong sexual influence on Maggie. However, there are other reasons, or possible reasons, for Maggie's elopement: through it she avenges herself on Lucy, as several critics have noted, metaphorically re-enacting her childhood revenge of pushing Lucy in the mud. Maggie knows that Tom is in love with Lucy, and her reaction when she hears this information is suspiciously calm, given the intensity of her love for and jealousy of Tom (II: 193). It is here that Maggie's earlier method of getting Tom's attention by infuriating him resurfaces.

The situation and action of a man and a woman in a boat is itself sexually suggestive, and Maggie's boat-ride with Stephen is described in strongly sexual terms. 'The delicious rhythmic dip of the oars' (II: 311) suggests that the boat-ride is the consummation of their love rather than the journey toward that consummation. When Stephen hails the Dutch ship, he refers to Maggie as his wife, and the two of them sleep side by side on the deck of the ship. Maggie wakes up with the harsh mental clarity of post-coital disenchantment.

Before she wakes, Maggie dreams of another boat, St Ogg's boat with Lucy as the Virgin and Tom as St Ogg. The dream, by placing Tom and Lucy together in a boat, reveals to Maggie the sexual possibility between them that has been facilitated by her elopement with Stephen. Her desires to gain Tom's attention and avenge herself on Lucy have been accomplished by the elopement itself. Stephen has served his purpose, as Tom did before him in the confrontation with Philip. This view of Maggie's subconscious motives is supported by the story of St Ogg, in which a feminist Virgin Mary commends Ogg for yielding to her judgement without question, gratifying 'the heart's need' (I: 180). The story of Ogg is given at the beginning of the chapter telling of Maggie's flight to the gypsies, another childhood foreshadowing of her adult elopement. Here, Stephen is seen as St Ogg, a mere ferryman, following Maggie's instructions without question. Auerbach's analysis of the hypnotic effect of Maggie's eyes on Stephen could be used in support of this argument, which also explains Maggie's uncharacteristic reaction to Philip's prophetic joke in the Red Deeps:

'Well, perhaps you will avenge the dark women in your own
person, and carry away all the love from your cousin Lucy. She
is sure to have some handsome young man of St Ogg's at her

feet now: and you have only to shine upon him – your fair little cousin will be quite quenched in your beams.'

'Philip, that is not pretty of you, to apply my nonsense to anything real,' said Maggie, looking hurt. 'As if I, with my old gowns, and want of all accomplishments, could be a rival to dear little Lucy, who knows and does all sorts of charming things, and is ten times prettier than I am – even if I were odious and base enough to wish to be her rival. Besides, I never go to aunt Deane's when any one is there: it is only because dear Lucy is good and loves me, that she comes to see me, and will have me go to see her sometimes.'

'Maggie,' said Philip, with surprise, 'it is not like you to take playfulness literally.'

(II: 103)

Just before the elopement, Philip says what Maggie will 'be selling her soul to that ghostly boatman who haunts the Floss – only for the sake of being drifted in a boat for ever' (II: 304). The phrase 'selling her soul' gives Ogg's story a diabolic twist: no longer saintly, Ogg, and by implication Stephen, becomes associated with the Mephistopheles of Faust and the ferryman of the river Styx, which in turn reminds us of the early reference to Bunyan's Christiana crossing the river of death (I: 57–8). Being 'drifted in a boat for ever' unites with the novel's several references to Dutchmen[4] to suggest Wagner's *The Flying Dutchman*, the entire plot of which Marian Lewes had recorded in her article, 'Liszt, Wagner, and Weimar' (Pinney 1963: 105–10). In *The Flying Dutchman* also, love, water, and demonism are a deadly combination for the heroine. All these associations prepare us to receive the elopement in a negative light, and our foreboding is increased when Maggie's feelings during the boat-ride are described in terms of drowning, suspension of will, and paralysis:

Maggie listened – passing from her startled wonderment to the yearning after that belief, that the tide was doing it all – that she might glide along with the swift, silent stream and not struggle anymore.

(II: 313)

All yielding is attended with a less vivid consciousness than resistance; it is the partial sleep of thought; it is the submergence of our own personality by another.

(II: 315–16)

all the delicious visions of these last hours, which had flowed
over her like a soft stream, and made her entirely passive.

(II: 319)

The diminishment of consciousness and the passivity are not only
Maggie's. As Laura Comer Emery and Mary Ellen Doyle have
pointed out, the narrator is also infected by them (Emery 1976: 48–50;
Doyle 1981: 85). Both Emery and Doyle find this sudden abatement of
diegetic comment disturbing. Yet it is in just this interstice of
omniscience and analysis that I suggest the full subconscious fecundity
of *The Mill on the Floss* comes into its own.

The images of Stephen as ferryman, whether diabolic or saintly,
diminish his importance. Maggie's elopement is seen, through them,
as her own act, in which Stephen is merely a 'Guest', an assistant, the
variable *x*. The drowning images suggest that Maggie's act is essentially self-destructive which would seem to support Ermarth's interpretation of the novel as 'Maggie Tulliver's long suicide'. However,
in this novel, self- destruction is seen as better than compromising the
self, and therefore the vision yielded by Maggie's self-destruction is
not as unmitigatedly tragic as Ermarth suggests.

It is also perhaps not accidental that, through her elopement with
Stephen, Maggie carries out her father's death-bed wish for revenge
on Wakem far more effectively than Tom ever does, thereby avenging
herself against Tom for displacing her in her father's affections.
Wakem, having told his neighbours about his son's engagement to
Maggie, is sorely humiliated when his son is jilted. These motivations
are in direct contradiction to Maggie's avowed feelings. Nevertheless
the working of a vengeful subconscious beneath an apprently altruistic
and well-meaning consciousness is hinted at in the parallels between
Maggie's childhood and womanhood and is supported by the demonic
imagery. Whether or not Marian Lewes intended this, George Eliot
has sown the evidence for it throughout the text, evidence that would
seem to contradict the opinion, held by Karen Chase and other critics
before her, that 'Inarticulate desires, unconscious passions, do not
interest George Eliot' (Chase 1984: 141).

The relation between Maggie and Stephen is seen as combat: the
word 'rage' is used once of Maggie (II: 275) and five times of Stephen
in reference to their feelings for each other (II: 275, 314, 332, 335,
388). The two meanings of the word – fury and passion – are made
equally manifest by their repeated use in a situation in which both fury

and passion are strong. This is another instance in which George Eliot uses both strands of meaning in an ambiguous word, and it is also another example of the proximity in her fiction of love and murder.

If, for Maggie, elopement is perceived as paralysis, for Stephen it is triumph, possession, and stepping into command, as seen in the imagery used in the description of their argument:

'We will *not* part,' Stephen burst out, instinctively placing his back against the door.

(II: 328)

Maggie's eyes opened wide in one terrified look at the face that was close to hers, and she started up – pale again.

(II: 333)

In view of the recurring battle of wills between Maggie and the men she loves, her constant struggle to maintain her uncorrupted self in the face of male coercion and insistence, it is essential that Maggie leave Stephen in order to assert her complete, equal, and independent humanity. Pauline Nestor has remarked that in addition to societal restraints, Maggie (like other George Eliot heroines) also suffers from the vulnerability that results from what George Eliot perceived as women's greater capacity for love (Nestor 1985: 188). Below the surface of this is the belief that a woman's sexual need is actually the means of her oppression, that in order to overcome male domination from without she must first overcome the domination of sexual desire within her. This is parallel to Maggie's earlier renunciation: in order to free herself from the oppression of narrow and impoverished outward conditions, she must first free herself from the yearning to transcend those conditions. In both cases, paradoxically, freedom consists in ridding oneself of the desire for freedom.

This is why she denies herself the rational satisfaction of marrying Stephen, which would cause less pain than her return, alone, to St Ogg's. Tom and the family would suffer less disgrace; St Ogg's would have less to gossip about, as is clearly shown at the beginning of the chapter entitled 'St Ogg's passes judgement'. Joan Bennett points out that Maggie's elopement is unnecessary and the return is self-destructive, but she fails to see that the tragedy – in so far as there is one – is that a nature less passionately idealistic than Maggie's would have made neither mistake.[5]

The fact that Maggie's passionate idealism results in pain to all

68

concerned, with very dubious mitigating advantages, has been foreshadowed throughout the novel. Her childhood kisses give her doll's cheek a 'wasted unhealthy appearance' (I: 23); her embrace spills Tom's cowslip wine, ruining both Tom's drinking pleasure and Aunt Pullet's carpet (I: 141). Maggie's passionate desire to cause no pain to others, by concealing and renouncing her love for Stephen, results in her causing everyone much more pain than a more pragmatic woman would have caused. This is foretold by Philip in the Red Deeps. Maggie rejects Joan Bennett's advice as proffered by Stephen (II: 286); it is, in Philip's words, a 'rational satisfaction' that she denies herself, and because of this she elopes with Stephen – an eruption of the 'savage appetite' (II: 97). But her moralistic altruism, which expresses itself in her desire to cause no pain, is merely the conscious manifestation of a deeper and more radical idealism: a refusal to be or to accept anything that is unworthy of her. She expresses her idealism in terms of selflessness because, as a woman and the daughter of a shamed and impoverished family, she has been taught that selflessness is the only acceptable virtue for her. To revert to the terms of Myers's Nietzschean argument, she expresses herself in the language of slave-mentality, but the desire she expresses is characteristic of master-mentality: not humility but pride, not selflessness but a demand for excellence in the self and a refusal of anything but the best for that self, is at the root of Maggie's motivation.

The second denial of a rational satisfaction, in her refusal at Mudport to marry Stephen, is both a victory of self-assertion over male domination and an act of masochistic self-repression. The decision to return to St Ogg's is both a victory of Maggie's courage and self-assertion and an act of self-destruction. 'She had made up her mind to suffer', says the narrator (II: 327) – a clearly ironic outburst of exasperation with Maggie in the midst of a treatment that equally clearly perceives Maggie's strength as heroic.

When she returns to Tom, the true object of her love and one who is more equal to her love, more her spiritual equal than Stephen, Tom is looking at the 'rushing mill stream', deafened to Maggie's approach by the sound of rushing water (II: 340). This recalls Maggie's earliest memory of seeing the Floss while holding Tom's hand. The image is representative of what in the sonnets 'Brother and Sister' George Eliot calls 'the primal passionate store', the original well-spring of her sexuality, of the yearning that nothing in the present or future will assuage. Maggie does nothing to defend herself, does not hurry to explain, but simply offers herself to the embrace of fury as the only embrace possible to her (here again the word 'rage' is used). Her opening speech, 'Tom . . . I am come back to you – I am come home' is chilling. And yet this painful confrontation of brother and sister is still a confrontation of self and other, of two separate and therefore more fully equal individuals than the vision of life with Stephen we glimpse in the elopement, in which Maggie would be absorbed into his more trivial existence. In the conflict between men and women, it seems that the only resolution that George Eliot can see is the absorption of the woman's life and identity into those of her lover.

In the finale of *Middlemarch*, we are told: 'Many who knew her, thought it a pity that so substantive and rare a creature, should have been absorbed into the life of another'(*Middlemarch* III: 461). This is reminiscent of the postscript that Lewes wrote in a letter to Barbara Bodichon in 1859: 'you must not call her Marian Evans again: that individual is extinct, rolled up, mashed, absorbed in the Lewesian magnificence!'(Letters III: 65). Clearly Marian Evans was not 'mashed' in the Lewesian magnificence; her experience was transformed and made fruitful in the fiction of George Eliot. Whether or not Lewes expressed himself quite this plainly to her face, her fiction evinces a wariness of the way in which the love of men involves a desire to extinguish women. The yielding up of individual identity that is symbolized in the taking of the husband's name is the conventional prerequisite of satisfying a woman's need for love. The fact that Marian Evans, is becoming Marian Lewes despite legal nomenclature, adopted that symbolism is in significant conflict with the fact that marriage for her meant not the extinction of individual identity but the birth of her new identity as George Eliot.

In returning to Tom, Maggie chooses the renewal of conflict over a solution in which she loses herself. This reunion of Tom and Maggie is inevitable in the emotional scheme of the novel, and is in many ways the end and consummation of the elopement. As Tom and Maggie stand face to face by the mill stream, they present a dramatic tableau; they seem to stand as opposites or conflicting aspects of the same entity. Tom, the rational pragmatist, confronts Maggie, the passionate idealist, just as the pragmatic side of George Eliot, 'the man's brain' stood in opposition to the passionate 'woman's heart' in her. These terms, which Dinah Mulock used to describe George Eliot,[6] are problematic in that they separate the human personality into parts which are then labelled 'masculine' (intellect) and 'feminine' (emotion). They are inappropriate to a discussion of George Eliot because the intellect we are discussing is female. They are equally inappropriate to *The Mill on the Floss* because Maggie is characterized as more intelligent than Tom. Rather, there is a level at which George Eliot is modifying these ideas for her own purposes.

Even though Maggie is brighter than Tom, emotion plays a far more active part in her decision-making than it does in Tom's. This is in part due to the difference between Maggie's education as a girl and Toms's as a boy: boys are encouraged to develop their intellects, girls their emotions. However, Marian Lewes also believed that women are intrinsically more emotional and more capable of love than are men. In a letter to Emily Davies in 1868 she wrote: 'We can no more afford to part with that exquisite type of gentleness, tenderness, possible maternity suffusing a woman's being with affectionateness, than we can afford to part with human love' (Letters IV: 467–8). There are moments in her work where it is suggested that only by repressing this larger capacity for love can women gain power in the conflict with men. This need to repress woman's finest attribute is seen in the novels as tragic. The opposition between Tom and Maggie, then, is both suggestive of the internal war between opposing elements in one personality and of the external war between men and women.

George Eliot chose to represent the opponents in this war as brother and sister, rather than the more obvious choice of lovers, because brother and sister are together through the most important formative years of life. However, the mature sexual relation between men and women is the actual scene of battle, and therefore Maggie's incestuous love for Tom enables George Eliot to explore the dynamics of love relationships between men and women from their childhood manifestations to adulthood, without changing from one love object to another, which helps to maintain unity in the novel.

The brother/sister relationship also permits a vision of the lives of men and women as parallel but discrete human experiences, whereas the marital relation tends to eclipse the life of the woman in that of her husband. Tom and Maggie are seen as parallel voyagers. The narrator tells us that she is exploring the emmet-life of Dodsons and Tullivers in order to see 'how it has acted on young natures in many generations, that in the onward tendency of human things have risen above the mental level of the generation before them' (II: 6).

Many critics, ignoring this reference, consider Tom to be of a piece with the last generation of his family and Maggie alone to have 'risen above the mental level of the generation before'. Others admit that Tom has also risen but not to the same extent as Maggie. These views provide no explanation for the may instances where George Eliot has gone to some pains to show the contrast between Tom and Maggie in a light favourable to Tom, most notably when Tom talks to the aunts and uncles (Book Three, chapter 3) and when Tom pays the creditors (Book Five, chapter 6).

The process of rising above the last generation seems, in *The Mill on the Floss*, to be a dialectical one. In both Tom's case and Maggie's, an uneasy mixture of Dodson and Tulliver traits comes into conflict with a new infusion of intelligence. In Tom's case the conflict lasts into his teens. Sometimes the Dodson/Tulliver mixture gains ascendancy, and he seems a stupid boy; at other times his enquiring mind gains ascendancy, and he seems (to aunt Glegg) to be a dubious Dodson. However, the catalyst of the family's misfortunes triggers a sudden synthesis in Tom. This is possible because it gives him a role, as the new head of the family, which channels his conflicting energies into an effective confluence. He becomes a new creature: the intelligent Dodson.

Maggie's conflict meets with no such catalyst. When her family falls, she is powerless to redeem it and is rendered even less powerful than before, in so far as she is now deprived of the power to choose a husband. Moreover, the new infusion of intelligence is more substantial in Maggie than in Tom, so substantial that it cannot synthesize readily with the Dodson/Tulliver inheritance. Therefore Maggie remains throughout the novel in the dichotomic stage of the dialectic, at conflict with herself: 'one has a sense of uneasiness in looking at her – a sense of opposing elements, of which a fierce collision is imminent' (II: 49).

In a sense, then, Tom is further along in the dialectical struggle to rise above the mental level of the last generation. He has achieved synthesis while Maggie is still divided against herself. But the painful difficulty in resolving Maggie's dialectic stems from its greater complexity. Had Maggie lived to resolve her conflict, she would have become a George Eliot, a persona far more difficult to give birth to, because far rarer, than a Tom Tulliver or an Isaac Evans.

Maggie's internally conflicting and apparently perverse logic, which Auerbach sees as witchery, Ermath as failure, and Smith as neurosis, is the only way she has, given her circumstances, of remaining spiritually intact, of maintaining her own desires and beliefs in the face of coercion. Philip Fisher comes closest to appreciating Maggie's position when he claims that 'If she must be a failure by their standards – for reasons in the nature of things – she can at least grab the side of defiance and exaggerate the difference into a distinction' (Fisher 1981: 97). George Eliot is fully aware of the fruitlessness, even destructiveness, of Maggie's struggle. To understand her one must leave the path of rationalism. George Eliot knows that logic and the greatest concrete good lie with practical compromise, Stephen's arguments at Mudport, Tom's rather than Maggie's behaviour, but her idealistic nature rebels against this paltry pragmatism. Although Tom and Stephen are in every way more reasonable, more likely to find happiness and give it to others than Maggie, George Eliot insists that Maggie is the more admirable.

This explains more fully why the novel is riddled with madwoman images and their historical associations: attics, fetishes, witches, gypsies, idiots, demonic possession. George Eliot, the most consciously intellectual and academic of novelists, uses her utmost intellectual effort to assert that there is something finer than reason.

Gilbert and Gubar have pointed out the similarity between *The Mill on the Floss* and *Wuthering Heights* in their explorations of the wild, dark, passionate heroine (Gilbert and Gubar 1979: 492). The most significant similarity, however, lies in the use of Gothic imagery to describe a psychological landscape for which psychology had yet to find a descriptive vocabulary. Both Emily Brontë and George Eliot are wrestling with a reality that had not in their times, and has not yet in ours, been brought into the realm of the rationally comprehensible. Female psychology, which flummoxed Freud, has perhaps received no treatment as thorough and insightful as these two novels. The problem in writing them was the absence of a vocabulary, and the problem of interpreting them for us lies in the deciphering of a heavily metaphorical language designed to communicate ideas that disrupt and subvert the assumptions of Victorian and our own society, both as to gender politics and as to human possibilities.

As in *Wuthering Heights* passion and torpor replace good and evil as positive and negative values, so in *The Mill on the Floss* passionate idealism replaces rational pragmatism as a positive value. In life, Geroge Eliot espoused the value she rejects in this novel; she espoused the rational pragmatism necessary to facilitate her life and art. It would seem that George Eliot's ideal, and her self-realization as George Eliot are mutually exclusive. The difficulty in formulating an understanding

standing of *Wuthering Heights* is similar to the difficulty of forming a subversive thought in Newspeak. That passion is more important than goodness, torpor more despicable than evil is difficult to articulate in a language that developed symbiotically with Christian values. A similar problem impedes the understanding of *The Mill on the Floss*. In this case it is not the Christian values built into our language but rather its rationalism that makes it difficult to articulate the submerged but insistent idea of this novel: that a passionate idealism, fundamentally radical in its demands for excellence – but which, by reason of its volatile intensity, inevitably results in failure – is more admirable than an inherently conservative pragmatism, which desires to do the least evil and which, by reason of the mediocrity of its aspiration, attains its goal and supersedes the good achieved by the passionate idealist.

5

ROMOLA:
WOMAN AS HISTORY

In the critical heritage of *Romola* a persistent idea has surfaced again and again: the relation between the conception of *Romola* and George Eliot's interest in positivism. Leslie Stephen criticized Romola for being too modern, for being, in fact, a product of positivist thought (Stephen 1902: 138); U. C. Knoepflmacher noted positivist elements in *Romola* (Knoepflmacher 1965: 40); William Myers clarified the idea by observing that Romola was an attempt to embody human destiny in Positivist terms (Lucas 1971: 119); J. B. Bullen explored the structure of *Romola*, suggesting that the entire novel is a positivist allegory (Bullen 1975); and Felicia Bonaparte traced the correspondences and differences between Comte's theories and *Romola* (Bonaparte 1979). However throughout all this critical investigation, the question of why George Eliot uses positivist ideas in *Romola* and to what end has never been sufficiently elucidated.

Bullen's analysis suffers from a common misconception of George Eliot scholarship, which tends to see George Eliot as a passive mirror in which we can see reflected the ideologies of the men by whom she may have been influenced, in this case Comte. This tendency to look for the source of George Eliot's thought in male thinkers, Feuerbach, Spencer, Mill, Comte, Bain, Huxley, and most often, Lewes, is ironically commented upon by George Eliot herself in the finale of *Middlemarch*, where Fred and Mary are credited with one another's books. Bonaparte examines the points at which George Eliot's thought, as expressed through *Romola* and elsewhere, diverges from Comte's, but she comes to no conclusions in which the Comtean elements of *Romola* enrich and deepen its meaning, that is to say, in which they add to anything other than its encyclopaedic impressiveness.

My aim in this discussion is to re-examine the idea of *Romola* as a positivist allegory, going beyond the threshold of influence and correlation to ask whether George Eliot uses the positivist structure to articulate ideas that are other than or more than Comte's theories, and, if so, how these ideas can be relevant to modern readers for whom Comte's theory, although of historical interest, is unlikely to be of vital philosophical interest.

It is important to remember here that George Eliot was not wholeheartedly behind the positivist movement, although she acknowledged a great intellectual debt to Comte. In a letter to Maria Congreve in 1867, she wrote: 'my gratitude increases continually for the illumination Comte has contributed to my life' (Letters IV: 333). This, as Haight has pointed out, must be considered in its context: her correspondent's husband was a leader of the British positivist movement (Haight 1968: 301). A comment, quoted by Mathilde Blind, from reported conversation gives a somewhat different impression: 'I cannot submit my intellect or my soul to the guidance of Comte' (Blind 1883: 213). It is likely that both statements are true, and that her relation to Comte was of the kind she described in an 1849 letter to Sara Hennell:

> I wish you to thoroughly understand that the writers who have most profoundly influenced me . . . are not in the least oracles to me. It is just possible that I may not embrace one of their opinions, that I may wish my life to be shaped quite differently from theirs. For instance it would signify nothing to me if a very wise person were to stun me with proofs that Rousseau's views of life, religion, and government are miserably erroneous – that he was guilty of some of the worst basenesses that have degraded civilized man. I might admit all this – and it would be not the less true that Rousseau's genius has sent that electric thrill through my intellectual and moral frame which has awakened me to new perceptions, which has made man and nature a fresh world of thought and feeling to me – and this not by teaching me any new belief.
>
> (Letters I: 227)

It follows that her idea of Comte's third and future phase of historical development is not necessarily identical with the vision of positivism. As several critics have pointed out, it would have been virtually impossible for any female intellectual, much less one whose life work was a series of novels on the possibilities of women's lives, to have accepted Comte's view of woman's potentialities:

Now, the relative inferiority of Woman in this view is incontestable, unfit as she is, in comparison, for the requisite continuousness and intensity of mental labour, either from the intrinsic weakness of her reason or from her more lively moral and physical sensibility, which are hostile to scientific abstraction and concentration.

(Comte 1853 II: 136)

George Eliot is also unlikely to have approved of the role for women that Comte envisioned for his Utopia:

What the ultimate conditions of marriage will be, we cannot know as yet; and if we could, this is not the place to treat them. It is enough for our purposes to be assured that they will be consonant with the fundamental principle of the institution, - the natural subordination of women, which has appeared under all forms of marriage, in all ages, and which the new philosophy will place on its right basis, - a knowledge of the individual organism, and then of the social organism. . . . Sociology will prove that the equality of the sexes, of which so much is said, is incompatible with all social existence, by showing that each sex has special and permanent functions.

(Comte 1853 I: 135)

I suggest that, far from obediently following in Comte's intellectual footsteps, as critics from Willis Cooke (1883) to J. B. Bullen have suggested, she found Comte's tripartite vision appealing as a firm structure in which to ground her own very different speculations as to human possibility.

Comte proposed three stages of history: the polytheistic, the monotheistic, and the positivist. These three stages, as both Bullen and Bonaparte have remarked, are microcosmically reflected in Romola's life.

Romola's early life is spent in scholarly seclusion with her father, studying Greek and Latin, immersed in classical literature and culture, and father and daughter are therefore seen as the Oedipus and Antigone of Sophocles,[1] but this is only half of our image of classical polytheism; the other half, the satyrs and maenads, the wine and concupiscence, are introduced into Romola's life through her love for Tito, who therefore plays Bacchus to Romola's Ariadne. The Bacchus and Ariadne imagery has been discussed by Gilbert and Gubar (1979: 527).

This Bacchic part of Romola's life does not outlive the courtship: even on the evening of their betrothal, at the end of the first book of the novel, Romola is beginning to lean toward the second, monotheistic, stage of her history. Just as the Bacchic crowning of Ariadne is the high point of Book One, Romola's submission to Savonarola on the road out of Florence is the high point of Book Two. Romola enters her second phase with as much yearning sincerity as she brought to her life with her father and her love for Tito, and as the narrator is at pains to emphasize, her conversion is just as much a matter of personal attachment, in this case to Savonarola, as were those first two loves.

Book Three builds toward disillusionment, and, in its final stages, after 'Drifting away', strains imaginatively after the realization of the third and final stage, the positivist stage, the stage that in George Eliot's own time, as in ours, is still subjunctive. And 'strain', unfortunately but perhaps inevitably, is the operative word.

A threefold vision of history is explored in a novel made up of three books of which the central image is the triptych. A central character in the novel, who is also a central and defining figure in the period of which the novel treats, Savonarola, is seen as the spokesman of a vision curiously Comtean in its emphasis on the community and on the identity of the religious and the political:

> But the real force of demonstration for Girolamo Savonarola lay in his own burning indignation at the sight of wrong; in his fervent belief in an Unseen Justice that would put an end to wrong.
>
> (I: 320)

> 'The cause of my party *is* the cause of God's kingdom.'
> (Savonarola to Romola, II: 309)

> The warning is ringing in the ears of all men: and it's no new story; for the Abbot Joachim prophesied of the coming time three hundred years ago, and now Fra Girolamo has got the message afresh.
>
> (I: 32)

This last quotation is the most illuminating. Joachim of Fiore, who died in 1202, was the Abbot of S Giovanni di Fiore in Calabria. He maintained that history was tripartite: the age of the Father had ended with the coming of Christ; the age of the Son extended to the mid-thirteenth century; and the age of the Holy Ghost would begin in the year 1260. His theories had a large following until the year 1260 passed uneventfully.

Although this view of history as imitating the tripartite nature of the

Christian deity is tantalizingly close to Comte's vision, Savonarola is
not the positivist protagonist and cannot be, since his otherworldliness
leads ultimately away from human concerns. The parallel suggests,
however, that in Savonarola we have approached one step nearer to
the positivist ideal, since his monotheism, unlike Bardo's polytheism,
is a step towards involvement in the living human community:

> 'Your life has been spent in blindness, my daughter. You have
> lived with those who sit on a hill aloof, and look down on the life
> of their fellow-men.'
>
> (II: 104)

> The Church, in her mind, belonged to that actual life of the
> mixed multitude from which they had always lived apart.
>
> (I: 234)

> Slowly Romola fell on her knees, and in the very act a tremor
> came over her; in the renunciation of her proud erectness, her
> mental attitude seemed changed, and she found herself in a new
> state of passiveness.
>
> (I: 241)

Words like 'proud' and 'aloof' provide a nexus of meanings: class
prejudice; moral and intellectual loftiness, and George Eliot's notion
of noble womanhood, which is linked to monumentality and has positive feminist implications. When Savonarola tries to humble Romola
from her 'proud erectness' there is a tension between the positive
aspects of joining the community and the negative implications of
relinquishing independence, with its attendant negative feminist
implications.

In the opening of the 'Proem', the setting of the novel, distant both
in space and time from its Victorian English readership, is presented
to us in such a way as to mitigate its distance and exoticism:

> More than three centuries and a half ago, in the mid spring-
> time of 1492, we are sure that the angel of the dawn, as he trav-
> elled with broad slow wing from the Levant to the Pillars of Her-
> cules, and from the summits of the Caucasus across all the snowy
> Alpine ridges to the dark nakedness of the Western isles, saw
> nearly the same outline of firm land and unstable sea. . . . And
> as the faint light of his course pierced into the dwellings of men,
> it fell, as now, on the rosy warmth of nestling children. . . . The

great river-courses which have shaped the lives of men have hardly changed; and those other streams, the life-currents that ebb and flow in human hearts, pulsate to the same great needs, the same great loves and terrors. As our thought follows close in the slow wake of the dawn, we are impressed with the broad sameness of the human lot, which never alters in the main headings of its history – hunger and labour, seed-time and harvest, love and death.

(I: 1–2)

Changes in landscape are compared to changes in human culture, and the suggestion is that there has been little change in either. Yet the year, that in which Columbus discovered America, highlights the advances and changes of humanity in the same sentence in which the narrator assures us of its stability. Humanity, apparently, is changing and yet not changing. Our lives can be described under the same 'main headings' but we have somehow progressed within them.

Marian Lewes called herself a meliorist. James Sully defined meliorism as 'the faith which affirms not merely our power of lessening evil – this nobody questions – but also our ability to increase the amount of positive good', and he reached this definition in consultation with Marian Lewes (Sully 1877: 399).[2] Even if George Eliot believes that we are able to increase good, she seems sceptical about whether we have made use of that ability.

The similarity between *Romola*'s time and George Eliot's is underlined by the use of a Pre-Raphaelite style of description, as William Myers has noted (Myers 1984: 95). The Pre-Raphaelites 'sought to infuse art with moral qualities through a scrupulous study of nature and the depiction of uplifting subjects' (*The Oxford Dictionary of English Literature*, 468). These two means, 'scrupulous study of nature' and 'the depiction of uplifting subjects', seem mutually exclusive, and the effort to use them both in the writing of *Romola* probably contributed to its problems. George Eliot's interest in Pre-Raphaelitism dated from its earliest stages (the Brotherhood was established in 1849). In 1852 she wrote the Chapman: '[*British Quarterly* has] one subject of which I am jealous – "Pre-Raphaelism in Painting and Literature" '(Letters II: 48).

The following description seems influenced by the Pre-Raphaelites not only as to means but also in the similarities between Romola's appearance and the kind of model for which the Pre-Raphaelites showed so marked a preference.[3]

> The only spot of bright colour in the room was made by the hair
> of a tall maiden of seventeen or eighteen, who was standing
> before a carved *leggio*, or reading-desk, such as is often seen in
> the choirs of Italian churches. The hair was of a reddish-gold
> colour, enriched by an unbroken small ripple, such as may be
> seen in the sunset clouds on grandest autumnal evenings. It was
> confined by a black fillet above her small ears, from which it
> rippled forward again, and made a natural veil for her neck
> above her square-cut gown of black *rascia*, or serge.
>
> (I: 72)

Although what is described has the colouring, lighting, and detail one might expect in a painting by Holman Hunt, the way in which it is described is Raphaelesque rather than Pre-Raphaelite in that the idealization is heightened by the use of monumental images. Romola's hair, perhaps the most typically Pre-Raphaelite detail in the description, takes on grand proportions when it is compared to autumnal skies, and with that enlargement the image takes on a weight and scope quite alien to the delicate representations of women in most Pre-Raphaelite paintings. Raphael, Leonardo, and Michelangelo's application of the classical style of portraying the human form to Christian subject-matter provides an interesting parallel to George Eliot's search for a synthesis of the two. Classical (polytheistic) art was characterized by physical grandeur; medieval (monotheistic) art was characterized by spiritual depth at the expense of physical grandeur. The retention of spiritual depth without the sacrifice of physical grandeur would be an adequate description of what George Eliot attempts in her monumental representations of women, and is the subject of explicit discussion in *Middlemarch* (I: 287–9). One of her reviewers, almost certainly R. H. Hutton, writing in the *Spectator* in 1863, seems to sense this when he compares George Eliot's art to Raphael's:

> George Eliot's drawings all require a certain space, like Raffael's
> Cartoons, and are not of that kind which produce their effect by
> the reiteration of scenes each complete in itself. You have to
> unroll a large surface of the picture before even the smallest *unit*
> of its effect is attained.
>
> (Carrol 1971: 199)

This monumental Raphaelesque element in her writing is characteristic, whereas the Pre-Raphaelite seems to be a deliberate choice.
The Pre-Raphaelites were at their height in George Eliot's own time;
the time of which she writes was genuinely, if only just, Pre-
Raphaelite.[4] If the human condition was so nearly the same in Renaissance Florence and Victorian England as to elicit this comparison, and
if, as I shall argue, *Romola* is not so much a historical novel as the novel
its title would suggest,[5] why does the author choose to set her story so
far away in space and time?

One possibility is that the setting is metaphorical. Florence is seen
as at the geographical centre of the cultured world: ' "No, no" said
Bratti cordially; "one may never lose sight of the Cupola and yet know
the world, I hope" '(I: 35).

Seen in the light of Comte's threefold view of history, the temporal
setting, in the Renaissance, is also centrally placed: the polytheistic
phase is definitely passed – the power of Savonarola marks the height
of monotheism – yet it is an uncomfortable turbid stage of flux, and
final synthesis is still a long way off:

> Our resuscitated Spirit was not a pagan philosopher, nor a
> philosophising pagan poet, but a man of the fifteenth century,
> inheriting its strange web of belief and unbelief; of Epicurean
> levity and fetischistic dread; of pedantic impossible ethics uttered
> by rote, and crude passions acted out with childish impul-
> siveness; of inclination towards a self-indulgent paganism, and
> inevitable subjection to that human conscience which, in the
> unrest of a new growth, was filling the air with strange
> prophesies and presentiments.

(I: 9)

Given the lapse of time between the height of the first phase, the
ancient Greek and Roman empires, and the height of the second
phase, the Renaissance, a similar lapse would be necessary between
the height of monotheism and the height of positivism, if the symmetry of the Comtean time model, and the corresponding symmetry of
George Eliot's image of the triptych, is to be borne out. In light of this,
it is arguable that *Romola* is as much a Utopian as a historical novel, in
so far as the life of its heroine reflects in microcosm a history of which
the last part must still be described in the future tense, which explains
why it is so strained and unconvincing in its final stages.

The mystical evocativeness of the number three pervades *Romola*.

Comte uses it; Christianity uses it to describe its God as three persons in three tenses: Father, Son, and Holy Spirit; is, was, and ever shall be. The Holy family has three members, and any family must have three members before it can claim the name. Hegel and Marx describe the dialectical movement of history as tripartite: thesis, antithesis, and synthesis. Marx describes history itself as divided into three parts: feudalism, capitalism, and communism. In one lifetime, generally speaking, we see three generations as we do in this novel.

All these accociations find their echoes in *Romola*. I have already discussed the Comtean, Christian, and time-tense uses. Felicia Bonaparte has discussed the focus on families in *Romola* (Bonaparte 1979: 73). Positivism as a synthesis of polytheism and monotheism rather than as the end of a linear progress, is shown in both the story itself and the symbolism of the triptych and the cross. Tito hides Dino's crucifix in the triptych and locks it in. The pain of monotheism is concealed within polytheistic hedonism. A synthesis is necessary, as indicated by the ambivalent ending of Book One:

> 'Nay, Romola, you will look only at the images of our happiness now. I have locked all sadness away from you.'
> 'But it is still there – it is only hidden,' said Romola, in a low tone, hardly conscious that she spoke.
>
> (I: 309)

The centrality of Nello, Bratti, and the Mercato underline the concern with economic evolution as the base on which the philosophic evolution from polytheism to monotheism has taken place. Bonaparte points out that Bratti is based on an actual merchant whom George Eliot found in the course of her research, and that this original Bratti died a very wealthy man (Bonaparte 1979: 164).

Finally, if the older generation of Bardo, Baldassarre, and Bernardo is polytheistic, and the middle generation of Dino, Tito, and Romola is in flux and change between polytheism and monotheism, what miserable uncertainty we are left in as to the future generation, given the utter vapidity of Lillo and Ninna. George Eliot tries to envision a final synthesis in the future, but she cannot do so.

In positivist terms, the structure I have been describing is peculiar to this novel. However, in the wider terms of seeking a solution to egoism (here represented in both Bardo's ambitious and Tito's hedonistic polytheism) without falling into masochistic self-sacrifice (here represented by Savonarola's self-martyring monotheism),

Romola's problem is the one central and recurring problem of the George Eliot canon. If this is tenable, the solution, the synthesis struggled for in the course of the novel, is not the actualization of Comte's religion of humanity, with which George Eliot was not entirely in agreement, but rather the hazily-envisioned better world towards which, throughout the canon, George Eliot gestures.

Surely in *Romola* George Eliot is describing another variation upon the common problem of which Dinah's, Maggie's, Dorothea's, and Gwendolen's are also variations, but his time on a historic scale. All those other heroines battle against egoism while trying to resist needless self-sacrifice, but, in each of their cases, the problem is seen mainly as personal or as a problem or gender.

This question of when to rebel met with various answers from George Eliot at various stages in her life and over various issues. At times, as in the 1865 letter to Clementia Taylor in response to a request for a donation to the Mazzini fund, her answer seems to create so many impediments to rebellion as to be effectually indistinguishable from an untroubled resolution never to rebel. It is only when we consider such answers as these in the context of her own rebellions that we can appreciate the complexity of the issue in her life and work.

> Now, though I believe there are cases in which conspiracy may
> be a sacred, necessary struggle against organized wrong, there
> are also cases in which it is hopeless, and can produce nothing
> but misery; or needless, because it is not the best means
> attainable of reaching the desired end; or unjustifiable, because
> it resorts to acts which are more unsocial in their character than
> the very wrong they are directed to extinguish: and in these
> three supposable cases it seems to me that it would be a social
> crime to further conspiracy even by the impulse of a little finger,
> to which one may well compare a small money subscription.
>
> (Letters IV: 200)

In *Middlemarch*, this same issue is seen as a problem common to all people of both genders. Lydgate and Dorothea both need to see the equivalent centre of self in others, particularly in their respective spouses. Lydgate's realization of Rosamond's needs, and his consequent resignation to the inevitability of relinquishing his vocation in favour of meeting those needs is seen as a positive thing, a victory over egoism, but Dorothea's refusal to continue Casaubon's work after his death is also seen as a positive thing, a refusal to sacrifice herself needlessly. However, in *Middlemarch* the issue is never raised to historic proportions, as it is in *Romola*.

The historic proportions of *Romola* allow the literal staging of a comparison that is implicitly explored to varying extents in all George Eliot's subsequent novels. By painting monumental women thwarted by the pettiness of the female lot, George Eliot, in the later novels, repeatedly suggests a world of unexplored possibility. The reader is invited to speculate about what might have happened had the heroine been born with the freedom and power of a man and to imagine a comparison between the heroine we have and her male equivalent, a hypothetical male embodiment of her strength of character, who, because of this maleness, can use that strength of character to its full potential.

In juxtaposing Romola with Savonarola, George Eliot portrays this comparison literally. This is something more adventurous than George Eliot's usual discussions of the interpenetration of the personal and the political, although it does grow out of the same conviction that produces not only the diegetic commentary about the correlation between private and public life but also the meticulous attention to the larger community that we find in all the novels.

In a letter of 1863, George Eliot told R. H. Hutton that the great problem of Romola's life 'essentially coincides with the chief problem in Savonarola's' (Letters IV: 97). This is explicitly stated in the text:

> It flashed upon her mind that the problem before her was
> essentially the same as that which had lain before Savonarola –
> the problem where the sacredness of obedience ended, and where
> the sacredness of rebellion began.

(II: 273)

Savonarola's conflict is of enormous historic moment; the fate of Florence will be deeply influenced by Savonarola's decision. In Romola's life, the issue is purely personal, a question of when to leave her husband or when to leave, for moral reasons, a church that will not be affected by her absence. Had she been a real citizen of fifteenth-century Florence, as was Savonarola, she would still not be, as he is, a historic figure, inasmuch as history is not the past itself but the written record of the past, and her story would not have been recorded. This difference between the lives of exceptional men and exceptional women, which is as much a problem in Victorian England as in fifteenth-century Florence, is ironically reflected in the fact that Savonarola is actually a character from history, whereas Romola is a fictional construct. Historic man confronts hypothetical woman; the subject of history confronts the object of fiction. And yet George Eliot uses the life of this hypothetical woman as the model and microcosm for her drama of history. This is something more radical than the positivist claim that only woman can represent humanity, because, as I shall try to establish, woman here is not representing man but displacing him.

The portrayal of Savonarola is particularly interesting in its ambivalence and in the many levels of purpose he serves in the novel. He is, as I have said, the exponent of monotheism within George Eliot's Comtean scheme, and as such he represents a stage to be transcended, though not completely. Savonarola overcomes Romola's elitism – an elitism that had been fostered by her father's intellectual snobbery – and awakens in her a sense of the political. His description of the divine life is very close to the language of the Prelude to *Middlemarch* when it refers to the need to escape self:

> '[Your wisdom] has left you without a share in the Divine life which quenches the sense of suffering Self in the ardours of an ever-growing love.'
>
> (Savonarola to Romola, *Romola* II: 109)

> some illimitable satisfaction, some object which would never justify weariness, which would reconcile self-despair with the rapturous consciousness of life beyond self.
>
> *Middlemarch* I: 2)

This seems ironic when we remember that Savonarola is in the process of persuading her not to go out, as St Theresa went out from Avila, in search of the very thing that, the Prelude to *Middlemarch* insists, will provide that necessary escape from self: a vocation.

Savonarola's argument against her flight is that she does not already have a vocation that would overrule the claims of personal bonds. This seems rather a weak argument, given that Dino's vocation (which is discussed as a contrasting example) might very well have come in part because of a desire to escape the pressures of Bardo's overbearing ambition. It seems enough that Romola wants to find a vocation and has come up with a plan that sounds promising. That plan would have made a radical change in Romola's life, in that it would have put her under the protection of a woman, Cassandra Fidele, rather than of a man.

The word 'power-loving' is used twice of Savonarola:

Savonarola had that readily-roused resentment toward opposition, hardly separable from a power-loving and powerful nature, accustomed to seek great ends that cast a reflected grandeur on the means by which they are sought.

(I: 576)

and with that immediate response to any appeal from without which belongs to a power-loving nature accustomed to make its power felt by speech, he met Tito with a glance as self-possessed and strong as if he had risen from resolution instead of conflict.

(I: 615)

The narrator's ambivalence towards him grows as the narrative proceeds. 'An arresting voice' is ambiguous: a voice that 'arrests' in that its dramatic power stops the hearer in her tracks, or the voice of one who 'arrests' in the policing sense, by force or coercion. The latter suggests that perhaps Savonarola's love of power is an element in his motivation here.

The love of power is not Savonarola's only fault; his ecstatic offers of self-sacrifice are presented as masochistic fantasies:

'let the thorns press upon my brow, and let my sweat be anguish – I desire to be made like thee in thy great love. But let me see the fruit of my travail – let this people be saved!

(I: 350)

'Come, O blessed promise; and behold, I am willing – lay me on the altar: let my blood flow and the fire consume me; but let my witness be remembered among men, that iniquity shall not prosper for ever.'

(I: 350)

George Eliot is at pains to inform us that these are her words, not a translation from Savonarola's original sermons.[6] When Savonarola sobs at the end of his sermon, we are reminded of Marian Evans's early religious passions and of Mr Brooke's reaction to Dorothea having sobbed upon hearing religious organ music, 'that kind of thing is not healthy, my dear' (*Middlemarch* I: 96).

The ambivalence, the mixture of admiration and disapprobation that George Eliot clearly feels for Savonarola leaves that brief idea of going to Cassandra Fidele up in the air; it flutters through the novel, is produced out of thin air and then vanishes as if by sleight of hand. Like the suggestion of a vocation for Gwendolen in *Daniel Deronda*, it seems to be ridiculed and made light of, as if George Eliot's heroines, all of whom are asking for a vocation, are being told by George Eliot, as Romola is told by Savonarola, 'Get back to your place!'

The introduction of Cassandra Fidele also destabilizes the opposition I referred to earlier, between Savonarola as subject of history and Romola as object of fiction. Just as in *Middlemarch* the invisible presence of George Eliot as female vocational success casts doubt on the historical and biological determinism of Dorothea's failure to find a vocation, so in *Romola* the mention of a female historical figure pre-empts deterministic conclusions. Romola remains the object of fiction because the odds are stacked against her but we are reminded that another woman might have overcome those odds. This is one possible correlative of the modification of Novalis's dictum in *The Mill on the Floss*: gender is destiny, but not all our destiny.

In an attempt to give Romola the scope necessary to withstand the comparison with Savonarola, George Eliot is particularly generous in her use of monumental images. This too is facilitated by the exoticism of a distant setting: Romola can be compared to Ariadne and to the Madonna without any of the mitigating mundane details that more nearly contemporary English heroines have to endure. Romola's epic yearning to be of use is met by the plague; Dorothea's, on the other hand, is met by the deflating fact that nobody's pig has died (*Middlemarch* III: 416). And yet, it is just this tragi-comic opposition of greatness and trivia that helps Maggie and Dorothea to appear more convincingly impressive than Romola. Dorothea has the 'impressiveness of a fine quotation from the Bible, – or from one of our elder poets, – in a paragraph of to-day's newspaper' (*Middlemarch* I: 7). If she had the impressiveness of a quotation from the Bible in the Bible, the tragedy, the comedy, the piquancy would be lost.

However, the problems with *Romola* cannot be fully accounted for by the lack of ironic counterpoint. The ending of the novel, especially the plague-stricken village scene, is embarrassing and unconvincing, as is the flood scene of *The Mill on the Floss*. Both scenes involve boats, water – that is to say, George Eliot's recurring network of images of desire – and rescue by a fearless woman who heroically risks her own death. In both scenes there is an attempt to transcend the realism meticulously cultivated elsewhere in the novels. According to Laurence Lerner, in the plague-stricken village scene, realism is not transcended but abandoned (Lerner 1967: 249), and the same might be said of the flood scene in *The Mill on the Floss*. While this criticism can hardly be refuted, I suggest that the reason these scenes fail is that they are straining to envision that which cannot yet be seen.

In *A Vindication of the Rights of Woman*, Mary Wollstonecraft wrote about the cultivation of fear in women:

> Fragile in every sense of the word, they are obliged to look up to man for every comfort. In the most trifling dangers they cling to their support, with parasitical tenacity, piteously demanding succour; and their *natural* protector extends his arm, or lifts up his voice, to guard the lovely trembler – from what? Perhaps the frown of an old cow, or the jump of a mouse; a rat, would be a serious danger. In the name of reason, and even common sense, what can save such beings from contempt; even though they be soft and fair?
>
> These fears, when not affected, may be very pretty; but they shew a degree of imbecility that degrades a rational creature. . . . I am fully persuaded that we should hear of none of these infantine airs, if girls were allowed to take sufficient exercise. . . . further, if fear in girls, instead of being cherished, perhaps, created, was treated in the same manner as cowardice in boys, we should quickly see women with more dignified aspects. . . . they would be more respectable members of society, and discharge the important duties of life by the light of their own reason.
>
> (Wollstonecraft 1792 I: 133–4)

The 'lovely trembler', being familiar from actual experience, is described with minute concreteness, but the fearless woman is vaguely conjured by abstract nouns. The essay form allows of abstractions and generalities to cover what is indistinctly perceived. We are asked to consider 'rational creatures', 'dignified aspects', 'respectable members of society', and 'the important duties of life'.

The 'lovely trembler' does not seem to have changed much over the seventy years that separate *A Vindication of the Rights of Woman* from *Romola*. She is recognizable from many a Victorian novel. Amelia in *Vanity Fair*, and Lucy in *A Tale of Two Cities*, for example, each share some of her attributes. The image of the fearless woman has also changed little; she is still difficult to envision, and when George Eliot approaches the task in fiction, where there can be no protection behind barricades of abstract nouns, she meets with strain and often with failure.

> In the excitement of getting into the other boat, unfastening it, and mastering an oar, Bob was not struck with the danger Maggie incurred. We are not apt to fear for the fearless, when we are companions in their danger, and Bob's mind was absorbed in possible expedients for the safety of the helpless indoors. The fact that Maggie had been up, had waked him, and had taken the lead in activity, gave Bob a vague impression of her as one who would help to protect, not need to be protected. She too had got possession of an oar, and had pushed off, so as to release the boat from the overhanging window-frame.
>
> 'The water's rising so fast,' said Bob, 'I doubt it'll be in the chambers before long – th'house is so low. I've more mind to get Prissy and the child and the mother into the boat, if I could, and trusten to the water – for th'old house is none so safe. And if I let go the boat – but *you*,' he exclaimed, suddenly lifting the light of his lanthorn on Maggie, as she stood in the rain with the oar in her hand and her black hair streaming.
>
> (*The Mill on the Floss* II: 393)

The attempt to envision 'dignified aspects' and 'the important duties of life' has fallen flat; the melodramatic, almost Wagnerian, image of Maggie at the end is false to the painstaking realism of her prior characterization and development. She becomes emblematic and unconvincing. And yet George Eliot must surely be admired for the attempt. No writer, except Sophocles and Shakespeare, has succeeded where she failed. The only convincing and positive images of women as powerful, fearless, and independent, show them excelling in their traditional domain, as in the scene where Tess christens her baby in *Tess of the D'Urbervilles*.

George Eliot is trying to get at something else. She, like Wollstonecraft, senses that the problem of women's oppression is very much to do with the timidity of women and that if this fear could be overcome not only would women's lives improve in consequence but society in general would benefit. Anna Jameson, in her introduction to *Legends of the Modonna*, touches on the same idea:

In the perpetual iteration of that beautiful image of THE
WOMAN highly blessed – *there*, where others saw only pictures
or statues, I have seen this great hope standing like a spirit
beside the visible form; in the fervent worship once universally
given to that gracious presence, I have beheld an acknowledge-
ment of a higher as well as a gentler power than that of the
strong hand and the might that makes the right, – and in every
earnest votary, one who, as he knelt, was in this sense pious
beyond the reach of his own thought, and 'devout beyond the
meaning of his will.'

(Jameson 1852: xix)

For Jameson, apparently, the significance of this image of female
power lay in its beneficence and gentleness. The amount of references
to Jameson in George Eliot's notebook as she wrote *Romola* suggest
that Jameson's idea of the madonna, and not just Comte's idea of the
human madonna which must replace the saintly as an object of worship, was in George Eliot's mind as she wrote (Wiesenfarth 1981:
183–8). Jameson's idea must have appealed to George Eliot, although
once more George Eliot is unlikely to have accepted it unquestioned.
The unqualified optimism of Jameson's image probably struck
George Eliot as naïve. In the George Eliot canon, women's power
has its dark side, is perhaps, like other forms of power, predominantly
dark. Gwendolen's monumentality is a product of her Lamia qualities;
Mrs Transome's is inextricable from her sin and her bitterness;
Maggie's is closely associated with her demons. One reason for the
failure of Maggie's flood scene and 'Romola's waking' is that in both
George Eliot is trying to suppress that dark side.

The strain of an idealized ending is not the only similarity between
the two novels. In *Romola*, as in *The Mill on the Floss*, the heroine is
introduced to us as her father deprecates the efficacy of her intelligence
and deplores the fact that that attribute was not manifest in a son
instead (*The Mill on the Floss* I: 24; *Romola* I: 77–8). The gulf between
Romola and Dino (I: 244) reminds us of that between Maggie and
Tom. But more importantly, Romola's relation to Baldassarre suggests a vengeful subconscious below the altruistic consciousness, very
similar to that suggested by the demon imagery surrounding Maggie.

In chapter 42, Romola saves Baldassarre's life:

She felt an impulse to dart away as from a sight of horror; and
again, a more imperious need to keep close by the side of this old

man whom, the divination of keen feeling told her, her husband
had injured. In the very instant of this conflict she still leaned
towards him and kept her right hand ready to administer more
wine, while her left was passed under his neck.

(II: 125)

Ostensibly the conflict is between the righteous impulse to save
Baldassarre's life and the unworthy impulse to let him die because he
is a threat to her husband. However, that husband is an object of
loathing for Romola, so the impulse to keep his potential murderer
alive can be seen in a rather more equivocal light. This suggestion is
developed on the second meeting of Romola and Baldassarre:

Romola started as [Baldassarre's] glance was turned on her, but
her immediate thought was that he had seen Tito. And as she
felt the look of hatred grating on her, something like a hope
arose that this man might be the criminal, and that her husband
might not have been guilty towards him. If she could learn that
now, by bringing Tito face to face with him, and have her mind
set at rest!
'If you will come with me,' she said, 'I can give you shelter and
food until you are quite rested and strong. Will you come?'
'Yes,' said Baldassarre, 'I shall be glad to get my strength. I
want to get my strength,' he repeated, as if he were muttering to
himself, rather than speaking to her.
'Come!' she said, inviting him to walk by her side.

(II: 141–2)

Later in the same interview Romola gives Baldassarre money that he
spends on a knife with which to kill Tito:

'Can I do nothing for you?' said Romola. 'Let me give you
some money that you may buy food. It will be more plentiful
soon.'
    She had put her hand into her scarsella as she spoke, and held
out her palm with several *grossi* in it. She purposely offered him
more than she would have given any other man in the same
circumstances. He looked at the coins a little while, and then
said –
'Yes, I will take them.'
She poured the coins into his palm, and he grasped them tightly.
Tell me,' said Romola, almost beseechingly. 'What shall you –'

But Baldassarre had turned away from her, and was walking again towards the bridge.

(II: 143–4)

Actually, George Eliot does not follow this through: Tito, like Captain Wybrow of 'Mr Gilfil's love story' and Grandcourt in *Daniel Deronda*, does not die by the knife that has been appropriated for that purpose. Tito and Baldassarre's deadly embrace in water is like Tom and Maggie's 'embrace never to be parted' – a powerful image used later by D. H. Lawrence in *Women in Love*. In this and other parallels between Baldassarre's murderous desire and erotic desire, George Eliot again suggests the affinity between the two. Even though the knife is not used to murder Tito, Romola's money buys the knife, and the wooden and repetitive dialogue gives the impression that both Romola and Baldassarre are in a half-dazed or entranced state – the state in which all murders take place in George Eliot's fiction. All this implicates Romola in Tito's murder.

The questionable relationship between Romola and Baldassarre develops in the same chapter, 'The visible madonna', in which George Eliot is apparently trying to establish her heroine as the positivist ideal, the human madonna. On the next page we find the following description:

the children trotted or crawled towards her, and pulled her black skirts, as if they were impatient at being all that long way off her face. She yielded to them, weary as she was, and sat down on the straw, while the little pale things peeped in to her basket and pulled her hair down, and the feeble voices around her said, 'The Holy Virgin be praised!' 'It was the procession!' 'The Mother of God has had pity on us!'
. . . 'Bless you, madonna! bless you.'

(II: 146)

This peculiar juxtaposition would seem to support a reading in keeping with my analyses of *Adam Bede* and *The Mill on the Floss*. The traditional image of the madonna is one of a helpmate and handmaiden to God and mother to Christ, that is to say, traditionally her power is used to support and comfort the divine patriarchy. Comte's glorification of the human madonna is likewise fundamentally partriarchal in that it provides a dignified and 'important' role for women while reserving all real political power for men. By contrast,

Anna Jameson's image of the madonna, which I quoted earlier, sees the madonna's power as an *alternative* to patriarchal power and this seems to be the version George Eliot has espoused in her portrayal of Romola. The juxtaposition seems otherwise inexplicable, as is the similar evidence of conscious altruism in conflict with subconscious vengeance in Dinah and Maggie.

All the missing fathers of other George Eliot heroines seem to be clustered around Romola. The natural fathers of Hetty, Dinah, Esther, Dorothea, and Gwendolen are all dead and, as U.C. Knoepflmacher has pointed out, are replaced somewhat ineffectually by uncles (Knoepflmacher 1975). Their ineffectuality is crucial – it means that Mr Poyser and Mr Brooke, for example, are not only literally uncles but they also have avuncular personalities: they can never transcend that affable, well-meaning, but somehow impotent role to become father figures. Mr Gascoigne, Gwendolen's uncle, tries to assume the authority of a surrogate father, but the peculiar impermeability of Gwendolen renders this impossible, and his efforts assume an aspect of irrelevance that they could never have assumed had he been her real father. Maggie Tulliver has a father, but only until her mid-teens.

On the death of her own father, in 1849, Marian Evans wrote to her friends Charles and Cara Bray,

> What shall I be without my Father? It will seem as if a part of
> my moral nature were gone. I had a horrid vision of myself last
> night becoming earthly sensual and devilish for want of that
> purifying restraining influence.

> (Letters I: 284)

In light of this, the autobiographical resonances of *The Mill on the Floss*, and the demonic imagery with which Maggie is surrounded, it seems unlikely that the determining event of Maggie's life, her elopement with Stephen Guest, could have happened if her father had been present, just as it is unlikely that Marian Evans would have become Marian Lewes, or indeed George Eliot, had her father lived.

Mr Tulliver, significantly, is nothing like Robert Evans. Robert Evans never went into litigation, never lost his property, seems, from his curt journal entries, to have had none of Mr Tulliver's volatility, and also seems, in a letter of 1848 from Cara Bray to Sara Hennell, to have been far less affectionate than the representation of Mr Tulliver:

[Robert Evans] takes opportunities now of saying kind things to M. A. contrary to his wont. Poor girl, it shows how rare they are by the gratitude with which she repeats the commonest expressions of kindness.

(Letters I: 272)

Dianne Sadoff has speculated about Marian Evans's relationship with her father (Sadoff 1982: 68–9). She agrees with Ruby Redinger's belief that the affectionate Mr Tulliver is more likely a fantasy father (Redinger 1976: 166). Sadoff then goes on to interpret 'Amos Barton', with this in mind, as a daughter's incest fantasy. Sadoff quotes selectively from the final paragraph of 'Amos Barton', ignoring the clear indications of sadness and sacrifice in Patty and the contrasting image of Dickie as having been able, by virtue of his masculinity, to live his life normally, without any matching sacrifice to his father. Sadoff's analysis is based on the female seduction-fantasy theory of Freud, which may well itself have been a father's – Freud's own – fantasy.

The conspicuous absence of fathers from George Eliot's fiction suggests the opposite of Sadoff's picture of the quietly compliant and doting daughter: it shows signs of decided father-fatigue. Her fiction was both the fruit and the defining feature of the life that began for her after her father's death. Robert Evans had dominated the first half of her life; perhaps she decided not to let him or his like into the second half. In George Eliot's two fictional portraits of Robert Evans, his paternal potency has been subtly removed: Adam Bede is described before he enters into the role of father; and Caleb Garth's fatherhood is relegated to the margins of *Middlemarch* in that he is Mary's father, not Dorothea's. George Eliot leaves Dorothea the freedom of fatherlessness, which, however, Dorothea abuses by immediately marrying an imagined father figure with disastrous consequences.

Romola is the exception. Perhaps George Eliot felt that fifteenth-century Florence was distant enough to allow the intrusion of fathers and fatherhood as an issue. Bardo, Bernardo, and Baldassarre are echoes of each other: Bardo's name is included in Bernardo's, just as the name of his role, father, is included in the name of Bernardo's role, godfather; Baldassarre, like Bardo, is a scholar, deserted by his son; Bernardo ends his life a prisoner, like Baldassarre; Baldassarre tells Romola, 'you would have been my daughter!' (II: 239) just as Bernardo, a few pages later, tells her, 'I am your father' (II: 248).

Their three names, each beginning with 'B', echo the Florentine 'Babbo' which we hear in reference to Tito (II: 264).

As Felicia Bonaparte, among other critics, has noted, Romola's fourth father is Savonarola (Bonaparte 1979: 198). A spiritual and intellectual father, he is chosen because of his influence, as opposed to the unchosen fathers in nature (Bardo), in the church (Bernardo), or in law (Baldassarre). Nevertheless, the desire for a father is operative in her choice. The way to conversion is opened by Romola's impulse to call Savonarola 'father':

> Yet she could not again simply refuse to be guided; she was constrained to plead; and in her new need to be reverent while she resisted, the title which she had never given him before came to her lips without forethought.
> 'My father . . .'

(II: 102)

The narratorial insistence on the idea that Romola's conversion was instigated by personal attachment to Savonarola underlines this affinity. In her movement from the polytheistic to the monotheistic stage of her history, Romola transfers her devotion from one father to another:

> 'I would rather have no guidance but yours, father,' said Romola, looking anxious.

(II: 113)

> Her trust in Savonarola's nature as greater than her own made a large part of the strength she had found.

(II: 149)

> Romola's trust in Savonarola was something like a rope suspended securely by her path, making her step elastic while she grasped it; if it were suddenly removed, no firmness of the ground she trod could save her from staggering, or perhaps from falling.

(II: 150)

Savonarola too is placed in momentary relation to each of her other fathers: his voice is the external echo of Baldassarre's vengeful desire (I: 345); his life ends at the hands of Florentine justice, as does Bernardo's; his influence bends Romola's life to a pattern of joyless self-sacrifice as does Bardo's. But the most striking common characteristic of all these fathers is the force of ego, manifested as will to

96

power in various ways: Bardo desires his name to be remembered forever; Baldassarre wants his injury avenged at all costs; Bernardo goes as far as conspiracy in order to maintain the rank he held under the Medici; and Savonarola's will to power has no bounds, as becomes apparent when he tells Romola that the cause of his party is the cause of God's kingdom (II: 309).

This throws some light on the striking *ménage* at the end of the novel. In it, as in the earlier stages of other George Eliot novels, the father figure is conspicuously absent; Romola herself has taken on that role. This has been prepared in Romola's earlier visit to Tessa's house:

> She sat down in Tito's chair, and put out her arms toward the lad, whose eyes had followed her. He hesitated: and, pointing his small fingers at her with a half-puzzled, half-angry feeling, said, 'That's Babbo's chair,' not seeing his way out of the difficulty if Babbo came and found Romola in his place.
>
> (II: 264)

The idea of Romola being in Babbo's 'place' is set in opposition to Savonarola's protestations on the road out of Florence, 'come, my daughter, come back to your place!' (II: 111) and the title of chapter 42, 'Romola in her place'. The scene between Romola and Lillo continues as follows:

> 'But Babbo is not here, and I shall go soon. Come, let me nurse you as he does,' said Romola . . .
>
> Tessa, who had hitherto been occupied in coaxing Ninna out of her waking peevishness, now sat down in her low chair, near Romola's knees, arranging Ninna's tiny person to advantage, jealous that the strange lady too seemed to notice the boy most, as Naldo did.
>
> (II: 264–5)

With Tessa and Ninna in their wonted places and postures, the family tableau is complete, but with Romola in place of Tito.

In the epilogue, this temporary substitution has become a permanent one. We are told that Tessa's face 'wore even a more perfect look of childish content than in her younger days' (II: 442) and that 'there was a placidity in Romola's face which had never belonged to it in youth' (II: 443). It seems that Romola and Tessa have gained, from the formation of this unusual partnership, something that overrules the obvious disadvantages of denying their sexual needs (I am assuming that Romola and Tessa are not lovers). Out of the heterosexual context, each woman can relax into a calm unselfconsciousness; neither is placed in anxious tension with an emotionally or physically elusive husband whose invulnerable ego renders her sense of her own value precarious.

The union with Tessa is the final overthrow of the elitism of which Savonarola accused Romola. Romola's proud 'aloofness' might be styled class prejudice or intellectual elitism; in either case, it must be overcome in order to live with and care for Tessa, a witless *contadina* who spends most of her time asleep (I: 37, 223; II: 19, 261, 442).

The Comtean scheme of *Romola* was used by George Eliot as a means toward the end of envisioning what is possible but as yet not only unachieved but unarticulated in human communities and individual lives. Romola seems rather forlorn and disappointed at the end of the novel. Her new-found peace of mind has not restored her to beauty and vigour, but she has defeated the elitism within her and the patriarchal control without.

6

LANGUAGE AND DESIRE
IN *FELIX HOLT*

Peter Coveney, in his introduction to the Penguin English Library edition, implies that the writing of *Felix Holt* was the painful and faltering rehearsal to the polished performance of George Eliot's mature art.[1] Coveney cannot explicitly espouse this position because he still wishes to recover *Felix Holt* as a major work. Far from doing a service to George Eliot (the impulse to defend *Felix Holt* is clearly motivated by protectiveness toward her) this kind of procrustean effort on behalf of a novel tends to blur the very distinctions which make us acknowledge her genius.

The commentaries of many leading critics of all political colours, from F. R. Leavis to Raymond Williams, agree about the weaknesses of *Felix Holt*. Terry Eagleton has defined the 'radicalism' of Felix Holt:

> [Felix's] 'radicalism' . . . consists in a reformist trust in moral
> education and a positivist suspicion of political change – a
> combination heroically opposed by the text to an unsavory
> alliance of opportunist Radical politics with the insensate
> irrationality of the masses.
>
> (Eagleton 1976: 116)

Raymond Williams has located the class bias at the root of such a definition of radicalism:

> [Cobbett] believed, moreover, what George Eliot so obviously
> could not believe, that the common people were something
> other than a mob, and had instincts and habits something
> above drunkenness, gullibility, and ignorance. He would not
> have thought Felix Holt an 'honest demagogue' for telling the
> people that they were 'blind and foolish'. He would have

thought him rather a very convenient ally of the opponents of reform.

(Williams 1958: 105)

And David Craig has analysed the prose through which this dubious radicalism is presented. Having quoted the description of Felix stepping up to speak after the trade union man in chapter 30, Craig demonstrates its stylistic weakness:

> We are not told by what mesmerism or miracle of elocution Felix draws people from afar. The association of 'clear' eyes with moral loftiness is of course sentimental pot-boiler's stock-in-trade, and that blurred 'somehow' is quite unlike George Eliot's typical good prose.

(Craig 1973: 136)

F. R. Leavis makes the same complaints on aesthetic grounds:

> Felix is as noble and courageous in act as in ideal, and is wholly endorsed by his creator. That in presenting these unrealities George Eliot gives proof of a keen interest in political, social, and economic history, and in the total complex movement of civilization, and exhibits an impressive command of the facts, would seem to confirm the deprecatory view commonly taken of the relation between intellectual and novelist.

(Leavis 1948: 66)

Yet despite this common aversion to the Felix and Esther part of the novel, most modern critics, again regardless of their political persuasion, seem to agree that the Mrs Transome chapters of the novel are among George Eliot's finest achievements. Leavis goes so far as to date George Eliot's graduation into his 'great tradition' from her creation of Mrs Transome:

> The beneficent relation between artist and intellectual is to be seen in the new impersonality of the Transome theme. The theme is realized with an intensity certainly not inferior to that of the most poignant autobiographical places in George Eliot, but the directly personal vibration - the directly personal engagement of the novelist - that we feel in Maggie Tulliver's intensities even at their most valid is absent here. 'The more perfect the artist, the more completely separate in him will be the man who suffers and the mind which creates': it is in the part of

Felix Holt dealing with Mrs Transome that George Eliot becomes one of the great creative artists. She has not here, it will be noted, a heroine with whom she can be tempted to identify herself.

(Leavis 1948: 69)

Eagleton also acknowledges Mrs Transome's centrality:

If Felix is in this sense a 'false' centre, the novel has a real but displaced centre in Mrs Transome. Both characters are historically obsolete; Mrs Transome is presented as a pathetically outdated feudalist whose pieties are ridden over roughshod by her Radical son. Yet if the novel mourns in her the death of traditional society, that mourning must be refracted in the case of the equally obsolescent Holt to a 'progressive' position. The Mrs Transome scenes are nothing less than the aesthetic betrayal of this ideological contradiction at the novel's heart – the unabsorbed region of bleakness, nostalgia and frustration with which nothing can be politically done, which is thereby forced to the work's ideological margins, but which protests by its sheer artistry against such relegation.

(Eagleton 1976: 117)

But why should an author choose, as her exponent of feudalism, a woman and an adulteress, whose family is not even the genuine feudal lineage? The most obvious answer – that she wishes to represent feudalism as devoid of true power, decadent, and built upon bogus claims – would imply such hostility to feudalism on George Eliot's part as to make nonsense of the ending, in which 'long possession'[2] is left undisturbed, even though tortuous plot convolutions have been devised in order to threaten it. In fact, the narrator clearly fears any radical disturbance or change and in this resembles Mrs Transome, whose conviction that 'the best happiness [she] shall ever know, will be to avoid the worst misery' (I: 43) amounts to a desire for things to continue as they are. The narrator's affinity with and sympathy for Mrs Transome is recognized by Eagleton, and with that recognition comes the recognition that an analysis of Mrs Transome's place in the novel (since the tentative political allegorical explanation has failed to convince) lies outside the terms of Eagleton's critical approach and, he suggests, outside the novel's system of values: 'The artistic power of the Mrs Transome scenes suggests the residual presence of an ineradicable "personal" disillusionment which refuses to be totalised and absorbed by the novel's official progressivist ideology' (Eagleton 1976: 117).

Mrs Transome, it seems, is a character without a novel. Eagleton was not the first to remark her homelessness. Although Holmstrom and Lerner tell us that George Eliot's reviewers did not see Mrs Transome as 'central and brilliant' (Holmstrom and Lerner 1966: 73), Henry James clearly had an inkling of her significance as he made this tentative stab at the same idea: 'Mrs Transome seems to us an unnatural, or rather, we should say, a superfluous figure . . . She is nevertheless made the occasion . . . of a number of deep and brilliant touches' (Haight 1966: 42).

The question, then, is why is Mrs Transome in this novel? She is clearly, as James and Eagleton remark, out of place. Her story is the creation of a far subtler and more generous side of George Eliot, yet it is neither substantial nor integrated enough to create a balance and tension with the rest of the novel, as, for example, the Gwendolen part of *Daniel Deronda* does with the Jewish part.

Rather than trying to excuse the greater part of *Felix Holt*, or on the contrary damning it and its author, I would like to examine the novel as symptomatic of various strains and changes in George Eliot and her work. The didacticism and naïvety of *Felix Holt* can then be seen not as the true George Eliot, briefly exposed by a dropping of the artistic guard, but rather as one of several identities which have been struggling within George Eliot's art and personality, one which we have seen before and will see again but never quite so completely ascendant over her other identities. Mrs Transome's presence in the novel is a strongly self-critical reflexive element, which in the excellence of its artistry and the complexity of its vision overrules and denies that ascendancy. Nevertheless, her part is so small, her story so static, that she cannot compensate for, but on the contrary exacerbates, the structural inadequacies of this novel.

At the time of writing *Felix Holt*, when she was 46 years old, Marian Lewes was suffering from dyspepsia and worrying about Lewes's health. Her recent publications, *Romola* (1862–3) and 'Brother Jacob' (1864), were not her best. The research for *Romola* had left her exhausted. She was also on the verge of producing the finer, more complex and sophisticated art for which she was to be remembered.

The strains of this particular moment in her life and career took their toll on her state of mind. On 25 March 1865, she wrote in her journal, 'About myself I am in deep depression, feeling powerless, I have written nothing but beginnings since I finished a little article for Pall Mall on the Logic of Servants'. Four days later she wrote, '*I have begun a novel*' (Letters IV: 184). The article to which she refers is perhaps the most unpleasant and embarrassing that she ever wrote[3] (with the possible exception of 'Address to working men, by Felix Holt'). Riddled with sneering class prejudice, 'Servants' logic' shows clearly the kind of condescension, aversion, and, at bottom, fear that would soon produce Felix Holt and his political platitudes.[4] But perhaps it is no accident that this nadir in her political generosity and philosophical sophistication should coincide with deep depression and with physical illness. By October that year, she had only reached page 74 of the novel, and she complains that, 'the last fortnight has been almost unproductive from bad health' (Letters IV: 205). The following April, in a letter to Barbara Bodichon, she writes, 'I am finishing a book, which has been growing slowly like a sickly child, because of my own ailments' (Letters IV: 236).

It is unlikely to be pure coincidence that Mrs Transome is constantly fiddling with medicines.[5] This is not the only indication that she is not as distant from her author as Leavis, in the passage quoted above, supposes. Another striking similarity is Mrs Transome's concern that she might not be invited to dinner:

> She had never seen behind the canvas with which her life was hung. In the dim background there was the burning mount and the tables of the law; in the foreground there was Lady Debarry privately gossiping about her, and Lady Wyverne finally deciding not to send her invitations to dinner.
>
> (II: 210)

Earlier, the narratorial irony about who gets invited to dinner betrays a certain bitterness on behalf of Mrs Transome and of Marian Lewes:

> Even in the days of duelling a man was not challenged for being a bore, nor does this quality apparently hinder him from being much invited to dinner, which is the great index of social responsibility in a less barbarous age.
>
> (I: 300)

The references are reminiscent of Marian Lewes's letter to Cara Bray in 1855:

> Light and easily broken ties are what I neither desire theoretically nor could live for practically. Women who are

satisfied with such ties do *not* act as I have done – they obtain
what they desire and are still invited to dinner.

(Letters II: 214)

Mrs Transome's Toryism is simply a more honest expression of the
political philosophy touted in the Felix part of the novel, in which the
proletariat is seen as subhuman, universal franchise is seen as opening
the doors to anarchy, and 'long possession' is seen as legitimizing the
ownership of any amount of property. But the narrator is strongly
critical of Mrs Transome for the ungenerosity of her politics:

> Mrs Transome, whose imperious will had availed little to ward
> off the great evils of her life, found the opiate for her discontent
> in the exertion of her will about smaller things. She was not
> cruel, and could not enjoy thoroughly what she called the old
> woman's pleasure of tormenting; but she liked every little sign of
> power her lot had left her. She liked that a tenant should stand
> bareheaded below her as she sat on horseback. She liked to insist
> that work done without her orders should be undone from begin-
> ning to end. She liked to be curtsied and bowed to by all the
> congregation as she walked up the little barn of a church. She
> liked to change a labourer's medicine fetched from the doctor,
> and substitute a prescription of her own. If she had only been
> more haggard and less majestic, those who had glimpses of her
> outward life might have said she was a tyrannical, griping
> harridan, with a tongue like a razor. No one said exactly that;
> but they never said anything like the full truth about her, or
> divined what was hidden under that outward life – a woman's
> keen sensibility and dread, which lay screened behind all her
> petty habits and narrow notions, as some quivering thing with
> eyes and throbbing heart may lie crouching behind withered
> rubbish.

(I: 43)

Mrs Transome's mental landscape here is very similar to that
betrayed in 'Servants' logic', and the narrator's disapprobation could
almost be a response to that article. William Myers has contrasted
what he calls the 'cheap sneers' of 'Servants' logic' with the sympathetic representation of labourers in chapter 56 of *Middlemarch* (Myers
1984: 119). Myers's analysis overlooks the difference between Victorian attitudes towards the labouring class and the servant class. It also

overlooks the very personal tone of 'Servants' logic', which leaves the impression that the writer is a hypersensitive woman reacting splenetically to the intimacy of daily contact with servants, a consideration that would not enter into her attitude toward labourers. The last part of the passage quoted above – 'a woman's keen sensibility and dread' – is as resonant of that splenetic reaction as it is of Mrs Transome's situation. There is certainly a disparity between the sensibility of Marian Lewes and that of George Eliot in regard to class bias, and within George Eliot's narration there are further divisions and clashes of sensibility. The clash between this narratorial disapprobation of Mrs Transome's attitude to the social strata beneath her and the narratorial mirroring of that attitude elsewhere in the text is but one example of this.

Mrs Transome is at the extreme right of the political spectrum represented in the novel. Sir Maximus Debarry and his son Philip are the novels representatives of the genuine ruling class, but both are quite liberal in their class sensibilities when compared to Mrs Transome. We are told that Philip is more polite to his valet than to an equal, and Sir Maximus espouses Harold's cause when the latter's illegitimacy has been exposed. The bitterest irony of Mrs Transome's situation is that no one in the community would judge her as harshly as she judges herself.

There are several startling inversions in *Felix Holt*: we expect patriarchy to be the order of the day in Transome Court, but we discover the reverse; the lofty Transomes turn out not to be genuine; the lowly Tommy Trounsem turns out not to be, by rights, lowly; the extravagant exterior of Transome Court conceals a pinched and threadbare interior; Harold reverses expectations by turning Radical, thus betraying his class; Felix, meanwhile, is from the class true radicalism would represent, yet his thinly veiled conservatism is a more serious betrayal of the working class than Harold's cosmetic radicalism is of the gentry.

Foremost of these inversions is the one in which the arch-Tory of the novel emerges as its only genuine Radical. Mrs Transome is a radical not in class but in gender politics. Before Harold's return, she has succeeded in seizing power in a male world, though only, it must be said, because her husband is feeble-minded. By conceiving Harold outside the law and her husband's family, she has appropriated the lineage, made it her own. It is a bitterly ironic nemesis, then, that makes Harold inherit his natural father's capitalistic mentality, so that, on his return, he divests Mrs Transome of the power of which his own conception was but a symbol. The very features that distinguish Mrs Transome as an aristocrat are those that distinguish her as an exceptional beauty and also as a woman not to be ruled by men:

> And you shall wear the longest train at court,
> And look so queenly, all the lords shall say,
> 'She is a royal changeling: there's some crown
> Lacks the right head, since hers wears nought but braids.'
>
> (I: 14, motto to chapter 1)

There is another apparent clash between the class-consciousness that places johnny-come-latelies in Transome Hall and makes an illiterate bill-sticker of the true Transome line and that which insists that members of the aristocracy are physically more beautiful than those of other classes to the point of being distinguishable even in fallen circumstances. These implications attach not only to Mrs Transome but to Esther, the novel's true fallen aristocrat:

> It was a pity the room was so small, Harold Transome thought: this girl ought to walk in a house where there were halls and corridors.
>
> (I: 260)

> 'Then she is a born lady?'
> 'Yes; she has good blood in her veins.'
> 'We talked that over in the housekeeper's room – what a hand and an instep she has, and how her head is set on her shoulders.'
>
> (II: 203)

This can only be adequately accounted for if we see it as essential to George Eliot's metaphoric structure in the novel. Sexual and political power are represented as residing in the same place so that each kind of power can illuminate the other. Denner says to Mrs Transome, 'you've such a face and figure, and will have if you live to be eighty, that everybody is cap in hand to you before they know who you are' (I: 39). 'Cap in hand' is a sign of deference, both to rank and to female beauty. Throughout the novel this interpenetration of the sexual and the political is what lends Mrs Transome her monumentality: 'On the 1st of September, in the memorable year of 1832, some one was expected at Transome Court' (I: 14). Here the radical nature of Mrs Transome's adultery is suggested by the construction of the sentence, in which the fruits of reform and the fruits of adultery are both about to present themselves. Through these juxtapositions, the sexual delinquent, she who refused to obey the dictates of patriarchy, expands to fill a larger symbolic space than her literal role in the novel would ordinarily deserve.

> She had a high-born imperious air which would have marked her as an object of hatred and reviling by a revolutionary mob. Her person was too typical of social distinctions to be passed by with indifference by any one: it would have fitted an empress in her own right, who had had to rule in spite of faction, to dare the violation of treaties and dread retributive invasions, to grasp after new territories, to be defiant in desperate circumstances, and to feel a woman's hunger of the heart for ever unsatisfied.
>
> (I: 40)

It is hard to remember, when reading this passage, that its subject is merely an adulterous wife. The metaphor monumentalizes her adultery, which then becomes an incident of international importance: rather than marginally affecting a few insignificant lives in Treby Magna, Mrs Transome's adultery seems to determine the lives of nations, to alter history. This suggests what a similar will to power might have been capable of had it been the attribute of a male character. In Mrs Transome we are simply shown the consequences of a woman's adultery, but we are continually reminded of the impotence of her actual situation in comparison to a man's situation or to the situation of certain women in other epochs.

This last idea will be raised again in the Prelude to *Middlemarch*. In another time, another culture, Dorothea could have been a Saint Theresa, and Mrs Transome, similarly, could have been an 'empress in her own right', a Cleopatra, perhaps, or a Boudicca, not a saintly figure but nevertheless an admirable and powerful one. This is another instance of George Eliot's insistence that the difference between exceptional men and exceptional women in her own time is that the women's lives are necessarily thwarted and trivialized.

Whereas the political metaphors monumentalize Mrs Transome, the economic metaphors tend to highlight the rather squalid nature of her situation and her experience: 'But heir or no heir, Lawyer Jermyn had had *his* picking out of the estate' (I: 11). The opening clause of this sentence reminds us, on a second reading, of Harold's illegitimacy and therefore suggests that the main clause of the sentence refers not only to the financial but also to the sexual fringe-benefits of his position. Mrs Transome herself realizes the squalid parallels between love and money: ' "I might almost have let myself starve, rather than have scenes of quarrel with the man I had loved, in which I must accuse him of turning my love into a good bargain" ' (II: 243).

We are told that the Transomes' marriage was arranged on the basis of a good bargain: ' "Forty years ago, when she came into this country, they said she was a pictur'; but her family was poor, and so she took up with a hatchet-faced fellow like this Transome" '(I: 11). The weaknesses of Mr Transome's character and person are themselves humiliating to a wife of Mrs Transome's stature, but the humiliation is extenuated by the fact that such marriages can be expected in the feudal situation, where the suitability of a potential husband's station and fortune is likely to take precedence over his personal suitability. The true humiliation comes when Mrs Transome finds that the man she has taken as a lover is also unworthy of her, in this case not because of physical and mental feebleness but because of a vulgarity of soul compared to which physical and mental feebleness begin to look quite attractive.

> He chose always to dress in black, and was especially addicted to
> black satin waistcoats, which carried out the general sleekness of
> his appearance; and this, together with his white, fat, but
> beautifully-shaped hands which he was in the habit of rubbing
> gently on his entrance into a room, gave him very much the air
> of a lady's physician.
>
> (I: 51)

The image of the lady's physician is perhaps the most chilling in all George Eliot's descriptions of sexual aversion. It suggests a man who has a licence to probe into a woman's physical privacy, no matter how much aversion the woman might feel for him. The most interesting aspect of this image is that it refers only to the present time: Jermyn, formerly the object of love and desire, has metamorphosed over the years into someone who can be compared to a lady's physician; his carnal knowledge of Mrs Transome, which was acquired when he was an object of love, can never be erased from his memory and for that reason he has become like the lady's physician, whose intimate knowledge of one's body is intolerable in proportion to his repulsiveness. Not even Grandcourt can make us shudder like this, although his *alter ego* Lush, the man who kicks Grandcourt's dogs for him, is made in the same mould as Jermyn. Our aversion to Jermyn is exacerbated by the paucity of our knowledge of him: we learn most of what we know of him by proxy, through his son Harold. Harold also has fat hands, which he habitually rubs together in the mercantile manner of his natural father, and, like his father his mercantile mentality extends to personal as well as business relations:

> [Harold] had a way of virtually measuring the value of
> everything by the contribution it made to his own pleasure.
>
> (II: 257)

> 'And I don't look languishing enough?'
> 'O yes – rather too much so – at a fine cigar.'
>
> (II: 272)

This consumeristic attitude to women[6] is not restricted to Harold and his father; Felix betrays a very similar attitude when he says, ' "I had a horrible struggle, Esther. But you see I was right. There was a fitting lot in reserve for you. But remember you have cost a great price – don't throw what is precious away." ' (II: 295). Jermyn and Harold are simply extreme examples of a pervasive masculine attitude, and that Harold's son was born of a slave is its logical conclusion.

This line of argument suggests a revision of Eagleton's claim that 'the novel has a real but displaced centre in Mrs Transome' and of James's claim that she is a superfluous figure. Mrs Transome is certainly a centre, but, rather than the displaced centre of the entire novel, she is the centre of a reflexive and critical element flourishing in the interstices of the novel. This element may be described as self-critical in two quite separate ways: in it George Eliot criticizes Marian Lewes; and in it the text deconstructs itself.

In its explorations of reactionary behaviour, self-hating egoism, and ostracism or the fear of ostracism, George Eliot interrogates and evaluates Marian Lewes. Mrs Transome's bitterness, conservatism, and obsessive self-hatred are not unfamiliar from the George Eliot essays and letters. Mrs Transome wallows in self-disgust and hopelessness.

> 'I am a hag!' she said to herself (she was accustomed to give her
> thoughts a very sharp outline), 'an ugly old woman who happens
> to be his mother.'
>
> (I: 30)

'I undid it [her hair] to see what an old hag I am. These fine
clothes you put on me, Denner, are only a smart shroud.'

(II: 199–200)

Haight tells us, in his biography of George Eliot,

In her letters to the Brays there are never more references to her
'ugliness' than during the months of her involvement with
Spencer. 'I am a hideous hag now,' she will write, 'sad and wiz-
ened', 'haggard as an old witch', 'like one of those old hags we
used to see by the wayside in Italy – only a little worse, for want
of the dark eyes and dark hair in contrast with the parchment'.

(Haight 1968: 115)

As Haight's opening sentence suggests, references to what she perceived as her ugliness are frequent, though never quite so extreme, at
other times in her life.[7] After she settles down to life with G. H. Lewes
and the writing of fiction, the self-castigation abates, but a remnant
always lingers on as a sort of warning. It is probably because of this
that George Eliot spent her entire career thinking and rethinking the
problem of realizing the equivalent centre of self in others. The interest is in no way academic: she sees the constant concern for that
equivalent centre as the only way of escaping from herself. Mrs
Transome's similar self-hating egoism is simply an extreme negative
example of what is implicit in the Prelude to *Middlemarch*: that we all,
men and women alike, not only want but *need* vocation in order to
escape from the prison of self-despair.

Mrs Transome has no vocation, neither has she an interest or occupation to take her mind off her own sorrows and fears. It is interesting
to note that Shakespeare, Wordsworth,[8] and George Eliot herself, in
Silas Marner, all suggest, as an answer to the problem of self-despair,
the rearing of a child. That, in a very literal and practical way, would
'reconcile self-despair with the rapturous consciousness of life beyond
self'. But in George Eliot's own life and in the Prelude to *Middlemarch*
vocation takes the place of child care as the medium through which the
self-hating egoist can at last forget herself.

Mrs Transome claims that she works as a farm bailiff: ' "You must
excuse me from the satin cushions. That is a part of the old woman's
duty I am not prepared for. I am used to be chief bailiff, and to sit in
the saddle two or three hours every day" ' (I: 28). But this role will be
undermined by the narrator when it is represented not as a means of

satisfying the need to be of service but as a means of satisfying the need to assert power (see p. 104).

Harold himself could have, in the past, been the means of escape; Mrs Transome could have played Silas to Harold's Eppie, but because of the secret of his illegitimacy, Harold severed Mrs Transome more completely from the community, rather than binding her to it. Therefore any beneficent effect that might have derived from the child would nevertheless have ended with his departure from the family home. But here again, Mrs Transome has missed an opportunity. She did not, even for the period of Harold's childhood, take advantage of the opportunity the child offered to escape from egoism: her ambition for Harold led her to wish for the death of her first son, a wish the narrator presents as self-destructive through an extended metaphor comparing the wish to gambling (I: 31).

A third opportunity for escape is offered to Mrs Transome in the person of Denner, her servant, and again Mrs Transome refuses. She seems to want her own destruction, to relish her pain, self-disgust, and isolation. As Laurence Lerner has pointed out, she is perverse enough to envy Denner's capacity for love, even though she herself is the object of that love (Lerner 1967: 238). Denner is a serving woman both literally and symbolically. On the symbolic level, her service is like that of Christ washing the feet of the apostles – it is Denner's capacity to serve that makes the fulfilment of her life; on the literal level, it is the reason for Mrs Transome's inability to reciprocate Denner's affection. Mrs Transome, in her hour of need, goes not to Denner but to Esther, a stranger, forty years her junior, but of her own class and therefore an acceptable confidante. That Denner has always known Mrs Transome's secret is a necessary evil of employing personal servants; the enormous resource that Denner's knowledge and sympathy could have been is lost on Mrs Transome because of her class prejudice. We are reminded again of 'Servant's logic', completed only a short time before Denner was conceived in the mind of her author. Once again it becomes apparent that George Eliot not only sees all Marian Lewes's faults but, in the selflessness of textual production, can overcome them. Unlike so many portrayals of servants in Victorian fiction, indeed unlike other portrayals of servants within this text, the characterization of Denner is free from ridicule, condescension, quaintness, and two-dimensionality.

Most of George Eliot's fictional egoists are complacent: Arthur Donnithorn, Tom Tulliver, Rosamond, Gwendolen (at the outset of her story), and Grandcourt, to name a few, all have high opinions of themselves. Only Mrs Transome has Marian Evans's (and to a lesser extent, Marian Lewes's) brand of egoism: the egoism that is morbidly obsessed with the deficiencies, rather than complacently confident of the excellences, of the egoist. Ironically, the very impulse to such severe and protracted self-examination is a perfect example of that same self-hating egoism, and this too is acknowledged by the text in the comic relief of Mrs Holt, who is a parody of Mrs Transome.[9]

Meanwhile, in the excellence of Mrs Transome's characterization, which, like the character herself, is both magnificent and thwarted, this reflexive element casts doubt upon the Felix/Esther part of the novel, that is to say, the finest part of the text is that in which the text criticizes itself. The happy ending, for example, in which we are told that Esther marries her hero, is put into question by the coexistence within the text of a heroine of far greater scope than Esther, who, because of her scope cannot be confined within the bounds of the traditional female role of faithful wife and loving mother.

The relationship between Mrs Transome and Esther cannot be described as fitting easily into the counterpoint categories that have been discussed in other chapters. The story of *Felix Holt*, as far as plot goes, is more Esther's story than Mrs Transome's. Nevertheless, the monumental metaphors normally kept for the heroines of the novels are here reserved for Mrs Transome, and Esther is described in the diminishing conventionally feminine terms usually reserved for the counterpoint characters (Hetty, Lucy, Tessa, Rosamond, and Mirah). If Mrs Transome were absent from this novel, we would be justified in arguing that Esther represents a complete reversal of George Eliot's ideas about women – ideas that are expressed not only before but also, and most forcefully, after the writing of *Felix Holt*. The following sentences might possibly have been written about Dinah, Maggie, Romola, Dorothea, or Gwendolen, but they could never have provided the unquestioned last word, the answer to the problems of the other heroines lives, as they do for Esther:

> In this, at least, her woman's lot was perfect: that the man she loved was her hero; that her woman's passion and her reverence for rarest goodness rushed together in an undivided current.
>
> (II): 313)

> Esther said all this in a playful tone, but she ended, with a grave look of appealing submission –

'I mean – if you approve. I wish to do what you think it will be right to do.'

(II: 355)

'Quite sure!' said Esther, shaking her head; 'for then I should have honoured you less. I am weak – my husband must be greater and nobler than I am.'

(II: 356)

The Esther story, in fact, bears a disconcerting resemblance to *The Taming of the Shrew*. In chapter 51, where Esther more or less places her hand beneath Felix's foot, the phrases used to describe Esther are saccharine and rather clumsily constructed: 'He looked at her still with questioning eyes – he grave, she mischievously smiling' (II: 353); 'with a pretty saucy movement of her head' (II: 354); ' "Oh yes," she said, with a little toss' (II: 356); ' "I call that retribution," said Esther, with a laugh as sweet as the morning thrush' (II: 356). Phrases used to describe the embraces of Esther and Felix are wooden and forced. Altogether, the ending of *Felix Holt* is characterized by poor prose, a rarity in the George Eliot canon. In fact, the prose of chapter 51 is so poor that it seems to be parodying itself. The saccharine descriptions of Esther can be read as a sardonic response to the abject slavishness of her submission to Felix.[10] The conscious conservative in George Eliot might have seized control of this ending, but the subconscious subversive is at work to sabotage it.

Take for example the sentence, 'She was not reading, but stitching; and as her fingers moved nimbly, something played about her lips like a ray' (II: 352). Everything after the semi-colon is poorly written and clichéd. Surely by 1866 the reading public was weary of the 'nimble fingers' of women sewing and of smiles 'playing about' women's lips like rays of sunshine, but quite apart from these clichés, the clumsy coyness of that 'something', like the 'somehow' to which Craig objects in the chapter 30 description of Felix (see p. 100), is symptomatic of a faltering and incomplete conception. However, the interest of the sentence lies in what comes before the semi-colon. Why put it negatively? Is the same sensibility that admires nimble fingers at work in the construction of that clause? Or is a conflicting element at work here, the same, perhaps, that inserted that little doubt into the sentence I quoted earlier: 'In this, *at least*, her woman's lot was perfect' (my emphasis). The opposition of reading and stitching is clear throughout the George Eliot canon: heroines read; counterpoint

113

women stitch. Earlier in the novel, Esther reads, but she reads Byron, to whom Marian Lewes had grown more and more averse over the years.[11] Nevertheless, the movement from reading, no matter how inadvisedly, to stitching, must, in the context of George Eliot's many sardonic comments on the pointlessness of needlework as mere occupation for women, be seen as a change for the worse. There is no solution to this contradiction. As in the prison scene in *Adam Bede*, meaning collapses, and the conflict is left without resolution except on a reflexive level. In this case, the bad writing and collapsing meanings of chapter 51 can be understood only as a playing out of George Eliot's trouble with language, and it is in this sense also that we can come to a clearer understanding of the role played by the novel's untamed shrew, Mrs Transome.

Mrs Transome is almost an abstraction, and this is why her part in the novel is so static. She personifies the strain her author is feeling, the strain to produce, through this unwieldy medium of language, the object of her desire, the catharsis of articulation, the delivery of George Eliot's mature thought and feeling, in their full lucid complexity. That delivery will not take place until the two final novels. To say this is not to unequivocally prioritize the final novels over the earlier work. It is quite possible to argue that *Adam Bede* and *The Mill on the Floss* are of equivalent stature. However, because the methods and concerns of the late novels were different from those of the early, George Eliot felt the strain of stretching her abilities to meet these new challenges.

What most binds Mrs Transome to her author is her hypersensitivity, the opposition in her of language and desire. George Eliot's life and work both demonstrate the problematic relationship between language and desire. George Lewes kept reviews from her; she preferred not to hear. Gillian Beer has discussed the issue of deafness in George Eliot's life and work (Beer 1986: 55–8). Time and time again, in her fiction and in her letters, George Eliot/Marian Lewes articulates a desire, in her heroines and in herself, to be deaf in order to shut out abusive, coercive, judgemental, or simply vulgar voices: the voices of the community in *The Mill on the Floss*, especially towards the end of the novel in 'St Ogg's passes judgment'; the voices of the community in *Middlemarch*, passing hasty, usually ungenerous, often mistaken judgement on Dorothea and on Lydgate; the heard thoughts of vulgar minds that oppress Latimer in 'The lifted veil'. All these voices are perceived by the narrators very much as Marian

Lewes perceived the voices of her critics, both literary and personal.

Therefore we find, in *The Mill on the Floss*, an opposition between voice and water. Water is used as a symbol of desire; it muffles language, judgement, maxims, and that is one reason why Maggie perceives her elopement, the gratification of her desire, as drowning, submersion, deafness.

Although, in most instances, language and desire are perceived as opposed to each other, language is not always perceived as oppressive – indeed, how could it be in the writing of a woman who gained the gratification of many of her desires through the artful use of language? An anonymous reviewer in *The Spectator*, probably R. H. Hutton, noticed the stress on language and text as an object of desire in *Romola*. Having quoted the passage in which Baldassarre suddenly regains his memory and has access to the hitherto indecipherable page of Greek before him, Hutton makes the following observation:

> This passage, taken with those which lead up to it, whether they refer to Bardo or Baldassarre, has the effect of reproducing one great feature in the age of the revival of learning with the finest effect – that sense of large *human* power which the mastery over a great ancient language, itself the key to a magnificent literature, gave, and which made scholarship then a *passion*, while with us it has almost relapsed into an antiquarian dryasdust pursuit. We realize again, in reading about Bardo and Baldassarre, how, for these times, the first sentence of St. John, 'In the beginning was the Word,' had regained all its force, to the exclusion, perhaps, of the further assertion that the Word was with God and was God.
>
> (Carroll 1971: 201)

Dinah's predicament toward the end of *Adam Bede* is the choice between Eros and Logos, love and preaching, and, since the preaching of the Word is Dinah's vocation, it is perceived as an opposition of two mutually exclusive goods. Similarly, the most explicit reference to the need for deafness in *Middlemarch* is in the need to block out tragically pathetic, not vulgar or antagonistic voices: the narrator of *Middlemarch* declares half-ironically, half-sincerely, that we need our partial deafness (insensitivity, stupidity, obliviousness) because we could not long survive full awareness of the pain around us:

> That element of tragedy which lies in the very fact of frequency, has not yet wrought itself into the coarse emotion of mankind;

and perhaps our frames could hardly bear much of it. If we had a keen vision and feeling of all ordinary human life, it would be like hearing the grass grow and the sqirrel's heart beat, and we should die of that roar which lies on the other side of silence. As it is, the quickest of us walk about well wadded with stupidity.

(*Middlemarch* I: 297–8)

The idea of the need for deafness suggests that the language that oppresses comes from without: other people's words militate against the desires of the subject. The subject's own words, on the contrary, are perceived as possible catharsis, release – ejaculation, if one can be allowed to include men in the ranks of those whose sexuality is smothered and oppressed by the language of others. The subject's desire to speak, which is often frustrated by the din of other speakers or by the subject's fear of being judged, is illustrated by George Eliot most clearly and frequently in her characters' pressing need for confession. The relation of language and desire in the George Eliot canon, then, is double-edged: we need to deafen ourselves to the articulation of others so as to make way for the effulgence of our own words: ' "Don't speak!" Mrs Transome said peremptorily. "Don't open your lips again. You have said enough; I will speak now" ' (II: 243). Tina in 'Mr Gilfil's love story', Mr Tryan and Janet in 'Janet's repentance', Hetty, Godfrey Cass, and Gwendolen all need to confess in order to relieve pent-up feelings of guilt and a consequent sense of alienation from other people.

Arthur Donnithorn tries to confess his desire for Hetty in order to elicit a response from Mr Irwine, a response that would thwart that desire. Had he told Mr Irwine about his feelings for Hetty, those feelings – vague, prelinguistic, fluid – would have been placed in a context of linguistic distinctions and hierarchies by Mr Irwine's response. Words like 'duty', 'honour', 'responsibility', 'station', 'rank', 'sin', would have been used in an attempt to discipline and regulate Arthur's sexuality.

The sympathy, even fondness, with which Mr Irwine is presented precludes the conclusion that such discipline and regulation would have been a bad thing. George Eliot acknowledges and yearns for the subjunctive, for a world in which it would be more possible to gratify desire without hurting other people, but she has a strong sense of the unpleasant necessities of the actual world, and especially of how often those unpleasant necessities entail the renunciation of desire.

The opposition between language and desire is not restricted to spoken language: at times George Eliot evinces an antagonism for written texts, a belief that written texts militate against desire. After Casaubon's death in *Middlemarch*, the question, for a time, is whether Dorothea is going to give her life to finishing his 'Key to all Mythologies', and this and the possibility of reawakening herself sexually with Will are seen as mutually exclusive. At the beginning of *Romola*, Bardo says that Romola fainted in the search for the references needed to explain a passage of Callimachus (*Romola* I: 78). Callimachus is famous for his dictum, 'A big book is a big evil.'

Above her recognition of the need to confess and the need to be deaf, the need to speak at the expense of other speakers, one senses in George Eliot a weariness and sadness that we must engage in the whole self-foregrounding, greedy, strife-ridden business. In her letters she sometimes expresses a desire to give up the enterprise of articulation, self-justification, and the assertion of self, as in this letter of 1852 to Herbert Spencer: 'I think of retiring from the world. . . . I should soon be on an equality, in point of sensibility, with the star-fish and sea-egg' (Letters VIII: 51). In this she anticipates that later Eliot, who, in 'The Love Song of J. Alfred Prufrock', a poem riddled with the problems of articulation and the irreconcilability of language and desire, wrote

> I should have been a pair of ragged claws
> Scuttling across the floors of silent seas.

Both these quotations suggest a peaceful and welcome silence not only through the metaphor of calm inarticulate life but also through the idea of that life passing under a soothing and muffling blanket of water – a suggestion that is spun out to its fullest extent in *The Mill on the Floss*.

The Mrs Transome chapters of *Felix Holt* are permeated by this issue of language and desire:

> But these things are often unknown to the world; for there is
> much pain that is quite noiseless; and vibrations that make
> human agonies are often a mere whisper in the roar of hurrying
> existence. There are glances of hatred that stab and raise no cry
> of murder; robberies that leave man or woman for ever beggared
> of peace and joy, yet kept secret by the sufferer – committed to
> no sound except that of low moans in the night, seen in no

writing except that made on the face by the slow months of
suppressed anguish and early morning tears. Many an inherited
sorrow that has marred a life has been breathed into no human
ear.

The poets have told us of a dolorous enchanted forest in the
under world. The thorn-bushes there, and the thick-barked
stems, have human histories hidden in them; the power of
unuttered cries dwells in the passionless-seeming branches, and
the red warm blood is darkly feeding the quivering nerves of a
sleepless memory that watches through all dreams. These things
are a parable.

(I: 13)

These are the final paragraphs of the author's introduction to *Felix
Holt*. Their effect on the reader is similar to that of the Prelude to
Middlemarch: they seem to encourage an expectation of a more
indubitable centrality for their subject than she achieves in the ensuing
pages; and they seem to contradict the quite different expectation
encouraged by the title.

The emphasis of the penultimate paragraph is not simply on suffering but on suffering in silence. Moreover, the silence is not surrounding silence but the silence of the sufferer herself amid external
din ('and vibrations that make human agonies are often a mere
whisper in the roar of hurrying existence'). The connection between
suffering and silence in the characterization of Mrs Transome is
in large part to do with her need for confession, but beyond that
immediate issue there is a sense in which her discourse is repressed
by the men around her. One is given the impression that this issue
of forced silence is not limited to adulteresses in need of confession
but is in fact common to women who live with men. It is a disturbing
fictional representation of what Sarah Ellis discusses, in *Wives of
England*:

I have listened much when men have been discussing the merits
of women, and have never heard any quality so universally
commended as quietness; while the opposite demerit of a tongue
too loud, too ready, or too importunate in its exertions, has been
as universally condemned. Thus I am inclined to think that
silence in general, and smooth speech when language must be
used, are ranked by most men among the highest excellences of
the female character; while on the other hand, those wordy

weapons sometimes so injudiciously made use of, are of all
things what they most abhor.

(Ellis 1843: 83)

The final paragraph of the author's introduction suggests that this
novel will be, in some way, a guided tour of hell, a suggestion which
has been made earlier:

The coachman was an excellent travelling companion and
commentator on the landscape: he could tell the names of sites
and persons, and explained the meaning of groups, as well as the
shade of Virgil in a more memorable journey.

(I: 9)

The hell we are visiting is one in which the sufferer cannot articulate
her suffering, where the inability to articulate, in fact, has become a
large part of the suffering itself, without which problem the pain could
long ago have been relieved by the catharsis of expression. (The
alliterated 'h' in 'have human histories hidden' imitates the broken
breathing of 'unuttered cries'). In the opening chapters, this kind of
suffering is seen in action:

She, poor woman, knew quite well that she had been unwise,
and that she had been making herself disagreeable to Harold to
no purpose. But half the sorrows of women would be averted if
they could repress the speech they know to be useless – nay, the
speech they have resolved not to utter.

(I: 56–7)

Mrs Transome desires to speak, but she also, and at the same time,
dreads speaking. The peculiar nature of her tragedy is that either
eventuality, the continuation or the breaking of silence, will cause her
intense pain. The dread of speaking stems from both the fear of
exposing herself and the fear of stimulating others, especially Jermyn,
to responding speech:

To-day she was more conscious than usual of that bitterness
which was always in her mind in Jermyn's presence, but which
was carefully suppressed: – suppressed because she could not
endure that the degradation she inwardly felt should ever
become visible or audible in acts or words of her own – should
ever be reflected in any word or look of his. For years there had
been a deep silence about the past between them: on her side,

119

because she remembered; on his, because he more and more forgot.

(I: 171)

But no sooner did the words 'You have brought it on me' rise within her than she heard within also the retort, 'You brought it on yourself.' Not for all the world beside could she bear to hear that retort uttered from without.

(I: 174)

When Jermyn does respond, we glimpse a perversity and volatility in language that will become central: 'Perhaps some of the most terrible irony of the human lot is this of a deep truth coming to be uttered by lips that have no right to it' (II: 242).

Mrs Transome's relation to this issue of speech becomes increasingly erotic as the silent years proceed; repression renders speech increasingly desirable and yet, at the same time, increasingly taboo, so that when Mrs Transome finally speaks, her utterance is spasmodic, uncontrolled, revealing: 'Jermyn turned to look in Mrs Transome's face: it was long since he had heard her speak to him as if she were losing her self-command' (I: 172). This unruliness of language, this view of language as something obscurely powerful and frightening because it is beyond our control, is a problem shared by other characters in the novel. Jermyn himself suffers from it, though he is too complacent to realize it: 'temper and selfish insensibility will defeat excellent gifts – will make a sensible person shout when shouting is out of place, and will make a polished man rude when his polish might be of eminent use to him'(II: 242). If Jermyn is unaware of his own lack of control over language, he certainly is aware of the dangers of uncontrolled language from Mrs Transome, as becomes apparent when we learn that, 'He almost felt inclined to throttle the voice out of this woman' (II: 244).

Rufus Lyon's uneasiness when he is restrained from speech is a comic inversion of Mrs Transome's tragic thirty-year silence:

But the little man suffered from imprisoned ideas, and was as restless as a racer held in. He could not sit down again, but walked backwards and forwards, stroking his chin, emitting his low gutteral interjection under the pressure of clauses and sentences which he longed to utter aloud, as he would have done in his own study.

(II: 8)

With a deftness worthy of Jane Austen, George Eliot turns the comic contrast to a tragic parallel later in Rufus's story. The parallel between Rufus and Mrs Transome is underscored by the use in both cases of a metaphor involving language and physical pain:

> Every sentence was as pleasant to her as if it had been cut in her bared arm.
>
> (I: 173)

> 'Then Miss Lyon is Annette's child?'
> The minister shivered as if the edge of a knife had been drawn across his hand.
>
> (II: 21)

Language is seen as the central weapon of power struggle in this novel: Rufus attempts to gain ascendancy over Augustus Debarry through debate; fear of a conflict of words leads Debarry's curate to run away; and Johnson, Felix, and the trade union man all use oratory to win the Sproxton workers. It is ironic, then that Harry and Mr Transome, the two least powerful figures in the novel (again ironically, since Mr Transome is the titular patriarch), have abandoned language and found happiness together in communal silence:

> 'He can talk well enough if he likes,' said Gappa, evidently thinking that Harry, like the monkeys, had deep reasons for his reticence.
> 'You mind him,' he added, nodding at Esther, and shaking with low-toned laughter. 'You'll hear: he knows the right names of things well enough, but he likes to make his own.'
>
> (II: 208)

The tremendous pressure building up behind the dam of Mrs Transome's silence is full of dramatic potential, and yet that potential is wasted: the breaking of her silence is not climactic; it takes place in a novel to which it is not central; it takes place only in the presence of Jermyn, whom time and its gradual action on his character have inured to the point that its power is lost on him. Her impotence is foreshadowed in her earlier conflict with Harold:

> Mrs Transome's rising temper was turned into a horrible
> sensation, as painful as a sudden concussion from something
> hard and immovable when we have struck out with our fist,
> intending to hit something warm, soft, and breathing like

121

ourselves. Poor Mrs Transome's strokes were sent jarring back
on her by a hard unalterable past.

(II: 165)

With this preparation from Mrs Transome's point of view, the narrator has gained space to tell the aftermath of the clash between Mrs
Transome and Jermyn from Jermyn's point of view, and this she does
brilliantly, recreating in the reader the utter frustration of a vulnerable
and sensitive mind in contact with the smooth impenetrable surface of
complacent egoism: 'In fact – he asked, with a touch of something
that makes us all akin – was it not preposterous, this excess of feeling
on points which he himself did not find powerfully moving?' (II: 246).

Frustration, unease, dissatisfaction are with the reader throughout
Felix Holt. The part of the novel over which Mrs Transome presides
makes a devastating reflexive comment on the novel's own failure to
articulate, to convince, to satisfy, but it is entirely possible that what is
best in *Middlemarch* and *Daniel Deronda* was facilitated by the writing of
Felix Holt, specifically by the creation of Mrs Transome, through
whom George Eliot explores her own conflicts, as writer and as
woman, with language, the recalcitrant and unwieldy instrument of
her art.

7

DIALECTIC AND POLYPHONY
IN *MIDDLEMARCH*

David Daiches has pointed out that the Prelude to *Middlemarch* raises
certain expectations in the reader that differ from those raised by the
title and subtitle of the novel: whereas the title and subtitle lead us to
expect a wide ranging exploration of the life of an entire community,
the Prelude leads us to expect a story focused on one woman and
ending with the tragic waste of her potentialities. His solution to this
problem is to discard the Prelude as misleading (Daiches 1963: 8).

I suggest that *Middlemarch* is both the novel of the title and the novel
of the Prelude. It maintains unity and integrity, despite this duality of
purpose, by a subtle and complex use of affinity and contrast, which is
developed by means of an extraordinary consistency of imagery.
Through this network of imagery, the reader is constantly reminded of
and kept in touch with Dorothea, no matter how far the novel has
strayed from her immediate story. Changes in our opinions of
Dorothea's character and situation take place in her absence.[1] Meanwhile, a host of characters and situations are developing, fulfilling the
promise of the title, and taking on a life larger than Dorothea's, so that
eventually Dorothea's problems and hopes are seen as particular
variations on universal issues, not because of an act of faith in the
reader, placing Dorothea in the allegoric role of Everyman, but
because of a painstaking, one might say scientific, exploration of
actual instances of affinity.

As many critics have remarked, affinities are shown between
Dorothea and Lydgate, but also between Dorothea and Rosamond,
and Lydgate and Casaubon. Featherstone is compared to Casaubon,
Fred to Will, and Mary to Dorothea. Gilbert and Gubar have traced
the less obvious affinities, and their discussion of Dorothea and Mary
is particularly illuminating (Gilbert and Gubar 1979: 513). Daiches

suggests that Mary, rather that Dorothea, embodies the moral centre of the novel:

> An important part of virtue, according to the view that emerges in the novel, consists in not making extravagant or vain claims upon life, and yet at the same time not lowering one's moral sights when one restricts any claim. . . .
>
> This is a very carefully balanced attitude and that the author's approval lies behind it there can be no doubt. In the light of it, what becomes of the Saint Theresa concept with which the novel opened? Surely it is now seen as a form of unreasonable claim on life, which it is the part of moral maturity to forego.
>
> (Daiches 1963: 57)

Daiches is mistaken in looking for a moral centre in the novel: *Middlemarch* is not a moral fable. The Garths are comparatively free from moral problems in the novel because they are simpler people than Lydgate and Dorothea; it is clear from the entire canon that George Eliot believes that intellectual and spiritual depth create rather than solve problems. Moreover, the finale reverts to the vocabulary of the Prelude, commenting bitterly on the defeat of those earlier ideals. The most one claim for it, along the lines that Daiches is pursuing, is ambivalence.

Middlemarch achieves the particularity of the feminist novel that the Prelude leads us to expect and simultaneously transcends that particularity, admitting that a man can also be a sexual victim, that vocational need might be 'a desire that by definition cannot be fulfilled' (Mintz 1978: 67) even if women did overcome the practical impediments to satisfying it, that, despite those impediments, apparently mediocre women may succeed in both work and love where the exceptional woman fails. The interplay between community and individual, Middlemarch and Dorothea, yields a subtle, tentative, and heavily qualified vision, dialectical in nature, in which every viewpoint has its say and tentative qualified conclusions are reached by a painstaking attention to consequences. Such a structure is very much open to misreading, in part because misreadings of this novel are easier to arrive at and express than the convolutions of its true structure, but mainly because misreadings are more fundamentally satisfying than the novel we have. The novel we have anticipates modernism in the tepidness of its ending. In Victorian novels, generally speaking, we leave protagonists either happy or dead. The assumption that *Middlemarch* conforms to this convention has led to the many misreadings of Dorothea's second marriage as a failed attempt by George Eliot to make a happy ending. The same assumption has produced various forced attempts to defend Ladislaw. Rather than setting a limit to the development of 'the old-fashioned English novel', as Henry James would have us believe (Carroll 1971: 359), *Middlemarch* looks forward to the encyclopaedic novels of modernism, not only in the complexity of its structure but also in its tentative conclusions.

Some critics have felt that the Prelude vacillates between a sincere espousal of and ironic stance towards the St Theresa theme. Certainly the writing is uneven, yet the tone of it as a whole is so sincere, so almost embarrassingly earnest in its partisanship of Dorothea, that interspersed irony at Dorothea's expense is highly unlikely. It is perhaps because of a feeling of embarrassment that critics seek irony in such painfully serious writing, but a stronger motive is possibly the desire to rescue the Prelude from disagreement with the clearly ironic first chapter of Book One. There certainly is disagreement, and it is deliberate. The technique George Eliot is employing here is one of systole and diastole: the demands made for Dorothea in the Prelude and the opening paragraph of chapter 1 allow the narrator the space for irony without risk of losing the reader's fundamental sympathy for Dorothea. This technique is one of the ways in which George Eliot develops the dialectic mentioned above, and is used throughout the novel. Such a claim as that Dorothea had 'the impressiveness of a fine quotation from the Bible – or from one of our elder poets – in a paragraph of today's newspaper', will sustain a reader's admiration through considerable detraction, and this first chapter is full of detraction and foreboding: 'there was even an ancestor discernible as a Puritan gentleman who served under Cromwell, but afterwards conformed, and managed to come out of all political troubles as the proprietor of a respectable family estate' (I: 8).

If Dorothea bears any resemblance to her ancestor, there will eventually be some relinquishing of saintliness. On a second reading of the novel, this reference seems to parallel Dorothea's career. Its interest lies in the reversal of values: whereas on the surface her marriage to Casaubon is seen as disastrous and ill-advised, and the subsequent marriage to Ladislaw is seen as at least an improvement, this parallel suggests the relinquishing of vocation and the settling for something unspectacular but comfortable that we feel brooding beneath the surface of Dorothea's story. The same effect is created by another ironic foreshadowing later in the same paragraph:

> she was enamoured of intensity and greatness, and rash in
> embracing whatever seemed to her to have those aspects; likely
> to seek martyrdom, to make retractions, and then incur
> martyrdom after all in a quarter where she had not sought it.
>
> (I: 9)

Although the first part of this excerpt obviously refers to Casaubon, the latter part traces her marriage to Casaubon, her disillusionment, and her marriage to Ladislaw. In light of this, the first part refers to Ladislaw as much as to Casaubon. Dorothea's misinterpretation of Ladislaw's feelings and motives, especially during their conversations in Rome, shows her propensity, once again, to attribute excellence where, the narrator steadily informs us, there is only mediocrity. Gillian Beer has pointed out that 'the boy in the legend' to whom Will compares Dorothea (I: 337) is a boy whose martyrdom was not to be a martyr (Adam 1975: 105). Both these references suggest an ending neither happy nor tragic, but simply disappointing and mundane, as does the reference to Dorothea's ancestor.

The oscillation between sincere admiration and critical irony discernible in this paragraph is reflected in the chapter as a whole. What Celia quite rightly interprets as inconsistency with regard to the jewels is a foreshadowing of inconsistency to come. Dorothea vacillates between extremes. She will either wear no jewellery at all, and distinctly condescend to the desire to wear jewellery, or she will choose something outlandishly exotic. The image of Dorothea bedecked with emeralds at the end of the chapter is slightly grotesque, which would not be the case had she chosen the cross or the amethysts. The emeralds are described as such sensuous excesses that they seem utterly incongruous on the wrist and hand so carefully described in the opening paragraph. This is another foreshadowing of her choice of Will. Light images in the novel are remarkably consistent: Casaubon's taper is placed in unfortunate juxtaposition to Dorothea's fire. Ladislaw, meanwhile, gives off a radiance that is not warm but glittering. The renunciation of the jewels followed by the impetuous choice of emeralds, a choice made against conscientious qualms, foreshadows her two marriages in a way by no means flattering to the second marriage (Celia tells us, ' "She said she *never would* marry again – not anybody at all" ' (III: 435)).

126

In his essay, 'Antique gems from *Romola* to *Daniel Deronda*', Joseph Wiesenfarth discusses the symbolic value of jewels in George Eliot's later fiction (Haight and Van Arsdel 1982). He points out that emeralds were believed to cure myopia. If the emeralds foreshadow Will, and given that myopia is Dorothea's greatest problem, Wiesenfarth's evidence would seem to bode ill for the argument I am developing that Will is not, nor is he designed to be, the solution to Dorothea's problems. However, if considered beside Dorothea's last vow to Will, 'I will learn what everything costs' (III: 427), the symbolism of the emeralds suggests that after the action of the novel, and through her marriage to Will, Dorothea does eventually learn to see clearly, but that clear-sightedness is not yet attained at the time of and therefore not operative in the foundation of her love for Will.

Her relation to the emeralds is echoed in her feeling about horse-back riding, revealing a conflict between extreme passion and extreme repression. The 'new current of feeling, as sudden as the gleam' (I: 17) corresponds to the 'pagan, sensuous way' in which she enjoys riding (I: 12). The effort to 'justify her delight in the colours by merging them in her mystic religious joy', corresponds to her decision to renounce riding, as does her later insistence that 'If I love him too much it is because he has been used so ill' (III: 420): in all three instances she denies her own sensuality.

That Dorothea has no father figure other than the patently inadequate Mr Brooke explains to some extent her feeling that 'the really delightful marriage must be that where your husband was a sort of father' (I: 12). Beyond this, she has grown up in an environment in which religion is the only outlet for both passion and intellect in a young woman. In *Woman in the Nineteenth Century*, Margaret Fuller tells us

> The women, shut out from the market-place, made up for it at the religious festivals. For human beings are not so constituted that they can live without expansion. If they do not get it in new way, they must in another, or perish.
>
> (Fuller 1844: 36)

The conflict between religion and sexual feeling and the conflict between the conventional lot of women and her desire for vocation divide Dorothea against herself, so that we find her, on the verge of accepting Casaubon's proposal, in front of the fire that is a symbol of her passion:

She threw off her mantle and bonnet, and sat down opposite
him, enjoying the glow, but lifting up her beautiful hands for a
screen. They were not thin hands, or small hands; but powerful,
feminine, maternal hands. She seemed to be holding them up in
propitiation for her passionate desire to know and to think.

(I: 54)

In George Eliot's characters, love and work are equal expressions of
one personality, and the same characteristics are manifest in both
halves of the individual's life: Casaubon is both sexually and aca-
demically desiccated; Lydgate's warmth affects both his love life and
his professional life[2]; Ladislaw is a dilettante both emotionally and
intellectually. Dorothea is both sexually and vocationally passionate;
she is sacrificing the former passion for the latter. The pathos lies in
the distance between the knowledge that narrator and reader share
and Dorothea's lack of awareness: she is not yet conscious that she is
making a sacrifice, and she has no suspicion, as we have, that her
sacrifice will be futile, that neither her sexual nor her vocational needs
will be satisfied by this marriage.

The parallel between sexual and vocational desire is suggested in
the choice of St Theresa of Avila, that is, as William Myers remarks,
of 'a Catholic saint who had been notoriously depicted by Crashaw
and Bernini in the throes of sexually compromising ecstasy' (Myers
1984: 238). Martin Svaglic, trying to unravel the St Theresa problem,
declares that 'George Eliot could admire the Theresa of Avila who
founded a religious order; but the Theresa of the ecstasy, whose
writings are one of the glories of Spanish literature, she cared nothing
for' (Haight 1966: 287). But why, in that case, did she not choose
Santa Clara, whose affinity with Dorothea she implies in Naumann's
choice of Dorothea as model for Santa Clara? Clara also founded a
religious order; she would have provided the vocational model without any tainting sexual implications or the gender-political associations which follow automatically from the choice of Theresa.

In *The Second Sex*, Simone de Beauvoir uses St Theresa as an example in much the same way as, and perhaps in part because, George
Eliot uses her:

There is hardly any woman other than St Theresa who in total
abandonment has herself lived out the situation of humanity: we
have seen why. Taking her stand beyond the earthly hierarchies,
she felt, like St John of the Cross, no reassuring ceiling over her

head. There were for both the same darkness, the same flashes
of light, in the self the same nothingness, in God the same
plenitude. When at last it will be possible for every human being
thus to set his pride beyond the sexual differentiation, in the
laborious glory of free existence, then only will woman be able to
identify her personal history, her problems, her doubts, her
hopes, with those of humanity; then only will she be able to seek
in her life and her works to reveal the whole of reality and not
merely the personal self. As long as she still has to struggle to
become a human being, she cannot become a creator.

(de Beauvoir 1953: 722–3)

Certainly if there exists the level of self-indentification that has been
commonly assigned to the characterization of Dorothea, Theresa, as
writer and impassioned woman, has far deeper affinities with the great
novelist and 'strong minded woman' of the Eliot biography than
would any other female saint. Svaglic's reaction is a product of the
'wise woman' image of George Eliot; it provides a classic example of
the kind of misreading that image has facilitated.

Theresa was chosen because she was passionate and dynamic: a
reformer, a writer, an erotically charged woman, she expressed, in
every aspect of her life, the energy and desire that obsesses George
Eliot throughout the canon and is conveyed by the images of flowing
water, currents, streams, rivers, and tides that Barbara Hardy has
elucidated so fully (Hardy 1959: 218–21). The culminating water
image of *Middlemarch*, seen in this light, is poignantly sorrowful: 'Her
full nature, like that river of which Cyrus broke the strength, spent
itself in channels which had no great name on earth' (III: 465). The
mitigating and qualifying sentence that follows, and provides the last
word in the novel, cannot overcome the powerful sorrow of that
image, partly because it is not metaphorically resonant; it is rather,
one feels, an effort on George Eliot's part to end on a positive note, to
fulfil what she took to be her artistic obligation to affirm.

Some Victorian critics seem to have understood this highly qualified ending far better than their modern successors. Edward Dowden,
for example, who is usually intensely conservative in his interpretations of George Eliot, summed up Dorothea's story in his 1877
review:

From her failure which is pain Dorothea only passes to her
failure which is happiness. From her vague ideal she lapses into

129

the common yearning of womanhood, the need to bless one
being with all good, and to receive the love of one heart. . . .
Saint Theresa becomes the wife of Will Ladislaw.

(Haight 1966: 114)

Dowden eventually uses this analysis to make the argument for
'sublime resignation'. Even so, he is clearly aware that Will is not a fit
mate for Dorothea and that George Eliot did not intend him to be.
That a conservative critic could see this, and its attendant implications
about sexual need, despite that fact that it was not in his interests to
do so, suggests the extent to which the sibylline image of George Eliot
has shaped criticism of her work. Dowden and his colleagues still
remembered the woman who had shocked London society; they
looked at her novels through the lens of Marian Lewes's earlier reputation, and saw a subversive George Eliot rather that the conservative
veneer with which she sought to protect herself and with which John
Cross protected her after her death.

Dorothea's critical illness on the birth of her son (and the sex of the
child is important here) seems a sort of desperate last protest against
the inadequacy of wifedom and motherhood as a response to her
potentialities. After the last physical recoil, Dorothea never regrets her
choice; she applies all her ardour to the modest work available to her
and, as Lee Edwards has pointed out, even gives away her adjective to
her husband who becomes 'an ardent public man' (Edwards
1984: 98).

I have already discussed the internal conflict within George Eliot's
treatment of the frustration of this yearning. At times it is attributed to
societal restraints; elsewhere the yearning seems to be by its very
nature impossible to satisfy. Clearly the immediate impediments to
the realization of Dorothea's vocational ideals are lack of education
and opportunity: she is limited by societal discrimination against her
gender, as Alan Mintz has remarked:

As a woman, Dorothea is not allowed the direct access to the
world possible to men. Despite this fact, what she wants most in
life is to do some great good for the world, and although there is
no adequate vehicle for this desire, it remains in George Eliot's
eyes unequivocally vocational. The impossibility of its
satisfaction does not change its nature. In fact, Dorothea's
womanhood, instead of being an anomaly, is simply the most
extreme example of the variety of constraints and contingencies

that frustrate the urge to alter the world. The intensity of her desire and the impossibility of her situation make Dorothea a kind of symbolic origin in relation to which the members of the crowded cast of *Middlemarch* locate themselves.

(Mintz 1978: 60–1)

The problem in this analysis is that it turns Dorothea into a symbol that illuminates the vocational troubles of the men in the novel, that is to say it sees the vocational troubles of men as the central issue which Dorothea, as symbol, can illuminate. The reverse is the more likely and interesting possibility: because Dorothea's problem is the absence of vocation, that negative space must be defined, investigated, understood by reference to the positive forms that surround it.

The description of Lydgate's discovery of his vocation (I: 216–18), for example, is written in such broad terms and with such obvious emotional involvement on the part of the narrator that it unavoidably suggests reflections on George Eliot's vocation. The clearest manifestation of this is the reference to literature that dwells on romance between men and women but ignores the romance of vocation (I: 218). There is a clearly reflexive element in this: the narrator of a novel of vocation discusses the need for a literature of vocation in the context of a description of the discovery of vocation.

Although Mintz notes this reflexivity (Mintz 1978: 100–1), he overlooks the automatic way in which it brings the reader back to Dorothea. Dorothea and Lydgate share the same virtues and vices: both are warm-hearted, intelligent, have a certain nobility of spirit; both are arrogant, self-righteous, and rash. These similarities give us the impression that had women been allowed the same educational and vocational opportunities as men, Dorothea would have found a vocation in very much the same way that Lydgate does. Yet the reminder of George Eliot's own vocation highlights the fact that certain women managed to overcome the limitations of the time, and, as Dorothea's story is the story of a fictional woman only eight years older than her author, the contrast between Dorothea's fictional life and Marian Lewes's actual life plants a seed of doubt in the reader's mind.

This is one of the instances, that I mentioned above, in which Dorothea is revaluated in her absence. We begin to think that perhaps Dorothea is a woman of average capabilities, which would make nonsense of the Prelude. But if we remember George Eliot's modification of the dictum she attributes to Novalis ' "Character is destiny." But not the whole of our destiny' (*The Mill on the Floss* II: 210), we begin to see that in the characterization of Dorothea, George Eliot portrays her own spiritual energy and vocational desire without the peculiar good fortune that befell her in her relationship to G. H. Lewes. The many dedications to Lewes indicate the extent to which George Eliot attributed her development as a writer to his encouragement and protection.[3] It is a fairly safe speculation, from what can be learned in the biographies and letters, that had Marian Evans spent her life with John Chapman or Herbert Spencer, George Eliot would never have existed.

Maggie's story in *The Mill on the Floss* is the investigation of one unrealized possibility of Marian Evans's life: what would have happened had she decided differently. Dorothea's story is the investigation of another unrealized possibility: what would have happened had external circumstances been different. All the discussions of vocation in the novel, of Caleb's quasi-religious relation to his work, of Will and Fred's dilettantism, of Lydgate's ambition, of Casaubon's sterility, reflect back on the unavailable possibilities of Dorothea's vocational yearning.

This is necessary because all the actual possibilities are so discouragingly petty: the prospect of marriage to Sir James provides an opportunity for philanthropic work by the manipulation of 'wifely influence' on a weak husband; marriage to Casaubon seems to provide an opportunity to act as 'lamp-holder', assisting, in a secretarial and wifely capacity, in the execution of a great work of scholarship; widowhood offers the opportunity for philanthropic work along Owenite lines, and tainted with Owenite problems; her second marriage offers the opportunity to pour her energies into the otherwise empty vessel of Will, so that he can accomplish what he never would have accomplished without her, and reap all the credit for that accomplishment.

Regarding the possibility of philanthropic widowhood, Mintz argues that,

> Dorothea's notions also closely resemble the projects of the Owenites, who could never quite reconcile their vision of classless egalitarianism with the desire to maintain some paternalistic control over the governance of undertakings they had originated and financed.
>
> (Mintz 1978: 109)

George Eliot's first impression of Owen, in 1843, was not positive (Letters I: 161). She anticipates the objections Mintz makes to Dorothea's kind of queenly philanthropy, and this is one reason why she rejects that role as an end for Dorothea. Gillian Beer has suggested that George Eliot rejects philanthropic widowhood as a solution because it ignores very real sexual needs (Beer 1986: 49). I would append that such a solution would be no solution at all in that it is only attainable by wealthy women whose husbands have been conveniently removed by death.

When Dorothea decides to marry Casaubon, she is already, at 19, accepting vocational compromise in aspiring to the role of lamp-holder. The reader and narrator share the knowledge that Dorothea lacks: the knowledge that even this modest aspiration will not be fulfilled. And yet Mr Casaubon's letter of proposal has not yet been produced as the final confirmation of our suspicions both as to his sexual aridity and his lack of sensitivity. The roots of our knowledge lie in the stated opinions of characters such as Celia, Mrs Cadwallader, Sir James, and Mr Brooke. The accuracy of their perceptions about Dorothea's first marriage makes us hesitate to dismiss their objections to her second. There has been considerable critical disagreement about the reliability of these voices. George Levine refers to 'James Chettam and other members of the community whose shallowness we know' (Levine 1981: 309) and William Myers agrees with him (Myers 1984: 196–7). Gillian Beer, however, commends us always to listen to Mr Brooke (Adam 1975: 94), while Gilbert and Gubar build a fascinating argument on the basis of an underlying truth in the gossip of the Middlemarch matrons (Gilbert and Gubar 1979: 522).

We are reluctant to believe that these voices may be right in their judgements: it offends our sense of the value of more spiritually developed characters, like Dorothea, if we have to admit that her philistine sister Celia, for example, actually perceives more clearly, in her facile self-satisfied way, than Dorothea. But this is clearly the case, not only of Dorothea who is characterized as short-sighted but of Maggie, in *The Mill on the Floss*, whose actions and decisions result in nothing but chaos and pain, even though she brings so much more intellect and spiritual depth to the making of those decisions than do the more conventional and limited characters in the novel. As Donald Stone has remarked (Stone 1980: 190), the implication is that intellectually original and spiritually developed characters in general are more likely to make mistakes than the ordinary person. This is perhaps because the independent thinker has only herself to rely upon, she takes all the risks of originality, whereas the conventional thinker relies on the inheritance of communal wisdom, which, though facile and narrow, has nevertheless been tested by the experience of generations and found adequate.

If we admit that we must pay attention to the conventional characters because they may be right, a larger problem arises: are they right sometimes, often, or always? They clearly cannot be right always or they would not seem conventional: they would emerge as oracular voices rather than as shallow trite voices of convention. It is only when we realize that they must be listened to sceptically but without prejudice that we come to appreciate how truly polyphonic, verging on the cacophonic, this novel is.

Dorothea, at the beginning of the novel, is vocationally thwarted and sexually repressed. We leave her, at the end of the novel, having resigned herself to the lack of vocational opportunity and pouring all her energies into marriage. This last is, at least, an advancement. In the opening chapter, her response to Celia's remark that Mr Casaubon is sallow evinces a deep-seated sexual aversion: 'All the better. I suppose you admire a man with the complexion of a *cochon de lait*' (I: 27). Dorothea's marriage to Ladislaw might be seen as a healthy revival of her capacity for sexual feeling, but the narrator does not even leave us this much without qualifying it. Whereas Stephen Guest, in *The Mill on the Floss* is , at least sexually, a man to complement Maggie's womanhood, Will is consistently characterized as childish and effeminate. That in itself would not be to his disadvantage, given George Eliot's Wordsworthian respect for the child and her clear bias towards women as the gender most capable of spiritual depth. However, Will's childishness is not Wordsworthian; it is reminiscent of Rosamond's 'infantine' quality: in both cases the egoism rather than the innocence of the child is being foregrounded. Similarly, Will is effeminate in that he has the vanity associated with women, not their power of loving. The choice of such terms as 'pouting' (I: 117), 'sulky' (I: 341), 'pettishly' (II: 246), 'petulance' (III: 17), 'defiant' (III: 108), and 'stubborn' (III: 139) to describe him cannot, in a writer of George Eliot's calibre, be attributed to inadvertency. They unite with the recurrent images of him 'shaking his curls', his frequent blushes, and his transparent girlish complexion to create a figure who cannot be seriously contemplated as the appropriate partner for a heroine of Dorothea's scope.

Ladislaw is a dilettante in a novel, in an entire body of work, where vocational yearning is a central positive value. The sincere admiration with which the narrator records Lydgate's discovery of his vocation stands in contrast to the irony of her account of Will's final choice:

> nevertheless, he was beginning thoroughly to like the work of which when he began he had said to himself rather languidly, 'Why not?' – and he studied the political situation with as ardent an interest as he had ever given to poetic metres or mediaevalism. It is undeniable that but for the desire to be where Dorothea was, and perhaps the want of knowing what else to do, Will would not at this time have been meditating on the needs of the English people or criticizing English statesmanship: he would probably have been rambling in Italy sketching plans for several dramas, trying prose and finding it too jejune, trying verse and finding it too artificial.

> (III: 285)

His dilettantism is reflected in the more personal aspects of his life. Reclining on the carpet and performing duets with Mrs Lydgate has implications not only for Rosamond herself but for the entire community and for Dorothea. In fact, the 'light gallantry' with which he treats Rosamond is reminiscent of Lydgate's accidental courtship, and, given the feelings he has elicited in Rosamond, Will's treatment of her on that and particularly on the second occasion of Dorothea's intruding upon them (chapter 77) seems rather brutal.

It is an index of George Eliot's sensitivity to nuance that she parallels the events of Lydgate's and Ladislaw's relations to Rosamond while casting them is opposing moral lights. Although Lydgate's condescension to women in general and his flirtations with Rosamond are perceived as 'spots of commonness', his reaction when he finds that she has built her hopes on him is seen as the rashly generous action of a warm heart. Ladislaw, in a similar situation, insults Rosamond, but later (III: 384) feels that his insult has bound him to submit to her will. This, since it is cold-blooded, lacking the warmth of heart that perpetrates Lydgate's submission, and since it involves paining and deceiving Lydgate, is seen as weakness in Ladislaw, and it is related to his general dilettantism.

At Featherstone's funeral, we are told that the scene 'always afterward came back to [Dorothea] at the touch of certain sensitive points of memory, just as the vision of St Peter's at Rome was interwoven with moods of despondency' (II: 79). The reference to St Peter's is a rephrasing of an earlier detail: 'in certain states of dull forlornness Dorothea all her life continued to see the vastness of St Peter's' (I: 297). Both these observations are made at junctures where Will is about to re-enter Dorothea's life. They not only inform us that the rest of her life is less than happy but imply that this forlornness is associated with the advent of Will.

Dorothea chooses Will because the alternative is widowhood, because she finds him sexually attractive, especially in contrast to Casaubon, because he satisfies her desire to be worshipped, and because she tends to believe the best of everyone. We are told in chapter 80 that she cried 'after her lost belief which she had planted and kept alive from a very little seed since the days in Rome' (III: 388). The image suggests the amount of imagination there is in her love for Will. Imagination, working on a few short interviews, has cultivated love. When we remember those interviews, how rife they were with misunderstanding on Dorothea's part, we begin to doubt the foundations of her affection.

During a conversation with Dorothea at Rome (chapter 22), Will, for the second time, finds her situation amusing, although this time his hilarity is vying with disgust. He smiles, and when asked the source of his amusement, quickly supplies a false explanation, which causes Dorothea to admire his good humour. In the following chapter, he again supplies a false motive, again making a positive impression on Dorothea:

> 'Mr Casaubon's generosity has perhaps been dangerous to me,
> and I mean to renounce the liberty it has given me. . . .'
> 'That is fine – I respect that feeling,' said Dorothea.'

(I: 340)

However, shortly afterwards the narrator tells us the true reason Will is giving up Casaubon's patronage is something that Dorothea would not respect: 'If he never said a cutting word about Mr Casaubon again and left off receiving favours from him, it would clearly be permissible to hate him the more. The poet must know how to hate, says Goethe; and Will was at least ready with that accomplishment' (I: 343).

Dorothea sees Will in contrast to Casaubon, very much as, in *The Mill on the Floss*, Maggie falls for Stephen in part because of his physical contrast to Philip. Dorothea first meets Will by the yew tree (I: 116), a

symbol of death associated with Casaubon who later dies in the yew
tree walk. Will is light against dark, radiant beside the rayless: 'The
first impression on seeing Will was one of sunny brightness. . . .
When he turned his head quickly his hair seemed to shake out light,
and some persons thought they saw decided genius in this coruscation.
Mr Casaubon, on the contrary, stood rayless' (I: 320–1).

The irony with which the narrator treats Will's genius tends to
discredit these unnamed 'persons':

> Genius, he held, is necessarily intolerant of fetters: on the one
> hand it must have the utmost play for its spontaneity; on the
> other, it may confidently await those messages from the universe
> which summon it to its peculiar work, only placing itself in an
> attitude of receptivity toward all sublime chances.
>
> (I: 123)

> [The example of Casaubon] seemed to enforce a moral entirely
> encouraging to Will's generous reliance on the intentions of the
> universe with regard to himself. He held that reliance to be a
> mark of genius; and certainly it is no mark to the contrary;
> genius consisting neither in self-conceit nor in humility, but in a
> power to make or do, not anything in general, but something in
> particular.
>
> (I: 124)

> 'To careful reasoning of this kind he replies by calling himself
> Pegasus, and every form of prescribed work "harness".'
> (Casaubon to Dorothea, I: 121)

The irony here is all the stronger in that the narrator uses the 'fetters'
and 'harness' imagery she applies to Lydgate. Whereas Lydgate considers the cessation of his true work fettering or harnessing, Will
objects to the commencement.

The irony used toward Will in this and most other instances has
been seen by some critics as affectionate: George Eliot treats him with
the indulgence one would use toward a wayward child. But when his
eventual relation to Dorothea becomes clear, the irony becomes
sharper. The description of Will on his way to Lowick church can no
longer be construed as affectionate. Here, as in the description of his
'coruscation', Will is one subject of a recurring ironic theme in
George Eliot's works: the actual absence of an assumed connection
between physical appearance and spiritual reality:[4]

and by this time the thought of vexing Mr Casaubon had
become rather amusing to him, making his face break into a
merry smile, pleasant to see as the breaking of sunshine on the
water – though the occasion was not exemplary.

(II: 300)

Hitherto, the image of Will smiling and sparkling has been used
sparingly and to rather winning effect, but in this scene it is protracted
to the point of seeming ludicrous and almost grotesque. The lyric that
Will sings exacerbates this feeling. Its tone is so playful as to again
seem to make light of Dorothea's very real suffering. The lyric can be
read in a very different way from that intended by Will, and this
alternative reading implies a much more acerbic author than the one
we are used to imagining behind George Eliot's prose:

> O me, O me, what frugal cheer
> My love doth feed upon!
> A touch, a ray, that is not here,
> A shadow that is gone:

II: 301)

If we read 'My love' as meaning Dorothea herself, rather than his
feeling for Dorothea, this first verse of the lyric anticipates Will's
'uncertain promises' ('a ray, that is not here') and also the idea that
Will's greatest virtue is that he is not Casaubon ('a shadow that is
gone'). These metaphors of ray and shadow have already been used of
Will and Casaubon (I: 321). We have been taught to sympathize with
Casaubon too much to excuse Will's childish and unnecessary disre-
gard for his feelings. In the description of him that follows the lyric, all
the gentle touches the narrator has used to show us how Dorothea
could be won to him are deployed together with jarring effect:

> Sometimes, when he took off his hat, shaking his head
> backward, and showing his delicate throat as he sang, he looked
> like an incarnation of the spring whose spirit filled the air – a
> bright creature, abundant in uncertain promises.

(II: 301)

In the culminating chapter of the Dorothea/Ladislaw love story
(chapter 83), Dorothea's naïvety, kindly treated as 'childlike' up to
this point, is also seen as ludicrous. The narrator seems, for a
moment, to lose patience with Dorothea. The irony of the description

138

of Dorothea's morning search for something to do is almost as cutting
as the treatment of Ladislaw on his way to Lowick church:

> What was there to be done in the village? On dear! nothing.
> Everybody was well and had flannel; nobody's pig had died.[5]
>
> (II: 416)

> She looked amusingly girlish after all her deep experience – nod-
> ding her head and marking the names off on her fingers, with a
> little pursing of her lip, and now and then breaking off to put her
> hands on each side of her face and say, 'Oh dear! oh dear!'
>
> (III: 418)

These are painfully diminished descriptions of the heroine whose
'grand woman's frame' moved us to both pity and respect in the
description of her night spent crying on the floor (chapter 80). That
George Eliot can allow her narrator this distance without alienating
the reader is another instance of her dialectical method: the unadulter-
ated sympathy of her description of Dorothea's pain in chapter 80
allows room for this criticism, just as the passionate advocacy of the
Prelude allowed room for the ironic distance of chapter 1.

At the beginning of chapter 83, Dorothea explains her love for Will:
'If I love him too much it is because he has been used so ill' (III: 420).
George Eliot often seems to suggest that love or seduction is more a
matter of pity than desire. Arthur is seduced by Hetty's tears, Tito by
Tessa's, and Lydgate by Rosamond's. Maggie pledges herself to
Philip out of pity, and Dorothea, like Gwendolen, falls in love with the
man who has been disinherited by her husband, as if her love can act
as a charitable donation to the unfortunate.

Dorothea's sympathy for the underdog has been prepared for in her
championship of Lydgate. The reader, who has been worrying with
Lydgate, experiences Dorothea's reaction as heroic and feels, with
Dorothea, some disappointment in Farebrother. Yet Farebrother,
though himself far from perfect in practice, is nevertheless a reliable
voice throughout the novel: 'she felt rather discontented with Mr
Farebrother. She disliked this cautious weighing of consequences,
instead of an ardent faith in efforts of justice and mercy, which would
conquer by their emotional force' (III: 308). As readers familiar with
Lydgate's story, we feel with Dorothea here, and yet Dorothea has
nothing to go on but her instinct, which, as we know from her relation
to Casaubon, is not always infallible. Even though in the specific case

of Lydgate, Dorothea's attitude is seen as heroic, we get an uneasy sense that in other cases this 'ardent faith' could be mistaken and dangerous to Dorothea herself.

These are the accumulated impressions that attend the reader as Will enters the library, in chapter 83. The library, haunted by the memory of Casaubon, again places Will in the advantageous position of contrast to that first and less desirable husband. The detail of Will laying his hat and gloves on the leather chair is expressive of his easy familiarity, his claiming place, knowing that he is loved.

There seems to be a reluctance on Will's part to consummate his relationship with Dorothea. This is not altogether surprising considering the chivalric nature of his love. He enjoys longing for the unattainable and seems rather nonplussed when his beloved turns out to be attainable after all. Several critics have pointed out that it is Dorothea who proposes to Will, and in this she resembles Catherine Arrowpoint of *Daniel Deronda*. However, the melodrama of Will's side of their conversation betrays a certain enjoyment of playing the star-crossed lover ('you may think of me as one on the brink of the grave' (III: 424)). He argues against her long after it has become obvious that she loves him above all monetary considerations. Her cry to him, 'Oh, I cannot bear it – my heart will break' (III: 426) is, as Gilbert and Gubar have noted (1979: 530), an echo of Lucy Snove's cry to Paul Emanuel, another evasive lover, who seems to have gone to the trouble of getting himself killed in order to evade Lucy.

The scene takes place during a thunderstorm, and though the narrator has playfully hinted that this might be a manifestation of Mr Casaubon's posthumous spleen,[6] George Eliot's disbelief in the supernatural encourages us to look for a metaphoric explanation. The 'angry spirit' in the rain is possibly attributable to the pathetic fallacy, which has been used throughout the novel to illuminate Dorothea's state of mind, but which, in this case, echoes not Dorothea's feeling but George Eliot's and our own discontent with the impending union.

Another explanation for the thunderstorm can be found in the novel's preoccupation with mythology. Mr Casaubon's research is an effort to find a key to all mythologies. In Rome, Will tells Dorothea that Mr Casaubon's work is pointless in that German scholars have already come up with the answer (I: 318). The school of German mythography to which Will refers had, by the time of the writing of *Middlemarch* (forty years after the time of its action), produced

Friedrich Max Müller, who was personally acquainted with George Eliot and whose work on mythology, suggesting that all myths are allegories of the sun, was known to and admired by her (Letters IV: 8). In summoning up this contemporary reference in the minds of her readers, George Eliot seems to confirm the notion that Will is intended as an adequate mate for Dorothea, and marriage to him as a positive ending, since Will is throughout the novel characterized by sun-god imagery.

However, Max Müller represented just one side of the mythology debate. Another viewpoint was represented by Adalbert Kuhn, another German, who maintained that all myths are allegories of thunderstorms.[7] Even though there is no reference to Kuhn in the letters and biographies, it is unlikely that such a meticulous scholar as George Eliot would discuss Max Müller's work and allude to the debate in her fiction without being aware of the strongest contemporary alternative interpretation. Given this, George Eliot's decision to set the final love scene between Will and Dorothea in a thunderstorm partakes of the same intellectual wit that William Myers has described in his discussion of *Silas Marner* (Myers 1984: 51).

Myers points out that the discussion in Raveloe about the theft of Silas's gold is a parody of the contemporary intellectual debate on origins, being likewise divided between the rational 'tinder-box and pedlar' theory and the mystic supernatural theory. The irony is that in *Silas Marner* neither of these theories proves to be true (even though Marian Lewes could be described as a member of the tinder-box and pedlar school).[8]

Similarly, in *Middlemarch*, the thunderstorm is introduced to put Will as sun god, that is Will as solution, into question once more. This supports the view, held by Gillian Beer and Alan Mintz, that there is no one key to all mythologies, and by extension, no one key to the problems presented by Dorothea's life, by Middlemarch society, or by *Middlemarch* the novel (Beer 1983: 165; Mintz 1978: 94–5). Mintz has developed a fascinating argument about taxonomy in *Middlemarch*, which is linked to the question of whether or not there is a key to all mythologies. Mintz's analysis takes us back to the idea of Farebrother as a reliable voice. In chapter 17, Farebrother tries to show Lydgate his insect collection. Mintz maintains that Lydgate's lack of interest stems from his rejection of taxonomic classification, which corresponds to his failure to transfer insight from his professional to his social life when he misjudges Rosamond (Mintz 1978: 205). When

Farebrother is trying in vain to draw Lydgate's attention to his trays of insects, Lydgate is absorbed in another specimen:

'You don't care about these things?'
'Not by the side of this lovely anencephalous monster.'

(I: 261–2)

If the anencephalous – brainless – monster is, as seems likely, an allusion to Rosamond, we once again glimpse a sharp-witted and caustic implied author who has little in common with the wise woman narrator.

David Daiches argues that Lydgate's search for one primitive tissue, and Casaubon's parallel search for one key to all mythologies, is approved by the narrator, who in Daiches scheme is reliably representative of the author, and whose own effort is also to find one tissue in the 'web' of community (Daiches 1963:N18). Quentin Anderson also takes this line (Haight 1966: 314). Gillian Beer maintains explicitly what is implicit in Mintz's taxonomy argument, that there is no one tissue, and that George Eliot knows this (Beer 1983: 105). Beer and Mintz are supported by George Eliot's own comments on diversity:

To discern likeness amidst diversity, it is well known, does not
require so fine a mental edge as the discerning of diversity
amidst general sameness. The primary rough classification
depends on the prominent resemblances of things: the progress is
toward finer and finer discrimination according to minute
differences.

(*The Impressions of Theophrastus Such*: 259)

This controversy has the widest possible implications for the interpretation of George Eliot's work: the belief that George Eliot is in search of the one tissue, that the aim and tendency of al her fiction is to discover a single key to all mythologies is the foundation without which no conservative and anti-feminist interpretation of her work can stand.

That 'angry spirit' in the rain looks forward to the 'thorns and thistles of the wilderness' mentioned in the finale (III: 455), the actualization which provides an unaccommodating sequence to the Eden of anticipation. One is reminded of the narrative comment on Dorothea's first marriage: 'Has any one ever pinched into its pilulous smallness the cobweb of pre-matrimonial acquaintanceship?' (I: 30). In light of this, Dorothea's final vow, 'I will learn what everything costs' (III: 427) has a poignant and ironic reverberation.

The finale bears this out. Its reversion to the language and imagery of the Prelude reminds us how far the 'home epic' is from the 'epic life wherein there was a constant unfolding of far-resonant action', Dorothea's critical illness on the birth of her son, the negative way in which the details of her life are related, and the last two paragraphs, summing up her life and deeds, leave us uneasy, dissatisfied, and remind us of those early references to 'certain states of dull forlornness'. It is also dispiriting to notice that of the three young women around whose careers the novel is built, Dorothea, Mary, and Rosamond, only Rosamond produces daughters, as far as we know. If Dorothea has any daughters, the narrator does not mention them. This seems pessimistic, seems to suggest that there is no point in reproducing women like Dorothea and Mary.

And yet we have already received a gleam of hope on this head, and indication that perhaps future St Theresas will succeed where Dorothea has failed. The word 'reform' has been used in many ways throughout the novel: St Theresa 'found her epos in the reform of a religious order'; Lydgate is working for medical reform; and the novel takes place against the backdrop of attempts to pass the First Reform Bill of 1832. Daiches and Jerome Beaty have both pointed out that the chapter after Dorothea's union with Will begins as follows: 'It was just after the Lords had thrown out the Reform Bill' (Daiches 1963: 65; Haight 1966: 312). George Eliot, in writing this novel, has also been looking at the possibility of reform. Her careful attention to likely consequences has forced her to resign herself to the knowledge that reform of women's opportunites is, at this point, unlikely. In chapter 83, George Eliot, like the Lords, throws out her own reform bill. Although at first glance this parallel seems to confirm the pessimism of Mary and Dorothea's daughterlessness, it is important to remember that the First Reform Bill was in fact passed a few weeks after the time of the end of the novel.

Another optimistic element of the ending is the fact that Dorothea manages to save three people from misery and mutual abuse. One thinks of Farebrother and the other clergymen in George Eliot's fiction, and of vocation in its religious sense. Even though Dorothea's rescue of Lydgate, Rosamond, and Will is the fruit of one morning's work, and the rest of her life is spent in more modest achievements, it could be considered, and might well be considered by a clergyman such as Farebrother, an achievement substantial enough to legitimize a life's ministry.

It cannot be denied that Dorothea's action is firmly on the side of self-interest. When she goes to plead with Rosamond, one cannot forget that, from Dorothea's point of view, if Rosamond can be persuaded to give Will up, he will again be free for Dorothea. Nevertheless, if pride had prevented Dorothea from doing this, the results would have been disastrous: Will has resigned himself to a joyless affair with Rosamond (III: 384), a step which would take him over the border from childish egoism and irresponsibility into a new territory of faithlessness and unhappiness. Rosamond would move from her similarly childish egoism into the hard and acquisitive sensuality, a kind of sexual imperialism, of which she has proven herself capable in her horseback riding with Lydgate's cousin; Lydgate himself, it is indicated, might well, under pressure of this degraded life, be moved to physical violence.

After Dorothea has smoothed the way between Lydgate and Rosamond, we are told 'He had chosen this frail creature, and had taken the burthen of her life upon his arms. He must walk as he could, carrying the burthen pitifully.' W. J. Harvey objects to this conclusion: 'But Lydgate's image of a parent cradling a child is wrong; and we know how indestructibly tough this "fragile creature" really is' (Hardy 1970: 178). Certainly Rosamond is psychologically indestructible, but throughout the history of this marriage there have been dangerous images of Lydgate's physical bulk in juxtaposition with Rosamond's physical fragility:

There was a tone in the last sentence which was equivalent to the clutch of his strong hand on Rosamond's delicate arm.

(III: 180)

he wanted to smash and grind some object on which he could at least produce an impression, or else to tell her brutally that he was master, and she must obey.

(III: 193)

The mediocrity of Lydgate's subsequent life is, in fact, a hard-won victory which might have been impossible without Dorothea's mediation. The greatest threat to Lydgate is not the loss of his vocation but the possible violence of his 'strong hands' in constant proximity to Rosamond's fragile and infuriating neck.

Gilbert and Gubar have defended Rosamond and damned Lydgate in a brilliant, if somewhat procrustean, feminist analysis of their marriage (Gilbert and Gubar 1979: 514–15). This is an instance of the way in which George Eliot's dialectical method can be manipulated to preconceived critical ends. Certainly the evidence that Gilbert and Gubar produce is strong and has been ignored in the critical heritage, possibly because most of the critics were men and had their own personal dread of Rosamond and her kind. But here again the most that can be claimed is ambivalence. The interplay between admiration and detraction is what lends *Middlemarch* its complexity and its atmosphere of unblinking honesty. Yet when all the evidence has been marshalled on both sides, it is clear that we are to sympathize with Lydgate and to shudder at Rosamond. The shudder, if we are careful readers, is part repulsion and part awe that this delicate young woman can exercise such power. There is something victorious as well as chilling in the ending of chapter 65: 'He wished to excuse everything in her if he could – but it was inevitable that in that excusing mood he should think of her as if she were an animal of another and feebler species. Nevertheless she had mastered him' (III: 205).

Below the surface of this ambivalence broods the suspicion that the deeper capacity for love, the attribute for which George Eliot most admires women, must be absent if women are to maintain themselves in the battle for power with men. George Eliot uses the kind of woman that most repels her as the only possible avenging angel.

In the finale we see Lydgate slaughtered off in his prime, and Rosamond surviving him. It seems almost cruel, especially in a Victorian novelist: after all, Lydgate's 'spots of commonness' have been purged – the progress of his story is the movement of a slow and painful cleansing. In his long interview with Dorothea (chapter 76) Lydgate is pure:

> 'God bless you, Mrs Casaubon!' said Lydgate, rising as if with
> the same impulse that made his words energetic, and resting his
> arm on the back of the great leather chair he had been sitting in.
> 'It is good that you should have such feelings. But I am not the
> man who ought to allow himself to benefit by them.'

> (III: 360)

This is the same chair on which Ladislaw, a few chapters later, somewhat smugly deposits his hat and gloves. The contrast between Lydgate's and Ladislaw's behaviour in these parallel scenes is revealing. Lydgate is no longer marked by the arrogance, the condescension, especially to women, which, though treated with gentle irony by

George Eliot in the early stages of his history, is nevertheless relentlessly punished by her. But punishment is problematic in George Eliot's work. She is not a Christian novelist and it would be inappropriate for her to take upon herself the privileges of a judgemental god. However, characters are certainly punished for their weaknesses and errors in her fiction. She justifies this by the assertion of belief in an almost mathematical sequence of events in which error is inevitably discovered, and in which repentance has no mitigating effect on the machinery of cause and effect. She follows consequences unflinchingly, with an agnostic's belief that wheels are set into motion by our deeds, and that this motion has a dispassionate logic, unaffected by considerations of mercy or justice.

Nevertheless, in her treatment of Lydgate one suspects another insistence of the fetish-bashing (see pp. 57–8) indulged in by the narrators of *Adam Bede* and *The Mill on the Floss*. In her own life, Marian Evans suffered greatly from the kind of commonness that flaws Lydgate at the beginning of his story. John Chapman and Herbert Spencer both rejected Marian Evans because of their conventional tastes in women. It is generally supposed that Herbert Spencer is referring to Marian Evans when, in his autobiography, he writes, 'Physical beauty is a *sine quâ non* with me; as was once unhappily proved where the intellectual traits and the emotional traits were of the highest' (Haight 1968: 115). And John Chapman, in his diary, records a revealing and painful exchange with Marian Evans:

> As we rested on the grass, I remarked on the wonderful and mysterious embodiment of all the elements, characteristics, and beauties of nature which man and woman jointly present. I dwelt also on the incomprehensible mystery and witchery of beauty. My words jarred upon her and put an end to her enjoyment. Was it from a consciousness of her own want of beauty? She wept bitterly.
>
> (Haight 1940: 172)

Ruby Redinger has pointed out the similarities between Lydgate and John Chapman (Redinger 1976: 471), but in his professional dedication and depth of thought on subjects other than women and furniture, Lydgate resembles Spencer more than Chapman. If Lydgate is a character drawn in part from both Spencer and Chapman, the harshness that he receives at the hands of George Eliot is easily explained. George Eliot, as powerful literary *alter ego* of the plain and powerless woman who was hurt by the same spots of commonness in both of Lydgate's originals, plays out in fiction what Marian Evans could not play out in life. Not only does she avenge herself on this fictional fetish but she brings him to realize the error of his common tastes in women and to worship the intellectual woman he once found insufficiently attractive. One is reminded of Armgart's description of her art:

> I carry my revenges in my throat;
> I love in singing, and am loved again.

The characterization of Lydgate is the strongest evidence against the argument that Ladislaw is intended to be an adequate mate for Dorothea. Counterpointing Lydgate's purity of feeling in chapter 76 is Ladislaw's egoism in chapter 83: 'You have never felt the sort of misery I felt' (III: 423). This is reminiscent of the egoism of Stephen Guest. We who have followed Dorothea through her night of suffering, feel this as an expression of a child's consciousness, perceiving itself at the centre of the universe, still, in his mid-twenties, 'taking the world as an udder to feel [his] supreme [self]', and hardly likely ever to achieve the consciousness of the 'equivalent centre of self' in others (I: 323) which stands as another central positive value of the novel. In this, too, he resembles Rosamond.

Lydgate and Will are set in parallel from the earliest chapters: both are outsiders in Middlemarch; both are confident of their genius and have high expectations of their destiny; both unintentionally inspire Rosamond's vulgar substitute for love; both eventually worship Dorothea as a saintly woman; and both go to London, in the end, to careers far short of their early aspirations. Every imperfection seen in Lydgate as a spot of commonness is matched in Ladislaw. Ladislaw is certainly 'a little too self-confident and disdainful' (I: 225), and his fear that he might fall into submission to Rosamond indicates that his 'better energies' are also 'liable to lapse down the wrong channel under the influence of transient solicitations'. But the clearest parallel lies in his attitude to women. His love for Dorothea is described in chivalric terms:

> And if Mr Casaubon had been a dragon who had carried her off
> to his lair with his talons simply and without legal forms, it
> would have been an unavoidable feat of heroism to release her
> and fall at her feet.

> (I: 320)

The remote worship of a woman throned out of their reach plays
a great part in men's lives, but in most cases the worshipper
longs for some queenly recognition, some approving sign by
which his soul's sovereign may cheer him without descending
from her high place. That was precisely what Will wanted. But
there were plenty of contradictions in his imaginative demands.
It was beautiful to see how Dorothea's eyes turned with wifely
anxiety and beseeching to Mr Casaubon: she would have lost
some of her halo if she had been without that duteous
preoccupation.

(I: 333–4)

Surely this is the commonnest sort of response, and the parallel with
Lydgate's response to Rosamond is underlined by the use of crystal
imagery in both cases, as Barbara Hardy has noted (Hardy
1959: 226):

It was as if a fracture in delicate crystal had begun, and he was
afraid of any movement that might make it fatal.

(III: 181)

To ask her to be less simple and direct would be like breathing
on the crystal that you want to see the light through.

(II: 144)

In the former quotation, crystal symbolizes Lydgate's love founded
on illusions about Rosamond, and that implication then seeps into the
crystal imagery of Will's love for Dorothea. The chivalric form of love,
involving a paradoxical attitude of both elevating and condescending
to the beloved, of imagining her both more and less than human, has
its ugly side:

The shallowness of a waternixie's soul may have a charm until
she becomes didactic.

(III: 177).

For the moment, Will's admiration was accompanied with
a chilling sense of remoteness. A man is seldom ashamed of
feeling that he cannot love a woman so well when he sees a
certain greatness in her: nature having intended greatness for
men.

(II: 176)

Not only is the criticism of Will's attitude to women more acid here, in that it is more permissible to be chilled by didacticism than greatness, but Will is never cleansed, as Lydgate is, of these flaws.

When *Middlemarch* first appeared, many readers, among them Henry James, thought that Lydgate and Dorothea should eventually marry:

> Lydgate is so richly successful a figure that we have regretted strongly at moments, for immediate interest's sake, that the current of his fortunes should not mingle more freely with the occasionally thin-flowing stream of Dorothea's. Toward the close, these two fine characters are brought into momentary contact so effectively as to suggest a wealth of dramatic possibility between them; but if this train had been followed we should have lost Rosamond Vincy – a rare psychological study.
>
> (Carroll 1971: 356)

In fact Rosamond would have been as essential to this possibility of *Middlemarch* as she is to the *Middlemarch* we have. Rosamond is the purgatory through which Lydgate must pass before he can be thought of as a partner for Dorothea, just as Dorothea must pass through her marriage to Casaubon before she can realize the imperative nature of her own sexual needs. Before his marriage, Lydgate does not find Dorothea attractive, and his attitude to women bears an unpleasant resemblance to Casaubon's. However, when, in the horseback riding accident, Rosamond's obstinacy proves capable of endangering her life, the possibility of freeing Lydgate, as Dorothea was freed, by the timely death of the undesirable spouse, is raised in the reader's mind and is unlikely to have been lost on George Eliot. That eventuality is certainly prepared for, not only in the foreshadowing of Rosamond's unrealized demise but in the constant correspondence and juxtaposition of Lydgate to Dorothea and to each of her husbands.

Barbara Hardy has noted George Eliot's attention to alternative destinies:

> There is nothing very startling in this method of trial and rejection in the inventive process, but it has a special interest in George Eliot because it draws attention to an interesting characteristic of her imaginative method. There is something very like the actual appearance of alternative destiny within the 'irrevocable and finished book'.
>
> (Hardy 1959: 136)

The Lydgate/Dorothea possibility is just such an alternative destiny. More recent criticism sweeps the evidence for it aside. Lerner and Fernando note the possibility but take it to no interpretative conclusions (Lerner 1967: 47; Fernando 1977: 46–7); Haight rejects it (Adam 1975: 36); Gilbert and Gubar note the possibility, but their analysis of Lydgate is so negative that it is difficult to make out how they can, in consistency, find it desirable (Gilbert and Gubar 1979: 519). Barbara Hardy argues against it:

> This possibility, if it is felt at all, is there as a faint stirring of irony asserting itself whenever Lydgate is made to reassess his first intellectual rejection of Dorothea or to make the contrast between the woman he wanted and the woman he did not want. It is certainly not felt at all on Dorothea's side. Both Dorothea and Lydgate are committed by their disastrous desires before they meet, but Dorothea plays a larger part in his reflections than he does in hers.

(Hardy 1959: 144)

The fact is that nobody plays a part in Dorothea's reflections until his love for her is declared. We have witnessed this in both Chettham and Ladislaw. (That Casaubon is an exception testifies to the asexuality of her feeling for him.) It is contrary to Dorothea's nature to speculate about romantic possibilities that have not been suggested to her. Yet the text does suggest the idea. We are made aware, for example, that Lydgate is what Dorothea imagines Casaubon to be – a great mind dedicated to great work. The narrator never uses irony to bring into doubt Lydgate's genius as she does Ladislaw's. Lydgate also has the warmth of heart, the capacity for love, that Dorothea finds so painfully absent in Casaubon.

Meanwhile, since Dorothea has sublimated all her vocational desire into a modest aspiration to be 'lamp-holder', she might well have been the supportive comforting resource that Lydgate, in his inexperience, imagined would only be found in a woman of Rosamond's intellect.

Given these impressions, a second reading of the novel renders the following passage even more ironic:

> Certainly nothing at present could seem much less important to Lydgate than the turn of Miss Brooke's mind, or to Miss Brooke than the qualities of the woman who had attracted this young surgeon. But any one watching keenly the stealthy convergence

of human lots, sees a slow preparation of effects from one life on another, which tells like a calculated irony on the indifference or the frozen stare with which we look at our unintroduced neighbour. Destiny stands by sarcastic with our *dramatis personae* folded in her hand.

(I: 141–2)

Much attention has been given to whether or not this 'destiny' is the personification of a deterministic fate. It seems unlikely: George Eliot's world moves on the cogs of large and small decisions. Destiny here is simply a personification of the future. But why should she attend Lydgate and Dorothea? Nothing in the action of the novel suggests that a glimpse into their actual futures would make their present mutual indifference ironic to them. Such prescience would certainly have made other relationships ironic to them, but not particularly their relation to each other. The choice of the strong word 'sarcastic' is justified only if the future will show them how misguided their present indifference is in light of other possible futures they might have had, but, at this juncture, and in ignorance of the consequences, have irrevocably precluded.

I am not suggesting that Dorothea, in her states of forlornness, is languishing for Lydgate but that she is missing things some of which, we know, Lydgate might have provided. The language used to describe the relationship between Ladislaw and Dorothea pales beside the few phrases describing Dorothea's brief contact with Lydgate. Whereas Will and Dorothea are characterized as 'two children' (III: 424), or as mother and child (the Solomon dividing the child metaphor used in chapter 80, III: 388–9), the description of Dorothea's appeal to Lydgate conveys something very different: 'this cry from soul to soul, without other consciousness than their moving with kindred natures in the same embroiled medium, the same troublous fitfully-illuminated life' (II: 27). There is, in the relationship between Dorothea and Lydgate, a sense of maturity and equality, of honesty and fundamental sympathy completely absent from her relations with Will.

Lydgate, however, could not have provided everything. Dorothea needs work. No 'home epic' could have given her the 'illimitable satisfaction' she sought. This is one of the reasons that the *Middlemarch* we have is a better though less satisfying novel than the one we would have had if George Eliot had chosen the obvious.

The other and more central reason for the ending we have is its plausibility. To unite Dorothea and Lydgate would have been to dismiss the issues raised in the novel in favour of a satisfying Christian optimism – an ending where characters emerge from purgatory purified and equipped with a ticket for heaven. *Jane Eyre* takes this route, though the literal fire that purifies Rochester has none of the subtlety and interest of Lydgate's purgatorial marriage. Once cleansed, Rochester is delivered into the arms of the heroine, who has been pure throughout the story. Dorothea is marred from the first by an innocence verging at times on stupidity and by its attendant short-sightedness. She and Lydgate are struggling from equally impure and short-sighted beginnings towards fuller awareness. Lydgate learns from his experience, but Dorothea learns regrettably little. Her obtuseness has many roots in her education, her available options, the medium in which she moves, and the psychological distortions likely to appear under such conditions.

Middlemarch is a study of cause and effect, remarkable in its sensitivity to the multiplicity of causes, meticulous in its faithfulness to likely effects. George Eliot navigates steadily between absolute tragedy and absolute fulfilment, relentlessly pursuing the likely, even though it goes against the Victorian taste for an artistically satisfying and morally sweeping conclusion. The result is a novel which is dissatisfying only in that it offers no solutions, no satisfaction of cathartic closure, but instead we are offered the open-ended satisfactions of its own orchestral polyphony.

8

THE OPEN-ENDEDNESS
OF *DANIEL DERONDA*

On the formal level, as a fictional structure, integrated and consistent both in quality and idea, *Middlemarch* is clearly George Eliot's master-piece. But these are not the qualities we have come to value in George Eliot. For these we would be happier in the company of Jane Austen or Henry James. We come to George Eliot not for perfect churches but for flawed cathedrals. Early commentators appreciated this. In 1866, E. S. Dallas wrote:

> Hitherto Miss Austen has had the honour of the first place
> among our lady novelists, but a greater than she has now arisen
> . . . George Eliot has not attained (Austen's) ease of story-
> telling because she has to deal with subjects far more difficult
> than Miss Austen ever attempted.
>
> (Carroll 1971: 263)

And Oscar Browning, in his biography of George Eliot, made the following remark about *Daniel Deronda*: 'If it fails in execution it is because the task cannot yet be accomplished. But if the work is ever to be done, the way must be paved by partial failure. It is better to have tried and failed than never to have tried.' (Browning 1890: 144).

Even *Middlemarch*, magnificent as it is, seems a shaky edifice when placed beside the works of Austen or James. The crossing of class boundaries, something that Austen and James never attempt, creates structural strain: we feel the effort of the author. This is never felt in Dickens because he crosses class barriers with his gloves in hand. Most of his working-class characters are flat in Forster's sense of the word: they are identified by a recurring idiosyncrasy that places them on the verge of caricature and they are incapable of change or development. George Eliot crosses boundaries of class and culture with as direct a novelistic interest as she brings to characters of her own class. Hetty the dairy-maid, Silas the weaver, Bulstrode the evangelical banker, Alcharisi the Jewish opera singer, Grandcourt the aristocrat, are all treated with the same depth. The resultant characterizations may be unequal, but the initial driving force of characterization, the effort to understand the equivalent centre of self in others, is the same despite differences of class, culture, and religion.

This conscientiousness sometimes results in embarrassing failures such as Felix Holt's interaction with the working men of Sproxton. It is easy to criticize George Eliot for failing in ventures which other novelists do not attempt. The failures have resulted in a critical mania for carving up the novels, usually along distinct class and cultural lines. Critics such as Leslie Stephen and F. R. Leavis want the Transome part of *Felix Holt* without the Malthouse Yard part, the Gwendolen part of *Daniel Deronda* without the Jewish part. The impulse is not always to cut away the lower part of the social scale: the same critics want the Dorlcote Mill part of *The Mill on the Floss* without the bourgeois St Ogg's part. The objection seems to be against the strain which results from the simultaneous and equal treatment of various social groups within one novel. Critics of this camp fail to see that the same elements that make George Eliot's novels structurally unsound also make them cathedrals; shaky, asymmetrical, problematic, but cathedrals none the less.

Carolyn Heilbrun has pointed out the irony of this critical carving up of *Daniel Deronda* when seen in the context of its influence: the Gwendolen and the Jewish halves of the novel, Heilbrun argues, provided the seeds for Isabel Archer and Leopold Bloom (Heilbrun 1973: 85–6). The suggestion is that, in this novel, George Eliot generated two major strands of fictional development. In light of this, the criticism she has received for intertwining two such disparate strands in one novel seems narrow-minded and time-bound, and Oscar Browning's words gain an added poignance.

Daniel Deronda crosses more boundaries, and is therefore more strained, than any other George Eliot novel. The English part of the novel is an England only recently familiar to George Eliot, the aristocratic world. She, like Balzac, paints drawing rooms into which she was never invited until the height of her success. The Jewish part is book learned, and it strains, like *Romola*, to seem lived. There are no Poysers or Garths in the novel, nothing of George Eliot's 'primal passionate store'.

Social barriers are not the only ones transgressed in this novel. The characterization of Gwendolen is a breakthrough in George Eliot's treatment of women, and a breakthrough in the treatment of women in fiction. Gwendolen's closest literary cousins are Becky Sharp, Emma Bovary, and Anna Karenina. These three characterizations, however, differ from that of Gwendolen in the clarity of narratorial judgement. Emma and Anna are both more sympathetic than Gwendolen, and Becky is less so. They fall more clearly into the traditional categories of the good and the evil woman.

In the characterization of Gwendolen there is a suggestion that any woman of personal power is bound to be bad; the conflict between her potential and the paucity of opportunity will inevitably result in evil. There were hints of this in the characterization of Maggie, but ultimately George Eliot's insistence on the conscious altruism, sexual innocence, and moral purity of Maggie constitutes a reluctance to face the issue on the conscious level; Maggie's demons are all subconscious. Dorothea is a more serious denial of the effect of environment on women. She is a madonna whose integrity is preserved despite the spiritual poverty of her milieu and the meanness of opportunity. Her faults are excesses of zeal rather than eruptions of evil. As such she is apparently a contradiction of George Eliot's belief that people do not develop fine personalities in limiting and repressive environments (Pinney 1963: 205). Celia and Rosamond are far more likely and believable products of the Middlemarch milieu. In *Middlemarch*, apparently, George Eliot was not yet ready to face this truth, and therefore to sympathize with these female characters. The argument for Rosamond is buried under a sediment of narratorial disapprobation similar to that with which Hetty Sorrel was presented. Narratorial sympathy is saved for Dorothea, who has inherited the ideal components of her nature from Romola and Dinah and is tainted, though to a lesser extent, by their lack of credibility.

This is one point at which *Daniel Deronda* transcends *Middlemarch* in its daring – crossing a psychological barrier that had hitherto resisted all George Eliot's probing. Even though she herself asserted, in a letter of 1860 to Barbara Bodichon, that 'the highest "calling and election" is to *do without opium*' (Letters III: 366, Marian Lewes's emphasis), she kept inviolate throughout her life and work a quasi-religious belief in the existence of wholly altruistic personalities who can act as beacons in the murk of everyday life and moral mediocrity. This belief, which she held in common with her contemporaries and was derived from

Christian idealism, no doubt fed the 'self-despair' to which Marian Evans Lewes was prone: had she admitted the impossibility of such personalities, she would not have resented herself so much for falling short of their imagined excellence.

On one level, all her novels are attempts to justify the ways of Marian Lewes to men. This has been attacked by Leavis as 'daydream self-indulgence' (Leavis 1948: 94) a phrase that suggests a transparent and embarrassing immaturity. For this reason the phrase is not helpful in determining the true reason for a certain aroma of untruthfulness in the earlier heroines. Leavis's condescension blinds him to the subtler psychological convolutions of a highly intelligent and mature personality battling with herself and her world; it leads him rashly to declare that Gwendolen is not a self-portrait simply because Gwendolen is not a fantasy (Leavis 1948: 116). Ellen Moers maintains that Gwendolen is not an idealized self-portrait, and further claims that 'Gwendolen is not a heroine; she is a victim, and also a villainess.' All this is rather confusing. One wonders what her definitions are (does being a heroine exclude her from being a victim? What about Clarissa or Tess?); she sees the characterization of Gwendolen as something new, in which for the first time George Eliot gives 'a realistic and tolerant appraisal of the difficulties of a woman's life' (Moers 1978: 196). Ruby Redinger recognizes the self-portraiture in the characterization of Gwendolen but sees it as a portrait of the vicious side of Marian Lewes (Redinger 1976: 473). This chapter will argue that Gwendolen marks a breakthrough in George Eliot's acceptance of herself.

Redinger's biography discusses 'the self that restrains self' (Redinger 1976: chapter 4: 161–224) – the personality George Eliot created or worked toward through self-discipline – a self she could live with. This is a sympathetic treatment of what Eliza Lynn Linton unsympathetically described as 'a made woman' (Linton 1899: 97). Eliza Lynn Linton's 'made woman' and Leavis's 'day-dream self-indulgence' both contain a grain of truth but fail to contribute significantly to the understanding of the woman and her work because the terms are oversimplified and dismissive.

Marian Lewes was painfully aware of her own personality flaws. She knew, as her letters and especially her fiction demonstrate, that she was vain, selfish, prone to hysterics, and at times insensitive. Her contemporaries condemned her for the irregularities of her life, and her novels, with their recurrent theme of a woman misunderstood by those around her, are repeated attempts at self-vindication. Many feminist critics have remarked that none of George Eliot's heroines is allowed the freedom that she won for herself: none of them finds a life-long vocation; none of them flouts the sexual conventions of her time; Dinah, Maggie, Romola, and Dorothea are all, on the surface level of the novels, unconvincingly selfless, in a way their author certainly never was. One gets the impression that although Marian Lewes considered herself innocent of the character her contemporaries had given her, she nevertheless felt that her true self was unworthy of forgiveness. Maggie, the most autobiographical of the heroines, is forced into an unconvincing altruism on the surface level of *The Mill on the Floss*, where we are asked to believe that a woman would give up what she perceived as her own happiness for the sake of keeping faith with others. Maggie's avowed motives at Mudport are implausible; we have to look below the surface to understand her, to see, in the metaphoric substructure of the novel, the psychology at work beneath Marian Lewes's anxious desire to vindicate herself to a world for which her true self was not good enough. Her feeling that she was not good enough is evident in her letters. In a letter of 1859 to Cara Bray, she wrote 'I have been blasphemous enough sometimes to think that I had never been good and attractive enough to win any little share of the honest disinterested friendship there is in the world' (Letters III: 22). And in a 1867 letter to Maria Congreve, 'Impossible to imagine the large charity I have for people who detest me' (Letters IV: 413).

In getting her contemporaries to sympathize with Gwendolen, George Eliot educated her audience and herself in the acceptance of human fallibility. When her audience accepted Gwendolen, they accepted, for the first time, not the 'made woman', the 'self that restrains self', but the part of Marian Evans that she had found it necessary to make over, to restrain. The self-portraitive element is as present in Gwendolen as in the other heroines, but in Gwendolen it is confession not cover-up, disrobing not disguise.

In this, George Eliot's last novel resembles Dostoyevsky's. *Daniel Deronda*, like *The Brothers Karamazov*, marks a release from psychological bondage that has constricted the writer for a lifetime. Freud's essay 'Dostoyevsky and parricide' may be inaccurate in its details and reductionist in its analysis, but its basic point rings true (Freud: XIV). In *The Brothers Karamazov*, Dostoyevsky finally faces the desire to kill his father – the guilt for having wished his father dead which tortured him after his father's actual death – and forgives himself. In *Daniel Deronda*, George Eliot can finally sympathize with a heroine who, like herself, is not earnestly and implausibly altruistic but humanly self-seeking and limited. In *Daniel Deronda*, as in *The Brothers Karamazov*, this breakthrough turns upon the idea of forgiving oneself for a murderous desire, and in both cases the murdered man is the patriarch, the male power figure at the apex of the social structure of the novel.

The political implications of this are far-reaching. Both writers spent their lives repressing the revolutionary elements of their personalities. Both, in their maturity, were avowed conservatives. Yet both end their long careers on this note of release and self-forgiveness: 'Who has not wished to kill his father?' asks Ivan in the courtroom, and Gwendolen goes free after murdering (in thought and arguably in fact) the male power figure. Not only is she unpunished, but the death of the male power figure is itself her deliverence: through the crisis it brings on, she manages, in Gillian Beer's phrase, to 'give birth to a livable identity' (Beer 1986: 223). At the end of both novels, there is a feeling of catharsis: the despot is dead; long live those released from his despotism. Grandcourt is a representative of the Victorian establishment, the class to which Marian Lewes had so long sought to justify herself. His coldness, his philistinism, his amorality are a comment on the unfitness of those who judged Marian Lewes to stand in judgement upon her. By creating Gwendolen and making her admirable, despite her faults, and by allowing her to kill Grandcourt and go unpunished, George Eliot at last flouts the establishment values that insisted that the only admirable woman was a selfless woman, a submissive woman, a woman without avowed sexual appetites and aversions.

Grandcourt, like Tom Tulliver, enjoys punishing. Gwendolen, like Maggie, must change but cannot be coerced into change. Whereas in the flood scene of *The Mill on the Floss* George Eliot evades the problem by bringing the coercive man to realize that coercion is inappropriate, in *Daniel Deronda* she destroys the coercive man and insists that the only path to change in Gwendolen is personal evolution with the guidance of an ideal, personified in Daniel.

Dinah, Romola, and Dorothea, the moral beacons of the earlier novels, were also the heroines of those novels. In *Daniel Deronda*, the role of beacon is relegated to Daniel, a man, and whether Marian Lewes intended it or not, a character of secondary importance to Gwendolen. This had been attempted before, in *Felix Holt*, another novel named for a secondary male character rather than the heroine at its centre. Felix is presented as a moral beacon and tutor to Esther, and perhaps in consequence, he is rather wooden and unconvincing; the characterization of Daniel suffers, though less seriously, from the same defect. The good and altruistic woman of *Daniel Deronda* is Mirah, and again we can see a precedent in an earlier Eliot novel: Lucy, in *The Mill on the Floss*, is the repository of traditional feminine virtues of lovingness, submissiveness, forgiveness, and patience, a constellation of virtues which is praised and given central place in *Romola* and *Adam Bede*, but which, in *The Mill on the Floss* and *Daniel Deronda*, is marginalized in secondary female characters.

In Gwendolen, George Eliot creates a figure whose motives are clearly and consciously self-seeking, but unlike her predecessors Hetty and Rosamond, Gwendolen is the indubitable heroine of the novel, and her vanity and selfishness are treated with a narratorial gentleness quite at variance with the apparent narratorial aversion to Hetty and Rosamond. The gentleness of the narrator's detraction, the affection behind her irony, betray an intellectual breakthrough that is the other side of the psychological breakthrough discussed above: George Eliot has overcome the last vestiges of her early Christianity. She accepts human nature as it is, relinquishing the longing apparent in her earlier novels for something better than the simply human. That longing was not easily relinquished; it had taken thirty-four years for her mode of thinking to adapt to her changed belief in this issue of religion. Like Feuerbach and Comte, she had denied the supernatural claims of Christianity but retained its forms, its ideals, and its morality. The characterization of Romola, for example, is set up as a positivist ideal, but, on the surface level, its forms, values, and iconography are indistinguishable from those of Christian hagiography. The positivist religion of humanity differed from other religions in that the object of worship was human, but worship of the truly human requires full understanding and acceptance of both the good and the bad elements of human personality, without which it is simply a secularization of Christianity wherein the worship of God is replaced by the worship of an impossibly virtuous Man, the difference being merely linguistic. William Myers has pointed out that George Eliot's novels are all open to these charges which Marx brought against Feuerbach (Myers 1984: chapter 6: 103–18), and this explains why it is possible for students who have no knowledge of George Eliot's life to read her earlier novels without realizing that she was not a believer. However, in *Daniel Deronda* we can see the beginnings of change, a tentative departure into not only a Godless but a Christless reality.

Even in this final novel, the longing for something finer than the
human is still evident in the characterizations of Daniel, Mordecai,
and Mirah, but a radical change has taken place. In removing what, at
risk of seeming cynical, I shall call superhuman virtue from the
realm of familiar English life, and locating it in an ancient and alien
tradition, in prophets and founding-fathers, in characters who seem
timeless and therefore almost mythical, George Eliot can discuss her
ideals of human possibility while at the same time admitting that, in
the workaday English world, they remain almost entirely in the realm
of the subjunctive. This division of actual and subjunctive, the 'realistic' and the 'visionary', can be interpreted deconstructively (Norris
1982: 133)), but, looked at from a slightly different angle, the Jewish
half of the novel enables George Eliot to be unblinkingly honest in the
portrayal of the actual English world, facing truths especially about
Gwendolen, that she had been unable to face in earlier novels, by
juxtaposing them with their opposites. The egoistic sadism of Grandcourt can only be admitted in contrast with the selfless sympathy
of Daniel; the obsequious opportunism of Lush can only be admitted
in contrast with the proud spirituality of Mordecai; the acquisitive
vanity of Gwendolen can only be admitted in contrast to the
passive humility of Mirah. The Jewish counterpoints are perhaps
unattainable, possibly undesirable in their pure form, but striving
towards them could save a world which, in this novel, is suffering from
death of the soul. In the Jewish half of the novel, George Eliot makes a
plea for what she perceives to be the vanishing spirituality of life.

Deirdre David has discussed imperialism in *Daniel Deronda* (David
1981: 176). I would add to David's comments that George Eliot sees
human and cultural values as dwindling in inverse proportion to the
growth of capitalism and imperialism. Having realized, in the creation of Gwendolen, that people are not like Dinah, Romola, and
Dorothea, spiritual in the extreme and to the point of implausibility,
she further realizes that the growing consumerism of British culture is
making it less and less possible for people to be spiritual to any degree
whatsoever. This is expressed in a remarkable series of images that
shows the human and spiritual being converted into commodities and
is chillingly prophetic of the Nazi prison camp manufactories of the
Second World War.[1]

> 'And, my dear boy, it is good to be unselfish and generous; but
> don't carry that too far. It will not do to give yourself to be
> melted down for the benefit of the tallow-trade.'

(I: 275)

Knowledge, through patient and frugal centuries, enlarges
discovery and makes a record of it; Ignorance, wanting its day's
dinner, lights a fire with the record, and gives a flavour to its
one roast with the burnt souls of many centuries.

(I: 340)

'No man,' says a Rabbi, by way of indisputable instance, 'may
turn the bones of his father and mother into spoons.'

(II: 156)

'the Gentile, who had said, "What is yours is ours, and no
longer yours," was reading the letter of our law as a dark
inscription, or was turning its parchments into shoe-laces for an
army rabid with lust and cruelty.'

(II: 386)

The gambling casino and the choir-stables are variations on the
same idea: the cannibalistic nature of the spreading capitalist ideology, and the way in which cultural, human, and spiritual values are
supplanted by commodity value. On the metaphorical level, the
description of the casino can also be seen as prophetic. In it, the
eroding of class and cultural barriers by the commonality of money-
lust under advanced capitalism is predicted with irony:

There too, very near the fair countess, was a respectable London
tradesman . . . conscious of circulars addressed to the nobility
and gentry, whose distinguished patronage enabled him to take
his holidays fashionably, and to a certain extent in their distinguished company. Not his the gambler's passion that nullifies
appetite, but a well-fed leisure, which in the intervals of winning
money in business and spending it showily, sees no better
resource than winning money in play and spending it yet more
showily – reflecting always that Providence had never manifested any disapprobation of his amusement, and dispassionate
enough to leave off if the sweetness of winning much and seeing
others lose had turned to the sourness of losing much and seeing
others win. For the vice of gambling lay in losing money at it.

(I: 6)

Gambling, like bourgeois individualism, both highlights individ-
uality and breaks down the divisive barriers of cultures and classes by
giving members of different cultures and classes the common and
uniting interest of competing for money:

But while every single player differed markedly from every
other, there was a certain uniform negativeness of expression
which had the effect of a mask – as if they had all eaten of some
root that for the time compelled the brains of each to the same
narrow monotony of action.

(I: 6–7)

The paradox implicit in this uniting to compete is both ironic and
profoundly discouraging: money-lust manages to achieve what belief-
systems, from Christianity to communism, have attempted with little
success:

Here certainly was a striking admission of human equality. The
white bejewelled fingers of an English countess were very near
touching a bony, yellow, crab-like hand stretching a bared wrist
to clutch a heap of coin.

(I: 6)

The image of choir-stables (chapter 35) expresses the same idea in
different form and links that idea into the dominant metaphoric network of the novel. Throughout the George Eliot canon, as elsewhere
in literature, attitudes to horse-riding are used as a metaphor for
sexuality. Here, as Barbara Hardy has pointed out, both Gwendolen
and Grandcourt see marriage as horse-riding (Hardy 1959: 228) – the
self in the role of rider and the other in the role of horse. Gwendolen
moves from a pleasant anticipation of mounting to the uncomfortable
realization of being mounted. This is a double-edged metaphor: on
the level of power struggle, Gwendolen is unpleasantly surprised to
find herself dominated where she had hoped to dominate; on the level
of sexual symbolism, the sexual aversion we witnessed in her repulse
of Rex (I: 117–19) becomes sexual terror as she realizes that Grandcourt's coldness does not, as she had thought, exempt her from sexual
obligations in marriage but rather obliges her to be subjected to cold,
power-seeking, and loveless sex. Meanwhile the jewel imagery which
has developed side by side with the horse-riding imagery fuses with it
brilliantly, as Lloyd Fernando has pointed out, when Gwendolen
realizes that the diamond necklace, which represents Grandcourt's
wealth and aristocracy and is associated with his illegitimate family by
Mrs Glasher (itself a privilege of his wealth and aristocracy), has
become the reins with which Grandcourt controls and dominates
Gwendolen herself (Fernando 1977: 59).

In this metaphoric context, the choir-stables suggests not only the decline of the church as it is displaced by a growing consumerism (Garrett 1969: 1–4) but also a parallel and related decline of the sacredness of marriage as it is displaced by a growing objectification of the marriage partner. Grandcourt sees Gwendolen as a commodity to be acquired and used for her sexual and ornamental value; Gwendolen sees Grandcourt as a commodity to be acquired and used for his monetary and prestige value. Deronda, by contrast, takes his hat off to the horses, suggesting reserves of reverence in him that have been eroded in everyone else: reverence for religion; reverence for human love; reverence for all the spiritual and human values that are being slowly usurped by the growing consumerism of English culture.

This is the dehumanizing cultural milieu in which Gwendolen is located. It bears no resemblance to earlier George Eliot worlds. Hayslope, St Ogg's, Raveloe, and Middlemarch may have had their faults, their narrow prejudices, harsh judgements, suffocating limitations, but they were nevertheless human communities for which it was possible to feel affection and even a grudging respect. The web imagery describing these communities suggests both suffocating restriction (as in spiders' webs) and a sense of security, belonging, and relationship (Beer 1983: 149–80). The broad international setting of *Daniel Deronda* and the consumerism which characterizes it preclude any feeling of community, much less of the kind of community that can be described as an organic mesh. This new world, a world that anticipates the alienated settings of modernism, poses new problems for George Eliot in both the characterization and the destiny of its heroine. Once this medium has been defined, it becomes obvious that no Dinah, Romola, or Dorothea could possibly inhabit it. It also becomes apparent that George Eliot's old solutions to the life problems of her heroines, the role of ministering angel in which we last see Janet, in 'Janet's repentance', and Romola, and the role of wife and mother in which we last see Dinah and Dorothea, depend upon the existence of an organic human community and a strong sense of family. Both these are absent from the English world of *Daniel Deronda*. In this novel, families are fragmented or malformed (Welsh 1984: 319). Of all the families in the novel, only the Meyricks and the Cohens give the impression of intimate and nourishing family life, but they are separated, both by the class structure of English society and by the structure of the novel, from Gwendolen's world: they inhabit a middle social stratum, which is still relatively untouched by the alienation that has infected the gentry and aristocracy, and they inhabit the Jewish half of the novel, in which George Eliot still allows herself to paint and believe in possibility of the ideal.

If Gwendolen, because of her own nature and the nature of the society in which she is located, cannot become a ministering angel or a wife and mother, the question is, what can she become? It is important to remember that for the only other George Eliot heroine who vaguely resembles Gwendolen, Maggie Tulliver, and for two of the three literary cousins of Gwendolen mentioned above, Emma Bovary and Anna Karenina, the only solution is death. The question of what Gwendolen can become is posed at the beginning of *Daniel Deronda*, and in the course of the novel, various tentative answers are tried and rejected. There are suggestions that she can and does on some level become a prostitute and a murderess, but by the end of the novel she has moved beyond these desperate identities, and the question remains unanswered. Gillian Beer has pointed out that Gwendolen, like Daniel, feels herself exceptional even though she has no particular gift (Beer 1986: 218), but despite her lack of a specific talent, one gets the feeling that had she been a man of similar intelligence and charisma something could have been done, something other than prostitution and murder, to redeem her family and give her life direction. Daniel is the proof of this. His vocation is determined by his relations to Mordecai, Charisi, and Kalonymos, all of which are relations of patriarchal descent, of spiritual father to son; Daniel's maleness provides him with a vocation.

Gwendolen, however, is also placed in opposition to Mirah and to Alcharisi, comparisons which erode any social–deterministic conclusions that the Gwendolen/Daniel contrast might have encouraged. Barbara Hardy has remarked that Mirah also tries to sing professionally and also has the opportunity to sell herself (Hardy 1959: 139), but, in contrast to Gwendolen, she succeeds in singing professionally and refuses to sell herself. This last contrast might suggest that the difference between Gwendolen and Mirah is the difference between the bad girl and the good girl, the harlot and the madonna, in which case it would be arguable that Daniel is handed as a prize to the good girl, but the situations of the two women are in fact very different. In Mirah's case, prostitution entails no mitigating good; in Gwendolen's, it allows her to save her mother and sisters from poverty. Mirah makes a firm and conscious decision on the side of right when she runs away from the prospect of prostitution, but Gwendolen makes no corresponding decision on the side of wrongdoing; her acceptance of Grandcourt and her failure to throw him the rope when he is drowning both take place when she is in a semi-conscious haze.

The differences between Mirah and Gwendolen are not simply differences of moral nature; they are differences of circumstance and most importantly, of scope. George Eliot's novels are like medieval paintings, in which some figures are constructed on a much larger scale than others. Dorothea, for example, is built on a larger scale than Celia and Rosamond. Difference in scope, as I argued earlier, does not necessarily coincide with difference in moral stature: Mrs Transome is built on a far larger scale than Esther, even though Esther can be seen as morally superior.

Leavis senses this when he identifies Gwendolen with Mrs Transome (Leavis 1948: 116), but he then goes on to dissociate Gwendolen from Dorothea, Rosamond, and George Eliot herself. In this he is mistaken. The monumentality of Mrs Transome, Dorothea, and Gwendolen is associated with George Eliot's sense of being exceptional. Marian Evans spent half her life aware that she was different from other women but unaware of the specific talent that would eventually vindicate and make a virtue of that difference. Mrs Transome, Dorothea, and Gwendolen are certainly not portraits of frustrated artists, but they are images of potential constricted, unrealized, and afraid of itself.

The ugly duckling metaphor used in the Prelude to *Middlemarch* encapsulates this idea. Marian Evans eventually realized her identity, her 'uncanniness' was eventually vindicated in her own and other eyes, but the Prelude posits an ugly duckling that never discovers its swan nature, a woman who never discovers that her oddness is the oddness that marks a potential leader:

> Mrs Transome had not the feminine tendency to seek influence through pathos; she had been used to rule in virtue of acknowledged superiority.
>
> *(Felix Holt* I: 22)

> a peerage will not quite do instead of leadership to the man who meant to lead; and this delicate-limbed sylph of twenty meant to lead.
>
> *(Daniel Deronda* I: 53)

The pain of constriction finds vent in adultery, domestic despotism, prostitution, manipulation, and murder. This sublimation of repressed energies is described through demonic imagery in *The Mill on the Floss, Daniel Deronda*, and most significantly, in the George Eliot letters. In her own life, before she found the true outlet for her creative and intellectual energies, George Eliot saw her own uniqueness as associated with evil. It is not surprising, therefore, that Mrs Transome and Gwendolen are monumental whereas their moral superiors, Esther and Mirah, are small.

If we compare scenes in which Gwendolen and Mirah are seen in similar situations or described with similar metaphors, the difference in the language used to describe the two women demonstrates the difference in scope of the two conceptions.

But in the course of that survey her eyes met Deronda's, and instead of averting them as she would have desired to do, she was unpleasantly conscious that they were arrested – how long? The darting sense that he was measuring her and looking down on her as an inferior, that he was of different quality from the human dross around her, that he felt himself in a region outside and above her, and was examining her as a specimen of a lower order, roused a tingling resentment which stretched the moment with conflict. It did not bring the blood to her cheeks, but sent it away from her lips. She controlled herself by the help of an inward defiance, and without other sign of emotion than this lip-paleness turned to her play. But Deronda's gaze seemed to have acted as an evil eye. Her stake was gone.

(I: 8)

apparently his voice had entered her inner world without her having taken any note of whence it came, for when it suddenly ceased she changed her attitude slightly, and, looking round with a frightened glance, met Deronda's face. It was but a couple of moments, but that seems a long while for two people to look straight at each other. Her look was something like that of a fawn or other gentle animal before it turns to run away: no blush, no special alarm, but only some timidity which yet could not hinder her from a long look before she turned.

(I: 280)

In both scenes, a woman is detected in a revealing moment by a man, Deronda. She meets his eyes, holds his gaze without blushing, then looks away. In the first case, the incident is seen from the woman's point of view, in the second, from Deronda's, and this contributes to the impression that the contrast between Gwendolen, in the first of these passages, and Mirah, in the second, is not only that between bad and good but also between a complex consciousness and an innocent, a woman and a child. The decisive contrast lies in the use of animal imagery. In the first case, Gwendolen imagines that Daniel sees her as an animal, 'a specimen of a lower order', but her complex speculations and reactions on this point demonstrate just the opposite: that she is not of a lower order than Daniel. The image of Mirah as a frightened fawn (not only animal but infant animal) is offered without irony and remains uncontradicted. Mirah succeeds where Gwendolen fails because she is a smaller and simpler soul. Her music is chamber music (Beer 1986: 224). She has not the scope to enter into the larger realm of conflict in which Gwendolen is so roundly defeated.

The affinities and contrasts between Gwendolen and Alcharisi are more problematic. Alcharisi is the only woman in all George Eliot's fiction who finds a vocation and sticks to it. She is the only woman in the novel with a personal power and presence equal to and indeed greater than Gwendolen's. As a successful singer, her destiny reflects on the lost possibilities of both Gwendolen's and Mirah's destinies, but the reflections are not what one might expect from an author whose professional excellence and personal happiness grew symbiotically.

When Gwendolen returns from Lebronn, having been informed of her family's ruin, she considers singing professionally in order to redeem her family's fortunes. The impulse behind this is that of a daughter trying to fulfil the obligations of what has become a husbandly relation to her mother. Dierdre David has discussed the psychological implications of Gwendolen's relation to her mother (David 1981: 193), but there are also gender-political implications here. Fanny Davilow's all-female family has all the characteristics of a self-sufficient unit. Gwendolen's desire to protect and provide for her mother differs from a man's desire to protect and provide for his family only in that Gwendolen has not been given the education and is not given the opportunity to do so in a healthy and satisfying way. She can and does provide for her family by selling herself to Grandcourt – and this is the only solution left open to her after she has been more or less told by Klesmer that such talents as she possesses are marketable only on the marriage market.

Both her desire to sing professionally and her decision to marry Grandcourt are in part motivated by an imperialistic mentality, the will to power over others, that surrounds and permeates her. In both cases, however, a tension is set up between the worthy and the unworthy motive. In the particular case of Gwendolen, the desire to provide for her family works in conjunction with her vanity to motivate her search for a position of power; we are nevertheless made aware that any woman wishing to provide for a family would be unable to do so by any means other than prostitution. That is, unless she was a woman of exceptional talent, and ironically, Alcharisi, the only kind of woman who could support a family, has rejected her family in order to pursue her vocation. At the centre of this is the impossibility, for most women, of love and duty flowing in one stream. Both love and duty, family and vocation, are insisted upon throughout the George Eliot canon as being essential to happiness, but whereas the most mediocre and talentless of men can find fulfilment in both, the most exceptional women have to choose one or the other, and lesser women are not given the choice.

Even Marian Lewes, though she came perhaps as close as a woman could to fulfilment in both hemispheres of her life, was unmarried and childless. If her marriage to Lewes had been legal, and if she had borne children, it is highly probable that she would never have become George Eliot. She might have become a Margaret Oliphant, as Oliphant herself implies in her autobiography (Oliphant 1899: 4-8), but she would have been unlikely to secure the peace and the scholarly atmosphere necessary to produce work of the highest quality. These necessities were made available to her as a positive by-product of ostracism. Marian Lewes acknowledged this herself in an 1859 letter to Barbara Bodichon discussing her joy at the reception of *Adam Bede*: 'I am a very blessed woman, am I not? to have all this reason for being glad that I have lived, in spite of my sins and sorrows – or rather, by reason of my sins and sorrows' (Letters III: 64). In 1869, again writing to Barbara Bodichon, she comments on the impossibility of Lewes obtaining a divorce:

I am not sorry. . . for myself I prefer excommunication. I have no earthly thing that I care for, to gain by being brought within the pale of people's personal attention, and I have many things to care for that I should lose – my freedom from petty worldly torments, commonly called pleasures, and that isolation which

really keeps my charity warm instead of chilling it, as much
contact with frivolous women would do.

(Letters III: 366–7)

Alcharisi's unloving nature and the bitterness of her old age suggest
that given the present relation between man and woman, no answer to
the question 'what can Gwendolen become?' will be adequate, that
frustration lies at the end of not only the realized but also the
unrealized possibilities of her life. As the novel draws to a close, we are
limply hoping that someone will marry her. No matter how much we
agreed with Gwendolen at the beginning of the novel about the dullness of the average woman's lot, that dullness begins to look like a
sanctuary after her disastrous marriage to Grandcourt, and after our
glimpse, in Alcharisi, of what becomes of the successful professional
woman. The best available candidate for marrying Gwendolen seems
to be Daniel.

The possibility of marriage between Gwendolen and Daniel is frustrated in much the same way as that between Dorothea and Lydgate,
although the possibility in this novel is allowed to emerge more
fully than that in *Middlemarch*. If my argument about the subjunctive nature of the Jewish side of the novel is a tenable one, it is
clear that the possibility cannot be realized. If it were, Daniel, who
hovers between the actual and subjunctive worlds of the novel and
must eventually move fully into one or the other, would, by moving
fully into the actual world, change that world for the better. We
would be left with hope for England. Daniel inherits the role of
beacon and the ideal elements of his nature from Dinah, Romola, and
Dorothea, and he, like them, could not possibly inhabit the English
world of this novel. That is why he feels alien in that world before
he knows that he is not of it; that is why he needs a new identity and
spiritual habitat before he can be released from the paralysis of passive
observation.

But beyond this purely structural objection, George Eliot suggests
that Daniel is not capable of sexual interaction. 'That she or any one
else should think of him as her possible lover was a conception which
had never entered her mind; indeed it was equally out of the question
with Mrs Meyrick and the girls'(III: 165–6). Both Gwendolen and
Mirah first encounter Daniel in a long mutual look, but neither
woman blushes, as the narrator takes pains to tell us. Daniel's effect is
not sexual.

'But *can* you marry?'

'Yes,' said Deronda, also in a low voice. 'I am going to marry.'

(III: 401)

His unsurprised response to this bizarre and rather insulting question indicates that Daniel is aware of his asexuality. Daniel's androgyny ('all the woman lacking in her was present in him', III: 176) has unsexed him, whereas the androgynous images of Gwendolen add to the dynamism and excitement of her sexual appeal.

Hans wants to paint Mirah as Berenice and Daniel as Agrippa, Berenice's brother, with whom she was suspected of incestuous relations. George Eliot originally called Mirah Miriam, the name of the sister of Moses, and Daniel is the Moses figure of the end of the novel. Deirdre David points out that through their marriage, Mirah gains the good Jewish father she never had and Daniel gains the good Jewish mother he never had (David 1981: 170). These details suggest a familial rather than sexual love between Mirah and Daniel. The larger implication is that masculine sexuality is inseparable from the assertion of the self, and that therefore a non-assertive, non-repressive man is also a non-sexual man.

There is also some indication that marriage between Gwendolen and Daniel would be bad for Gwendolen. Just as Lydgate was seen both in contrast and as parallel to Casaubon, Daniel is both the antithesis and the disguised twin of Grandcourt. This is again ironically prophetic, given the subsequent evolution of the Zionist movement that the novel foretells and of which Daniel is the representative into a power arguably as imperialistic as the power from which it originally rebelled and of which Grandcourt is the representative.

Myers has noted the similarity between Grandcourt and Daniel and suggests that the transference of the word 'submission' from Grandcourt's context to Daniel's implies that Daniel is 'a partner of the sadistic oppressor of [Gwendolen's] spirit' (Myers 1984: 179–80). This ignores the different uses of the word in the two contexts: Grandcourt applies 'the spiritual pressure which made submission inevitable' (III: 15), whereas Daniel, earlier in the same chapter, impresses her with 'the feeling of submission' (III: 4). Myers also seems to forget the fact that submissiveness is a positivist virtue. George Eliot carefully chooses these different uses of 'submission' to point out the difference between being forced to submit and being inspired with the desire to submit, between coercion and guidance, rape and love-making.

Yet the similarity is there. Gillian Beer has pointed out that Sir Hugo calls Daniel a kind of Lovelace (Beer 1986: 224). In light of this, it is possible that the similarity of the names Harlowe and Harleth is not accidental, and certainly an unsavoury sense of ownership is betrayed in Daniel's inability to answer Hans's accusation:

> 'You monster!' retorted Hans, 'do you want her to wear weeds
> for *you* all her life – burn herself in perpetual suttee while you are
> alive and merry?'
> Deronda could say nothing
>
> (III: 393)

The clearest evidence of Daniel's similarity to Grandcourt lies in his effect on Gwendolen. Throughout the novel, Gwendolen has been seen as a strong, assertive, combative, androgynous figure. These attributes have been seen ambivalently: they are both her faults and her virtues. The description of her relation to Grandcourt, for example, is very similar to the description of Lydgate's relation to Rosamond, and in both cases the desire for ascendancy is seen as a fault justly punished:

> Any romantic illusions she had had in marrying this man had
> turned on her power of using him as she liked. He was using her
> as he liked.
>
> (*Daniel Deronda* III: 80–1)

> but it was inevitable that in that excusing mood he should think
> of her as if she were an animal of another and feebler species.
> Nevertheless she had mastered him.
>
> (*Middlemarch* III: 205)

Similarly, when Gwendolen aspires to positions traditionally held by men, that aspiration is often seen as culpable:

> she had visions of being followed by a *cortège* who would worship
> her as a goddess of luck and watch her play as a directing
> augury. Such things had been known of male gamblers; why
> should not a woman have a like supremacy?
>
> (I: 8)

> 'Woman was tempted by a serpent: why not man?'
>
> (I: 11)

This potent charm . . . may seem so full a reason for
Gwendolen's domestic empire, that to look for any other would
be to ask the reason of daylight when the sun is shining. But . . .
I remember having seen the same assiduous, apologetic attention
awarded to . . . a very common sort of men. And the only point
of resemblance among them all was a strong determination too
have what was pleasant, with a total fearlessness in making
themselves disagreeable or dangerous when they did not get it.
Who is so much cajoled and served with trembling by the weak
females of a household as the unscrupulous male . . .?

(I: 56)

The knife that Gwendolen dreams of putting under her pillow
(III: 224) is another instance of her aspirations to the male role,
wishing to penetrate before she is penetrated, and again the instance is
a negative one.

However, there are also positive products of Gwendolen's
androgynous nature, and positive images to describe them. Her desire
to fend for her family is the other side of her domestic tyranny, and
Gwendolen does, after all, save her mother from penury. Her name is
that of an ancient British moon goddess, the equivalent of Artemis,
and her archery conjures not only images of Artemis but also of
Rosalind in *As You Like It* (David 1981: 184), which could have been
an ironic title for Gwendolen's part of the novel. These are the things
that monumentalize Gwendolen and enable her to inspire our admiration and interest more than Mirah does, even though Mirah is clearly
her moral superior.

Daniel's guidance helps Gwendolen through her crisis, but
the metamorphosis it affects in her is not all positive. It diminishes her, as marriage diminishes Dinah and Dorothea. The
Gwendolen of the opening scenes might have been vain, manipulative, deluded, and selfish but she was also powerful and monumental.
Consider Mackworth's opinion of her mouth, given in the opening
chapter:

'And her mouth – there never was a prettier mouth, the lips curl
backward so finely, eh, Mackworth?'
'Think so? I cannot endure that sort of mouth. It looks so self-
complacent, as if it knew its own beauty – the curves are too
immovable. I like a mouth that trembles more.'

(I: 12)

172

Up to the last sentence, we might agree with Mackworth. We have already seen evidence of complacency in Gwendolen, and it has been presented with some ironic disapprobation. But Mackworth's final sentence changes the lights for us. It is a crude expression of sadism, of the desire, inextricable in Mackworth's case from his sexuality, to subjugate, intimidate, to break the spirit and drain the strength of the object of his sexual desire. In this light, the mouth that a moment earlier seemed smug and repellent becomes heroic. Mackworth is a foreshadowing of Grandcourt, and throughout the description of their courtship, Gwendolen's smiling mouth is seen fascinating and challenging the lizard-like Grandcourt. But it is only at the end of the novel, in her final interview with Daniel, that we see Gwendolen conquered: 'She looked at Deronda with lips childishly parted'; 'Gwendolen's lip began to tremble. "But will you come back?" she said' (III: 396). Certainly her complacency has vanished, but so too has her strength, her monumentality. Daniel has achieved through gentleness what Grandcourt's sadism attempted but failed to achieve: he has wiped the smile off Gwendolen's face; he has made her mouth tremble.

Daniel resembles Grandcourt only in being a man. Intimate connection with a man, George Eliot seems to be saying, somehow inevitably entails subjection of the woman, unless the woman is completely insensitive, like Rosamond Vincy, or the man is weaker than the woman, as in the unrealized possibilities of marriage between Dinah and Seth, Maggie and Philip.

Gwendolen, like Dinah, is only attracted to men who are, in her opinion and their own, superior to her. This aspiration is seen as admirable in itself, and George Eliot uses sharp irony in her descriptions of the opposite situation, in which men like Mr Tulliver and Lydgate delight in the inferiority of their wives. However, the desire for a superior lover is seen as disastrous for women. We leave Dinah in a diminished state, having become an auxiliary to Adam. We leave Gwendolen in metamorphosis. She has been saved by Daniel's rejection; had Daniel accepted her, the novel would have ended with a diminished and eclipsed image of the heroine. As it is, we leave her in the process of absorbing what Daniel had to teach her, and therefore becoming more than she was before, not less. But we leave her solitary. The suggestion of Rex waiting in the wings is tentative, one of the many question marks with which this novel and the George Eliot canon closes. It takes us back to the early part of the novel, in which

Mr Gascoigne's offer of his pony for Gwendolen to ride foreshadows Rex's offer of love and elicits the response, 'I cannot endure ponies' (I: 47). We are reminded of the narrator's flight of fancy about Gwendolen and Rex:

> if only things could have been a little otherwise then, so as to have been greatly otherwise after! – if only these two beautiful young creatures could have pledged themselves to each other then and there, and never through life have swerved from that pledge! For some of the goodness which Rex believed in was there. Goodness is a large, often a prospective word; like harvest, which at one stage when we talk of it lies all underground.
>
> (I: 97)

The particulars that would have had to have been 'a little otherwise then' all pertain to Gwendolen's scope. A lesser woman would not have thought Rex a pony; someone like his sister Anna, for example, would have been able to find fulfilment in marriage with Rex and could therefore have been happy and good. The reminder reconciles us to Gwendolen's solitude. To wish her happy, fulfilled, and good is, in the logic of this novel, to wish that she had been a smaller and simpler soul.

The open-endedness of Gwendolen's story, set beside the expatriation of most of the repositories of spiritual values in the novel, Daniel, Mirah, and Mordecai, constituted a challenge to George Eliot's contemporaries, and remains a challenge to us today, since the problems it poses have yet to be solved. The only George Eliot novel to be set in its own time ends in suspension. At the end of the novel Gwendolen might have given birth to 'a livable identity', but we leave her in a spiritually impoverished landscape, with all available solutions to her life already tried and found inadequate. The question 'what can Gwendolen become?' can only be answered by the future.

9

GEORGE ELIOT
AND
TWENTIETH-CENTURY
FEMINIST PERSPECTIVES

Marian Lewes was not a feminist; she would not have called herself a feminist, she would probably have objected to being called a feminist, and no one familiar with her letters and the lukewarm support she gave to the women's movement of her day would venture so to call her. It is nevertheless true that George Eliot is feminist. In a sense, George Eliot is more 'feminist' because Marian Lewes did not identify herself as 'a feminist': her refusal to marginalize herself by making primary the identification with her gender, her implicit claim that she is human first and female second, that the problems of humanity are primary to her and those of women secondary, prefigures a state of post-feminism that is still far from realized, the state towards which Simone de Beauvoir gestured in her description of St Theresa (see pp. 128–9).

There are obvious problems with this. No one was more aware than George Eliot herself that the exceptional woman's escape does not alter the imprisonment of other women. As Gillian Beer has pointed out, this is explored in the contrast between Gwendolen and Alcharisi in *Daniel Deronda* and more explicitly in 'Armgart' (Beer 1986: 7: 200–28). However, when the fruit of those exceptional qualities changes our image of women, when the 'lovely trembler' with whom we are so familiar as a literary image of woman is replaced by a monumental image of passion and intelligence, of will and need, of full dynamic humanity, then perhaps the exceptional woman can be said to have provided what other women need most of all: a vision of how things might be, or be perceived, otherwise.

A clear example of this is Rachel, the French–Jewish opera star of the mid-nineteenth century who provided the inspiration for

Charlotte Brontë's Vashti, and, through Brontë, for George Eliot's
Armgart and Alcharisi:

> She was a study of such nature as had not encountered my eyes
> yet: a great and new planet, she was: but in what shape? I
> waited her rising.
>
> She rose at nine that December night: above the horizon I saw
> her come. She could shine yet with pale grandeur and steady
> might; but that star verged already on its judgment-day. Seen
> near, it was a chaos – hollow, half-consumed: an orb perished or
> perishing – half lava, half glow.
>
> I had heard this woman termed 'plain.' and I expected bony
> harshness and grimness – something large, angular, sallow.
> What I saw was the shadow of a royal Vashti: a queen, fair as
> the day once, turned pale now like twilight, and wasted like wax
> in flame.
>
> For a while – a long while – I thought it was only a woman,
> though an unique woman, who moved in might and grace before
> this multitude. By-and-by I recognized my mistake. Behold! I
> found upon her something neither of woman nor of man: in each
> of her eyes sat a devil. These evil forces bore her through the
> tragedy, kept up her feeble strength – for she was but a frail
> creature; and as the action rose and the stir deepened how wildly
> they shook her with their passions of the pit! They wrote HELL
> on her straight, haughty brow. They tuned her voice to the note
> of torment. They writhed her regal face to a demoniac mask.
> Hate and Murder and Madness incarnate, she stood.
>
> It was a marvellous sight: a mighty revelation.
> It was a spectacle low, horrible, immoral.
>   (Brontë 1853: I: 188–9)

This description from *Villette*, a novel that deeply impressed Marian
Evans and appeared only a few years before the beginning of her
fiction-writing career, is probably the only precursor, other than
Sophocles, Shakespeare, and Goethe,[1] of the monumental images of
women in the George Eliot canon. Charlotte Brontë uses the same
tools that George Eliot was soon to take up in the building of her
heroines: metaphors of physical enormity, sovereignty, androgyny,
and demonism. However, Vashti is not the heroine of *Villette*, and
Lucy Snowe is far from monumental (at times she is almost micro-

scopic). In fact, the description illuminates the effect 'an unique woman' might have upon an ordinary woman, and of how a sufficiently 'mighty revelation' as to the possibilities of power and passion in woman could provide a catalyst for the nascent female artist.

No matter how polemically unsound Marian Lewes and occasionally George Eliot herself might be, those heroines and their author affect us as Vashti affects Lucy, so that, for example, no matter how unfeminist or even anti-feminist some of the Esther episodes in *Felix Holt* might be, the creation of Mrs Transome overrules them. It is Mrs Transome we remember because of her scope, and her scope is enhanced by the contrast between Mrs Transome, the heroine, and Esther, the girl who marries her hero.

Zelda Austen has discussed the feminist objections of the 1970s to George Eliot:

> The application of the feminists' argument to *Middlemarch* is that
> George Eliot should have seen that while she was imitating
> reality in depicting the misery of the unconventional heroine and
> the placidity of the conventional wives and mothers, she was also
> sanctioning the norm and making it normative.
>
> (Austen 1976: 554)

This argument is difficult to refute in view of the fact that a century of conservative and anti-feminist criticism has based its interpretations on the equivocal ending of *Middlemarch* and similar ambiguities throughout the George Eliot canon. Zelda Austen argues that

> From the eighteenth century through the middle of the
> nineteenth century. . . the novel dwelt in the shackles of a
> censorship that insisted not on reality but on ideal behaviour.
> On these grounds it competed with sermons for the approbation
> of the Protestant middle class. By George Eliot's time, and
> indeed in part because of her, (and the French and the
> Russians), the novel had reached a stage where it no longer had
> to apologize for mirroring the world as it is. Feminist criticism,
> with its call for aspiring and achieving women, puts literature
> into similar shackles.
>
> (Austen 1976: 552)

Moreover, implicit in the feminist argument against George Eliot is a desire for a kind of feminist social realism that would be read by no one but feminists themselves. In fact, George Eliot did attempt a utopian kind of writing, with artistically unsuccessful results, in the woman-as-rescuer scenes in *The Mill on the Floss* and *Romola*. If such scenes had been characteristic of the entire George Eliot canon, it would, on aesthetic grounds alone, have been justifiably forgotten. George Eliot's value to feminism, which is derived from her artistic as well as her ideological worth, would have been lost. Her feminism is to be found in the tension between the monumental characterizations of her heroines and the inadequate options available to them, and in the tension between their fictional lives and the actual life of their author, which is constantly present in the reflexive elements of her novels and in the distance between the frames of reference of her heroines and her narrators. Behind those narrators we are constantly made aware of as a woman whose intellect and artistry render the bigotry of sexism self-evident. Those who happily sacrifice such an asset lay themselves open to Nina Auerbach's criticism:

> Feminist critics seem particularly reluctant to define themselves
> to the uninitiated. There is a sense in which our sisterhood has
> become too powerful; as a school, our belief in ourself is so
> potent that we decline communication with the networks of
> power and respectability we say we want to change.
>
> (Todd 1980: 258)

Auerbach is objecting to the strain of separatism that has become more and more characteristic of the feminist movement as it has matured and that recently, in conjunction with French theory, has become focused on the celebration of difference. An early and influential twentieth-century exponent of this idea was Virginia Woolf:

> [early nineteenth-century female novelists] had no tradition
> behind them, or one so short and partial that it was of little help.
> For we think back through our mothers if we are women. It is
> useless to go to the great men writers for help, however much
> one may go to them for pleasure.
>
> (Woolf 1929: 114)

I am not suggesting that the strain of separatism in feminist thought originates in Virginia Woolf, or that Woolf was herself a separatist, but rather that the tendency toward separatism draws strength from the idealization of 'feminine' characteristics combined with a strong emphasis on sexual difference. Woolf, both in her fiction and her essays, exhibits this combination, and it was through her commentary on George Eliot for the centenary celebration of 1919 that these ideas first entered George Eliot's critical heritage (Woolf 1919: 657). Woolf's meditations on the achievement of George Eliot are of particular interest because in them Woolf is herself 'thinking back through her mothers' and expressing all the quasi-Oedipal complications of that literary consanguinity.

Elaine Showalter has quite rightly taken exception to Woolf's emphasis: 'But a woman writing unavoidably thinks back through her fathers as well; only male writers can forget or mute half their parentage' (Abel 1982: 33). If we overemphasize the incompatibility of male text and female reader, of male teacher and female student, we radically diminish the possibility of there ever being an equal complement of female texts and female teachers from which and from whom a subsequent generation of male and female students can learn (the male students thereby being forced to think back through their mothers also). Precisely because men have throughout history controlled the production and interpretation of texts, any woman who aspires to intrude upon the area of male control must be both willing to learn from male teachers and able to compete with male colleagues. Both Mary Wollstonecraft and George Eliot found their greatest inspiration in their reading of and reactions against Rousseau. George Eliot's entry into the history of ideas and the 'great tradition' of English literature was through the appropriation of knowledge conventionally reserved for men.

The development of the strain of separatism, which has sustained feminist antipathy to George Eliot, has been supported by theory contending that men and women do not speak the same language. This too entered George Eliot's critical heritage by way of Virginia Woolf:

> The sentence that was current at the beginning of the nineteenth century was . . . a man's sentence; behind it one can see Johnson, Gibbon and the rest. It was a sentence that was unsuited for a woman's use. Charlotte Brontë, with all her splendid gift for prose, stumbled and fell with that clumsy weapon in her hands. George Eliot committed atrocities with it that beggar description. Jane Austen looked at it and laughed at

it and devised a perfectly natural, shapely sentence proper for
her own use and never departed from it.

(Woolf 1929: 115)

Jane Austen's sentences are more 'shapely' that George Eliot's in part
because what Austen is trying to express in her sentence is less complex, less intellectually weighty, and more traditionally feminine than
what George Eliot is attempting: Austen never touches on subjects
that would be 'better omitted from the scope of female meditation'.
Whereas it is perfectly reasonable and appropriate to evaluate Austen's
achievement in terms of the production of a 'feminine' discourse, it is
open to question whether such discourse is universally desirable for
female writers, and to criticize George Eliot for not concentrating her
efforts on the production of a 'shapely' sentence is to follow the
patriarchal example of censoring and limiting what women are permitted to say and how they are permitted to say it.

When I touched upon the differences between Jane Austen's style
and George Eliot's (p. 153), I considered it in terms of the strain
caused by George Eliot's crossing of class and cultural boundaries,
that is to say, as a subject of more interest to socialist than to feminist
criticism. Raymond Williams has made a similar argument comparing
George Eliot and Trollope:

And I think we have to remember this when we are asked by
several kinds of critic to abstract 'construction', 'organization',
'thematic unity', 'unity of tone', and even 'good writing' and
judge novels by those canons. On these abstract criteria – and
especially those of unity – we should have to find Trollope a
better novelist than George Eliot. What we have to emphasize,
on the contrary, is the creative disturbance which is exactly
George Eliot's importance: the disturbance we shall see also in
Hardy. That is where the life is, in that disturbed and
unprecedented time. And those who responded most deeply,
who saw most, had no unified form, no unity of tone and language, no controlling conventions, that really answered their
purposes. Their novels are the records of struggle and difficulty,
as was the life they wrote about.

(Williams 1970: 85)

The socialist and the feminist arguments for George Eliot are
inextricably entwined. Does not Virginia Woolf's preference for the

Austenian 'feminine sentence' bear a striking resemblance to the preference for Trollope's 'undisturbed' prose? Is there not something
calm and comfortable and therefore unrebellious and non-feminist in
that prioritization of the 'shapely sentence'? I am not suggesting that
either Virginia Woolf or Jane Austen is a reactionary writer but rather
that in criticizing George Eliot for not using Austen's feminine sentence, Woolf is disparaging the very 'disturbance' that make George
Eliot important to socialist and feminist critics.

Virginia Woolf's own fictional style aspires to Jane Austen rather
than George Eliot as its model, and therefore excels in the light
touch, the sudden shaft of perception, rather than George Eliot's
more analytic and exhaustive methods. It also aspires to the ideal of
the feminine sentence and is therefore impressionistic, associative,
drawing its comparisons from the immediate sensory perceptions of
the heroine rather than from art, history, science, and the immense
world of knowledge and reference that George Eliot commands, even
though it is clearly beyond the ken of her heroines. Implicit in Woolf's
discussion of male and female sentences is the yielding up of learning,
logic, and lucidity that has become most palpable in recent French and
French-influenced theory. An English exponent of this idea is Dale
Spender:

> The English language has been literally man made and . . . it is
> still primarily under male control. . . . This monopoly over
> language is one of the means by which men have ensured the
> invisibility or 'other' nature of females, and this primacy is
> perpetuated while women continue to use, unchanged, the
> language which we have inherited.
>
> (Spender 1980: 12)

Women like Mary Wollstonecraft and George Eliot used the tools of
patriarchal language – logic and lucidity – to undermine patriarchal
ideology, that is to say, they changed the ends to which logic and
lucidity were employed. However, many French thinkers would interpret the need for linguistic change in a far more drastic sense. John
Sturrock has discussed the theory behind the difficulty of Barthes's,
Derrida's, Foucault's, and especially Lacan's prose:

> Lucidity gives us the illusion that we have language firmly under
> our thumb, that we are making it do what we want. Lacan and
> the others . . . would remove that illusion. They would rather

show what a large degree of autonomy language enjoys, and that
there is infinitely more to be said on every topic than will ever be
said by those who believe that anything worth saying must be
said unambiguously. . . . The relationship between writer and
reader becomes more democratic when the writer no longer
hands down to us from on high his firm doctrine, in all its
illusory simplicity, but sets us to work picking our way through
his ambiguities, gathering meanings as we go. These are not
seminal but 'disseminal' works.

(Sturrock 1979: 17)

The painstaking lucidity of Sturrock's elucidation of the argument
against lucidity puts into question the degree to which these writings
are in fact 'democratic' and 'disseminal'. If what Sturrock says is true,
he is guilty of re-injecting the seminal and the undemocratic into the
texts he discusses by the very act of elucidating them. Moreover, it is
possible, and arguably more justifiable, to criticize writers, as James
Joyce and T. S. Eliot have been criticized, for elitism because of the
deliberate obscurity of their texts.

This rejection of lucidity is dangerous when adopted by feminist
theorists: the production of such 'disseminal' texts by feminist writers
would seem to offer confirmation of the patriarchal contention that
women are incapable of rationality, lucidity, and consecutive
thought – a contention that George Eliot spent her life disproving.
The difference between Raymond Williams's discussion of 'disturbance' and French post-structuralist antipathy to lucidity is that the
writers Raymond Williams is discussing, George Eliot and Thomas
Hardy, are lucid wherever possible. Their 'disturbance' lies in the
area where the demands of lucidity conflict with the demands of representing what they wished to represent. At these junctures, and these
only, the representation of that which is most difficult to represent is
purchased at the expense of lucidity. This is a form of dissident
expression – whether feminist or socialist or any other – which seeks
rather than declines communication with what Nina Auerbach calls
'the networks of power and respectability we say we want to change'.

Lucy Irigaray, by contrast, contends that:

[Women] must not pretend to rival [men] by constructing a logic
of the feminine that again would take as its model the onto-
theological. They must rather try to disentangle this question
from the economy of the logos. They must therefore not pose it

182

in the form 'What is Woman?' They must, through repetition-interpretation of the way in which the feminine finds itself determined in discourse – as lack, default, or as mime and inverted reproduction of the subject – show that on the feminine side it is possible to *exceed* and *disturb* this logic.

(Irigaray 1977: 75–6, Irigaray's emphasis)

Irigaray's objections to logic extend to embrace all search for similarity, the search for similarity being theoretically masculine and therefore oppressive and reactionary:

The interpreters of dreams themselves had only one desire: to find the same Everywhere. And it was certainly insistent. But from that moment, didn't *interpretation* also get caught up in this dream of an identity, equivalence, analogy, homology, symmetry, comparison, imitation etc. which would be more or less *right*, that is to say, more or less *good*?

(Irigaray 1974: 27, Irigaray's emphasis)

Yet her argument is itself based on an analogy between the interpreters of dreams and other interpreters. If she gave up her own search for 'the same', Irigaray would also give up her argumentative coherence.

George Eliot also stressed difference, as has been seen in the discussion of her uses of taxonomy and mythography (pp. 140–2), and as is implicit in the polyphony of her writings. She would certainly agree with Irigaray that the perception of sexual difference as lack and default is a distorted one, seeking to reject everything that is not identical with the writing (and ruling) subject. George Eliot, in her comparisons and contrasts of Maggie and Tom and of Dorothea and Lydgate, tries to escape the bonds of gender bias to a point from which she is able to celebrate the virtues and illuminate the weaknesses of both genders in such a way as to set them before her reader as equal figures bound in conflict in an unequal system that the weaknesses of both help to perpetuate. And it is this – the fact that she criticizes women as well as men – one suspects, that is at the root of feminist anger with George Eliot. This despite the fact that some of the most revered and influential works of feminist theory, for example Dorothy Dinnerstein's *The Rocking of the Cradle, and the Ruling of the World* (Dinnerstein 1978), do the same thing. The George Eliot canon constitutes an answer to Judith Stacey's remarks:

Instead of celebrating the feminine, we need to retain a vital
tension between androgynous and female-centered visions. We
need to recognize contradiction and to apply a critical
perspective that distinguishes between giving value to
traditionally female qualities and celebrating the female in a
universalistic and essentialist manner.

(Stacey 1983: 575)

If we accept Julia Kristeva's description of three broad stages of
feminist development – the imitation of the male, which claims equality; the glorification of the female, which celebrates difference; and a
synthesis of the two, which is more than and other than the sum of 'the
masculine' and 'the feminine' (Kristeva 1981: 33–4) – we realize that
in the middle stage we are bound to find George Eliot more problematic than Jane Austen or Virginia Woolf, simply because George Eliot,
in her person and in her characterization of women, is trying to erode
the difference.

The opening chapter of Toril Moi's *Sexual/Textual Politics*, however,
describes and confronts several feminist rejections of Woolf determined on much the same grounds used to reject George Eliot: the lack
of positive representations of women (Moi 1985: 1–18). In Woolf's
case, feminists have attacked characterization rather than plot. The
objection to a lack of diversity in the characterization of heroines
seems at first to be a firmer basis for criticism. For example, in
Virginia Woolf's novel *Mrs Dalloway*, we are told 'She cared much
more for her roses than for the Armenians'. Here, character, narrator, the female reader are all frozen in the stultifying apolitical
domesticity of conventional middle-class womanhood. Aesthetically,
it is a brilliant moment, one of those Austen-inspired shafts of perception that startle the reader. From a feminist point of view, however,
there is an uncomfortable sense that narrator and character are
together inviting the female reader to consider the prioritization of
roses quite seriously, are seducing the female reader into the torpor of
traditional middle-class feminine non-responsibility for analysis,
politics, and economics.

Such a moment could never happen in George Eliot's fiction. It is
not that George Eliot refuses to discuss the temptation to passivity –
she does so at length in *The Mill on the Floss* – but in Maggie's case
the issue of passivity is itself tortuous, dynamic, and strife-ridden.
Maggie is anything but passive by disposition; her frenetic fruitless

activity exhausts her, and therefore she is tempted to be passive. 'She cared much more for her roses than for the Armenians' suggests that Clarissa Dalloway is, on the contrary, passive by nature or preference.

The very shapeliness of this sentence produces the effect of complicity with conventional notions of the passivity of women. The term 'shapely sentence' itself borrows from those conventional notions in that it uses a metaphor of the female body. The aesthetic balance of Woolf's sentence rests in the fact she depicts a mind that is passive with respect to politics and concerns itself only with appearances, with the arranging of roses, and she depicts this mind with the light touch of an Austenian sentence the aesthetic requirements of which preclude the struggle necessary to escape the bonds of this passivity.

However, the strongest argument against Woolf's point about the shapely sentence, and simultaneously against at least some of the feminist antipathy to Woolf, is to be found in her own prose. Having declared a preference for the shapely and feminine sentence, Woolf goes on to 'commit atrocities' that owe much more to George Eliot than to any other literary parent and that actually save Woolf's prose, despite the passivity of her heroines, from being itself passive. The context from which I took that sentence in *Mrs Dalloway* is as follows:

> He was already half-way to the House of Commons, to his Armenians, his Albanians, having settled her on the sofa, looking at his roses. And people would say, 'Clarissa Dalloway is spoilt.' She cared much more for her roses than for the Armenians. Hunted out of existence, maimed, frozen, the victims of cruelty and injustice (she had heard Richard say so over and over again) – no, she could feel nothing for the Albanians, or was it the Armenians? but she loved her roses (didn't that help the Armenians?) – the only flowers she could bear to see cut.
>
> (Woolf 1929: 181–2)

The long final sentence of this extract is anything but shapely. It is a sentence with a broken back, a brilliant, dynamic, shattered sentence in which we can recognize what Judith Stacey calls 'a vital tension between androgynous and female-centered visions'. In its struggle to splice together Richard's and Clarissa's worlds it collapses, imitating in its own form the alienation between male and female, public and private spheres.

That struggle is characteristic of George Eliot's prose; it is an intense dynamic intellectual and emotional activity and thus pre-empts the use of metaphors of the shapely and (by conventional association) passive, female body. The evasion of that constellation of associations seems to me an enormous feminist achievement. So far are we from being able to reduce George Eliot to her body *only* that critics have had to strain to remember that she had a body *as well*. This is not, as I hope I have established, because the sexual and physical is absent from her work, but because, as readers bound by the assumptions of our culture, we have been unable to reconcile her dynamism and her femaleness: we see woman as matter, man as energy. In a male writer, dynamism is seen as identical with sexuality, whereas a woman's sentence must be shapely to be sexual.

It is vestigial patriarchal thinking, then, that leads feminist critics to reject George Eliot, or any other female writer, on the grounds that her writing is 'masculine'. The theory behind such rejection is explained here by Hélène Cixous:

> Most women are like this: they do someone else's – man's –
> writing, and in their innocence sustain it and give it voice, and
> end up producing writing that's in effect masculine. Great care
> must be taken in working on feminine writing not to get trapped
> by names: to be signed with a woman's name doesn't necessarily
> make a piece of writing feminine.
>
> (Cixous 1976b: 52)

Cixous herself is only too aware of the problems of using the terms 'masculine' and 'feminine', she embraces the phallic elemments of her own discourse, and here her use of 'feminine' is metaphorical in that 'feminine writing' need not necessarily be a woman's writing. Apparently conscious of all the risks of using such terms, she nevertheless continues to use them, disparaging the 'masculine', praising the 'feminine', and laying herself open to Toril Moi's criticism:

> In her eagerness to appropriate imagination and the pleasure
> principle for women, Cixous seems in danger of playing directly
> into the hands of the very patriarchal ideology she denounces. It
> is, after all, patriarchy, not feminism, that insists on labelling
> women as emotional, intuitive and imaginative, while jealously
> converting reason and rationality into the exclusively male
> preserve.
>
> (Moi 1985: 123)

'Celebrating the female in a universalistic and essentialist manner' has a further problem beyond the yielding up of reason and language. French feminists have inherited from the prominent French male theorists a tendency to let metaphors break their tropic bonds so that the tenor becomes indistinguishable from the vehicle.[2] The example of this that has done most damage to feminist theory is Barthes's use of the word 'body' to signify the unconscious. Feminist critics have talked about the 'body' as the instrument of writing and have lost themselves in a maze of Lacanian and Barthesian metaphors from which they emerge with a view of female writing as a literally erotic activity. This is dangerously close to the familiar perspective that women have no other being or value than the erotic. Monique Plaza has criticized this tendency in the work of Irigaray: 'Luce Irigaray pursues her construction, cheerfully prescribing woman's social and intellectual existence from her "morphology". . . . Her method remains fundamentally naturalist and completely under the influence of patriarchal ideology, (Plaza 1978: 31). Toril Moi makes a similar objection to Irigaray's use of a secondary nexus of metaphors, which is itself derived from the primary nexus of metaphors of the body: 'her mimicry of the patriarchal equation between woman and fluids (woman as the life-giving sea, as the source of blood, milk and amniotic fluid . . .) only succeeds in reinforcing the patriarchal discourse' (Moi 1985: 142).

The overemphasis on difference was intrinsic to sexism long before it was inherited by feminism, and it is this inheritance that makes the ecstatic writings of Cixous and Irigaray dangerously if inadvertently complicit with the sexism of their literary fathers. In *The Female Eunuch* – a book which belongs very clearly to the first stage of feminism – Germaine Greer has pointed out the dynamics of difference:

> What man feels for the very different from himself is fascination
> and interest, which fade when the novelty fades, and the
> incompatibility makes its presence felt. Feminine women chained
> to men in our society are in this situation. They are formed to be
> artificially different and fascinating to men and end by being
> merely different, isolated in the house of a bored and antagonistic
> being.

> (Greer 1971: 140)

It is partly because of this disturbing similarity between sexist and feminist uses of difference that socialist feminist theorists like Monique Wittig and Cora Kaplan have rejected the stressing of sexual difference

at the expense of wider political considerations: through this preoccupation with woman's sexual identity feminists have continued to put
off the realization of our human identity – the identity which sees, as
George Eliot saw, the problems of humanity as primary and those of
gender as secondary. Cora Kaplan conveys this without prioritizing
the socialist over the feminist:

> both [psychoanalytic and semiotically oriented feminist criticism]
> have been correctly criticized from a socialist feminist position
> for the neglect of class and race as factors in their analysis. If
> feminist criticism is to make a central contribution to the under-
> standing of sexual difference, instead of serving as a conservative
> refuge from its more disturbing social and psychic implications,
> the inclusion of class and race must transform its terms and
> objectives.
>
> (Greene and Kahn 1985: 149)

Feminist reason and reality are, as Dale Spender points out, very
difficult to articulate in man-made language. George Eliot knew the
difficulty of true articulation for women: she vividly depicted the
struggle with silence and self-contradiction in the reflexive element of
Mrs Transome and the demonic imagery surrounding Maggie
Tulliver. Yet overarching these depictions is the articulate excellence
of George Eliot herself, who shows us the problems but, in her own
abundantly passional and rational texts, provides us with encouragement and positive example.

NOTES

1 THE MAKING AND REMAKING OF GEORGE ELIOT

1 Gordon S. Haight, ed., *The George Eliot Letters*, I: 163. All subsequent references to *The George Eliot Letters* will be indicated in the text by 'Letters' followed by the volume and page number.

2 Haight's *George Eliot: A Biography* quotes Bray on p. 51; on p. 77 he writes 'But she leaned even more on Maman's little husband'; on p. 90: ' "She was not fitted to stand alone" '; but it was all too clear that John Chapman would never be the man she could lean upon'; p. 116: 'In 1842 at almost the same time the phrenologist was discovering that Marian Evans was "of a most affectionate disposition, always requiring some one to lean upon", another phrenologist, aptly named J. Q. Rumball, was "reading" Herbert Spencer's head'; p. 117: 'But any dream she may have had of Spencer as the man she could lean upon had fled'; chapter 6 is entitled, 'Some one to lean upon', and its opening paragraph ends with 'At last she had found some one to lean upon.' Bray's language disappears for the duration of George Eliot's union with G. H. Lewes but resurfaces after the account of Lewes's death, on p. 517: 'She had no one to lean upon.' This prepares us for George Eliot's impending union with John Walter Cross, which, when finally unveiled in the Beatrice letter on p. 530, is acknowledged by the single sentence: 'She was not fitted to stand alone.'

3 For example, Richard Congreve and Clementia Taylor (Haight 1968: 539–43).

2 RECONSTRUCTING GEORGE ELIOT

1 *'Jubal' and Other Poems* 75. This and all subsequent references to the works of George Eliot, unless otherwise specified, are from the *The Works of George Eliot*, Cabinet edition.

2 Sigmund Freud, *Civilization, Society, and Religion*, edited by Albert Dickson, translated by James Strachey, The Pelican Freud Library, XII: 312–13. All subsequent references to Freud will be indicated in the text by 'Freud', followed by the volume and page number.

3 HETTY AND DINAH: THE BATTLE FOR PREDOMINANCE IN *ADAM BEDE*

1 The *OED* defines 'agnostic' as follows:

> One who holds that the existence of anything beyond and behind material phenomena is unknown and (so far as can be judged) unknowable, and especially that a First Cause and an unseen world are subjects of which we know nothing.
> [Suggested by Prof. Huxley at a party held preview to the formation of the now defunct Metaphysical Society, at Mr James Knowles's house on Clapham Common, one evening in 1869, in my hearing. He took it from St Paul's mention of the altar to 'the Unknown God.' R. H. Hutton in letter 13 Mar. 1881.]

The *OED* traces the origin of the word 'atheist' back to 1571, then cites Gladstone, in *Contemporary Review* (22 June 1876), who defined an atheist as follows: 'By the Atheist I understand the man who not only holds off, like the sceptic, from the affirmative, but who drives himself, or is driven, to the negative assertion in regard to the whole Unseen, or to the existence of God.' Although George Eliot clearly did not fall into the latter category in so far as public assertion goes, it is difficult to ascertain what she might have privately believed in various periods of her development, and it is equally problematic to label her an 'agnostic', since the term did not exist at the time of her change in belief nor yet for more than half of her writing career.

2 'unsoaped' and 'lazy' suggest the first *OED* definition of 'slut': 'A woman of dirty, slovenly, or untidy habits or appearance; a foul slattern,' but the second definition is also suggested, and it is only this definition that establishes a parallel between Bessy and Hetty: 'A woman of a low or loose character; a bold or impudent girl; a hussy, jade.' Blackwood was nervous about readers construing according to the second definition when he assumed only the first was intended: 'The meaning of the proverb about Chad's Bess should be made clear or it may be taken to imply something more than I suppose it does' (Haight 1968: 253).

3 Myers says she is the risen Christ (Myers 1984: 34). Witemeyer sees her as the angel at the tomb of the risen Christ (Witemeyer 1979: 73).

4 Anonymous, *Edinburgh Review* 144 (October 1876), 442–70, 444; James, 'The novels of George Eliot' (Haight 1966: 50).

5 Joan Bennett (Bennett 1948: 29) notes the injustice of this notion but does not apply it to Hetty's story.

6 For further discussion of language and desire in *Adam Bede*, see pp. 115–16.

7 E. M. Forster, in *Aspects of the Novel* (Forster 1927: 163–75) notes other affinities between George Eliot and Dostoyevsky.

4 DEMONISM, FEMINISM, AND INCEST IN *THE MILL ON THE FLOSS*

1 *Daniel Deronda*: I: 3, 'Was the good or the evil genius dominant in those beams? Probably the evil; else why was the effect that of unrest?'; I: 11, 'Woman was tempted by a serpent: why not man?'; II: 125, 'Roulette was not a good setting for her; it brought out something of the demon'; II: 197, 'there seemed to be at work within her the same demonic force that had possessed her when she took him in her resolute glance and turned away a loser from the gaming-table'; II: 297, 'There may be a demon in her to match the worst husband'; II: 237, 'this light-haired one has plenty of devil in her'; III: 16, 'Grandcourt was not likely to be infallible in his judgments concerning this wife who was governed by many shadowy powers, to him non-existent.'

Letters I: 284, 'What shall I be without my Father? I had a horrid vision of myself last night becoming earthly sensual and devilish for want of that purifying restraining influence'; I: 335, 'It was some envious demon that drove me across the Jura to come and see people who don't want me'; II: 94, 'I am very hard and Mephistophelian just now'; II: 115, 'consequently I find life very glorious and myself a particularly fortunate diabolessa'; IV: 346, 'I am a good deal knocked up, and look very much like a persecuted witch.'

2 The scene in which Maggie tests Tom on the Eton grammar is at the centre of a network of imagery concerning gender. Mary Jacobus has discussed this scene in detail (Abel 1980: 49–50), yet one feels that its possibilities have by no means been exhausted. Tom keeps making a mistake in which he introduces *'ostrea'* before its time. *Ostrea* means oysters and is an epicene noun, but oysters are also a common vaginal symbol. The subsequent chapters 'Tom applies his knife to the oyster' (Book Three, chapter 5) and 'Showing that Tom had opened the oyster' (Book Six, chapter 5) deal with Tom's initiation into manhood via his entry into the business world. Again the implied author behind this wordplay is a rather acerbic one. The problem of astronomers hating women in general, also from the Eton Grammar, is discussed in the context of Maggie's encounter with a Latin teacher named Stelling, the Latin for 'star' being *stella*. (I am indebted to Becky Morris, a student at Queens' College Cambridge, for that last observation.) Whether or not there is, as I suspect, more to all this than has been hinted at here, George Eliot, as a female scholar who has mastered Latin, is making a fascinating comment here on gender, language, education, and power. When, in 1866, Swinburne was criticized for the obscenity of his *Poems and Ballads*, he replied that the objection must be not to the content itself but to the language in which it was presented, since all these issues (incest, homosexuality, sado-masochism) were treated in the Classics, which were available to every 13-year-old school boy of a certain class (Thomas 1979: 131). Marian Evans Lewes was of neither the class nor the gender for whom the initiation, through Latin and Greek, into this secret knowledge, primarily sexual, emblematized

their ruling status. In light of this, the feminist assertion that men and women do not speak the same language is quite literally true of Victorian men and women, but it is also true that the different classes in Victorian society were separated by the same linguistic barrier. Marian Evans, who should have been excluded on both counts of gender and class, overcame that exclusion through her own efforts, learned Latin and Greek, and thereby appropriated that secret knowledge. In this sense, she really did have 'the brain of a man and the heart of a woman' (see note 6 below).

Those who accept Francis Bacon's dictum 'Knowledge is Power' usually do so with the implicit qualification that the knowledge under discussion must be of obvious utility in the gaining or maintaining of power, for example a knowledge of Political Economy, which Dorothea despairs of acquiring in *Middlemarch*. However, Swinburne's remarks in defence of *Poems and Ballads* suggest, as indeed does the Book of Genesis, that sexual knowledge is power. George Eliot's obscure wordplay on knives and oysters, on supines, the genitive, and epicene nouns, in the context of a story deeply concerned with gender and education, would seem to suggest the same idea, and, in light of this, Maggie's later elopement with Stephen is simply another aspect of her desire for knowledge, her will to power.

3 A. S. Byatt, editor of *The Mill on the Floss*, Penguin Library edition, uses the manuscript version, which is quoted here (Penguin Library edition, p. 438). For the first edition 'low' was removed from the sentence. Similarly, in my second example (Penguin Library edition, p. 394), the manuscript reads 'lower deformed', and the first edition reads 'deformed'.

4 Maggie discusses Dutchmen with Luke (I: 40); the crew of the ship on which Maggie and Stephen travel to Mudport is made up of Dutchmen (II: 317); Bob Jakin finds a leg of pork that had fallen off 'one o' them round-sterned Dutchmen' (I: 378); and Bob's wife looks like a Dutch doll (II: 189).

5 I use idealistic here as opposed to pragmatic rather than as opposed to materialistic.

6 Elizabeth Barrett Browning originated this formulation in her poem, 'To George Sand: A Desire' (1844). Dinah Mulock adopted it to describe George Eliot in her review in *Macmillan's Magazine*, (3 April 1861), 441–8, (Carroll 1971: 158).

5 *ROMOLA*: WOMAN AS HISTORY

1 Piero di Cosimo paints Romola and Bardo as Antigone and Oedipus. This has been discussed by Barbara Hardy (Hardy 1959: 173).

2 Sully was under the mistaken impression, given him by Marian Lewes herself (Letters IV: 333–4) that the term had originated with her. According to the *OED*, 'meliorist' was first used by J. Brown, in his preface to *Horae Subsecivae* (1858).

3 An early example of this is Millais, *The Bridesmaid*, painted in 1851.

4 Raffaello Sanzio (1483–1520). The novel closes on the eve of Raphael's
   career as an artist. This, like the ending of *Middlemarch*, which is set a
   few weeks before the passing of the Reform Bill of 1832, contributes to
   the sense of life continuing after the end of the novel.

5 *Romola* is the only George Eliot novel named for its heroine, although
   she did consider 'Sister Maggie' as a possible title for *The Mill on the
   Floss*. The name is of interest as it has two sources, both of which seem
   to lend historicity to the unhistoric heroine: 'You have been rightly
   inspired in pronouncing Romŏla, and in conceiving Romolo as the
   Italian equivalent of Romulus. . . . There is a mountain named
   Romola in sight from Florence.' The last sentence of this quotation,
   which is taken from Gordon S. Haight's *Selections from George Eliot's
   Letters*, p. 392, was omitted from Haight's original transcription
   (Letters V: 174). In naming her heroine after a place, George Eliot
   seems to be playing with the idea of authenticating the legends about
   Romola which, in the novel, spring up in the area after she visited the
   plague-stricken village. This, together with the association with
   Romulus, gives Romola a legendary rather than fictional status.

6 George Eliot's footnote in *Romola*, Cabinet edition:

   The sermon here given is not a translation, but a free representation
   of Fra Girolama's preaching in its more impassioned moments.

6 LANGUAGE AND DESIRE IN *FELIX HOLT*

1 As a major novel, *Felix Holt, the Radical* has been remarkably
   neglected. It has never really attracted quite the general attention it
   deserves. . . . It does not of course reveal its major qualities easily.
   Qualities of a non-major kind are only too easily apparent. The
   adverse things, the idealization of Felix Holt himself and the largely
   unrewarding complexity of the plot, have inevitably coloured opinion against it. But beneath all that, and not really very far down,
   lies the very evident genius of the novelist whose organic powers
   were to produce *Middlemarch*, next indeed after *Felix Holt*.

Peter Coveney, 'Introduction', *Felix Holt, the Radical*, Peter Coveney,
ed., Penguin Library edition, p. 7.

2 Every day she was getting more clearly into her imagination what it
   would be to abandon her own past, and what she should enter into
   in exchange for it; what it would be to disturb a long possession,
   and how difficult it was to fix a point at which the disturbance
   might begin, so as to be contemplated without pain.

                                                        (II: 213–14)

3 'Servants' logic', *Pall Mall Gazette* (17 March 1865):

   Reason about things with your servants, consult them, give them
   the suffrage, and you produce no other effect in them than a sense
   of anarchy in the house, a suspicion of irresoluteness in you, the
   most opposed to that spirit of order and promptitude which can

alone enable them to fill their places well and make their lives respectable.

(Pinney 1963: 396)

4 This is not unique to *Felix Holt*. As John Goode has pointed out:

> The lower orders [as represented in *Adam Bede*] are animals making efforts to become human. The Poysers are higher up on the evolutionary scale, and thus the demands their environment makes are more sophisticated.

(Hardy 1970: 28)

William J. Hyde made the same point (Hyde 1957), as did Edward Dowden, describing the connection between conservatism and evolutionary theory (Dowden 1878: 115).

5 See pp. 31–2 above.
6 Harold and Jermyn's consumerism is not limited to women. Jermyn uses men for the information he can get from them and is used by Harold for political ends.

7   The people here are all so ugly: Almost as ugly as I am.

(Letters I: 65)

> The idea of making a study of my visage is droll enough.

(Letters I: 330)

> I confess I tremble a little at the prospect of your seeing me in the flesh. . . . Imagine a first cousin of the old Dante's – rather smoke-dried – a face with lines in it that seem a map of sorrows.

(Letters V: 437)

> I am a good deal knocked up, and look very much like a persecuted witch.

(Letters IV: 436)

8 Shakespeare, in sonnet II, 'When forty winters shall beseige thy brow'; Wordsworth, in 'Michael'.
9 See pp. 31–2.
10 Something similar is occurring in the description of Dorothea just before her final love scene with Will. See pp. 138–9.
11 In a letter to Sara Hennell (21 September 1869) she wrote:

> As to the high-flown stuff which is being reproduced about Byron and his poetry, I am utterly out of sympathy with it. He seems to me the most *vulgar-minded* genius that ever produced a great effect in literature.

(Letters V: 56–7)

7 DIALECTIC AND POLYPHONY IN *MIDDLEMARCH*

1 Peter Garrett (Garrett 1969: 29), points out that Harriet Bulstrode's forgiveness of her husband is a greater leap than Dorothea ever accomplishes in her marriage to Casaubon. The careful reader,

noticing this, re-evaluates Dorothea by the side of this unexpectedly heroic woman.

2 His relation to Rosamond is often seen as doctor and patient, and his relation to his patients borrows from the erotic: 'He cared not only for "cases", but for John and Elizabeth, especially Elizabeth' (I: 219).

3 For example, on the flyleaf of the copy of *Adam Bede* that George Eliot gave to Lewes is the following inscription:

> To my dear husband, George Henry Lewes, I give this M. S. of a work which would never have been written but for the happiness which his love has conferred on my life.

> (Haight 1968: 278)

4 Dorothea and Celia's deceptive appearances (I: 11), Hetty's deceptive eyelashes in *Adam Bede*, Tito's deceptive radiance in *Romola*. Hardy remarks that the images of light and pagan gods are transferred from Tito to Will (Hardy 1959: 62).

5 This irony is also directed against the pettiness of the life of philanthropic widowhood which is Dorothea's only alternative to marrying Will.

6 there might be large opportunity for some people to be the happier when he was gone; and if one of those people should be Will Ladislaw, Mr Casaubon objected so strongly that it seemed as if the annoyance would make part of his disembodied existence.

> (II: 223–4)

7 *Funk and Wagnall's Standard Dictionary of Folklore, Mythology, and Legend*, gives the following description of Adalbert Kuhn:

> Kuhn, (Franz Felix) Adalbert (1812–1881) German Indo-Germanic philologist and mythologist, one of the founders of comparative mythology. He was one of those 19th century nature mythologists who emphasized thunderstorms and lightning, as compared to the sun mythologists, such as Max Müller. Kuhn was co-founder and editor, beginning in 1851, of *Zeitschrift fur vergleichende Sprachforschung*, and the editor of several volumes of Brandenburg, North German, and Westphalian legends, myths, and customs (1843, 1848, 1859). He was also the author of works of Indo-Germanic archaeology and linguistic paleology, and of essays on mythology.

Kuhn's work on thunderstorms originally appeared as volume I of his *Mythologische Studien, Die Herabkunft des Feuer und des Göttertranks, Ein Beitrag zur vergleichenden Mythologie der Indogermanen*, Berlin, 1859, reprinted Darmstadt, 1968.

8 I have not discussed *Silas Marner* simply because it does not share the features that have been basic to my analyses of the other six novels (a heroine at the centre, another female character placed in counterpoint to the heroine, a preoccupation with the issue of vocational desire in women). However, *Silas Marner* is open to other kinds of feminist

investigation, and I highly recommend Jennifer Uglow's treatment (Uglow 1987).

8 THE OPEN-ENDEDNESS OF *DANIEL DERONDA*

1 This foreboding of barbarity to come was almost certainly the result of the Franco-Prussian war on George Eliot's sense of the direction in which history was moving. Before the Franco-Prussian war, she still found it possible to write the following lines to John Blackwood (25 July 1866):

> The care the Prussians are said to have for the wounded Austrians is one of the proofs one likes to register, that we are slowly, slowly, growing out of barbarism . . . one of the best compensations for dwelling on the barbarities of Spanish and Flemings in the glorious 16th century, is the sense that such horrors are no longer possible in any European nation.
>
> (Letters IV: 291)

9 GEORGE ELIOT AND TWENTIETH-CENTURY FEMINIST PERSPECTIVES

1 The strength of Sophocles' influence on George Eliot can be seen in Marian Evans's essay, 'The Antigone and its moral' (Pinney 1963). She notes in an early letter that Shakespeare's heroines often propose marriage, and this might have influenced her decision to have both Dorothea and Catherine Arrowpoint propose marriage. The possibility of Goethe's influence on Eliot's monumental representations of women is supported by the fact that G. H. Lewes wrote a book in 1867 entitled, *Female Characters of Goethe: From the Original Drawings of W. Kaulbach with Explanatory Text* in which he discussed the impressiveness of Goethe's heroines. Marian Lewes had translated passages of Goethe for Lewes's 1855 book, *The Life and Work of Goethe; With Sketches of his Age and Contemporaries from Published and Unpublished Sources*. Lewes's ideas about the Goethe heroines and George Eliot's notion of monumental heroines for her own work may well have emerged from conversations on Goethe during the writing of the *Life*.

2 In *Structuralism and Since*, Dan Sperber, John Sturrock, and Hayden White each note that the thinker under discussion (Levi-Strauss, Barthes, and Foucault respectively) allows his thought to be shaped by his favourite trope (Sturrock 1979: 25; 54; 82).

REFERENCES

Abel, Elizabeth, ed. (1982) *Writing and Sexual Difference*, Brighton: Harvester Press.

Adam, Ian, ed. (1975) *This Particular Web: Essays on Middlemarch*, Toronto: Toronto University Press.

Auerbach, Nina (1975) 'The power of hunger: demonism and Maggie Tulliver', *Nineteenth Century Fiction* 30: 150–71.

Austen, Zelda (1976) 'Why feminists are angry with George Eliot', *College English* 37: 549–61.

Bakhtin, M. (1981) *The Dialogic Imagination: Four Essays*, Michael Holquist, ed., translated by Caryl Emerson and Michael Holquist, Austin: University of Texas Press.

Barthes, Roland (1975) *The Pleasure of the Text*, translated by Richard Miller, New York: Hill & Wang.

Basch, Françoise (1974) *Relative Creatures: Victorian Women in Society and the Novel 1837–67*, London: Allen Lane.

Baxendall and Morowski, eds (1974) *Marx on Art and Literature*, St Louis and Milwaukee: Telos Press.

de Beauvoir, Simone (1953) *The Second Sex*, edited and translated by H. M. Parshley, London: Jonathan Cape.

Beer, Gillian (1983) *Darwin's Plots: Evolutionary Narrative in Darwin, George Eliot, and Nineteenth Century Fiction*, London: Routledge & Kegan Paul.

—— (1986) *George Eliot*, Brighton: Harvester Press.

Beer, Patricia (1976) *Reader, I Married Him: A Study of the Women Characters of Jane Austen, Charlotte Brontë, Elizabeth Gaskell, and George Eliot*, London: Macmillan.

Bennett, Joan (1948) *George Eliot, Her Mind and Her Art*, Cambridge: Cambridge University Press.

Blake, Kathleen (1983) *Love and the Woman Question in Victorian Literature: The Art of Self-Postponement*, Brighton: Harvester Press.

Blind, Mathilde (1884) *George Eliot*, London: W. H. Allen & Co.

Bloom, Harold (1973) *The Anxiety of Influence: A Theory of Poetry*, New York: Oxford University Press.

Bodichon, Barbara (1867) *Claim of Englishwomen to the Suffrage*, London: Social Science Association.

197

Bonaparte, Felicia (1979) *The Triptych and the Cross: The Central Myths of George Eliot's Poetic Imagination*, New York: University Press.

Bottomore, T. B., ed. (1963) *Karl Marx: Early Writings*, London: C. A. Watts.

Bray, Charles (1884) *Phases of Opinion and Experience during a Long Life: An Autobiography*, London: Longman.

Brontë, Charlotte (1853) *Villette*, London: Smith & Elder.

Browning, Oscar (1890) *Life of George Eliot*, London: Walter Scott.

Bullen, J. B. (1975) 'George Eliot's *Romola* as a positivist allegory', *Review of English Studies* 26: 425–35.

Carroll, David (1971) *George Eliot: The Critical Heritage*, London: Routledge & Kegan Paul.

Cecil, Lord David (1934) *Early Victorian Novelists: Essays in Revaluation*, London: Constable.

Chase, Karen (1984) *Eros and Psyche: The Representation of Personality in Charlotte Brontë, Charles Dickens, and George Eliot*, London: Methuen.

Cixous, Hélène (1976a) 'The laugh of the Medusa', *Signs* 1, Summer: 875–93.

—— (1976b) 'Le sexe ou la tête?' *Les Cahiers du GRIF* 13: 5–15, translated by Annette Kuhn (1981) 'Castration or decapitation?' *Signs* 7, I: 41–55.

Comte, Auguste (1853) *The Positive Philosophy*, 2 vols, condensed and translated by Harriet Martineau, London: Chapman.

Cooke, George Willis (1883) *George Eliot: A Critical Study of her Life, Writings and Philosophy*, Boston: J. R. Osgood.

Coveney, Peter (1972) 'Introduction', in *Felix Holt, the Radical*, Harmondsworth: Penguin.

Craig, David (1973) *The Real Foundation: Literature and Social Change*, London: Chatto & Windus.

Cross, John (1885) *George Eliot's Life as Related in her Letters and Journals*, 2 vols, Edinburgh: Blackwood.

Daiches, David (1963) *George Eliot: Middlemarch*, London: Edward Arnold.

Dallas, E. S. (1866) *The Gay Science*, 2 vols, London: Chapman & Hall.

David, Deirdre (1981) *Fictions of Resolution in Three Victorian Novels: North and South, Our Mutual Friend, and Daniel Deronda*, London: Macmillan.

—— (1987) *Intellectual Women and Victorian Patriarchy: Harriet Martineau, Elizabeth Barrett Browning, and George Eliot*, London: Macmillan.

Dinnerstein, Dorothy (1978) *The Rocking of the Cradle, and the Ruling of the World*, London: Souvenir Press.

Dowden, Edward (1878) *Studies in Literature 1789–1877*, London: Kegan Paul.

Doyle, Mary Ellen (1981) *The Sympathetic Response: George Eliot's Fictional Rhetoric*, East Brunswick, NJ: Associated University Presses.

Eagleton, Terry (1976) *Criticism and Ideology: A Study in Marxist Literary Theory*, London: New Left Books.

—— (1983) *Against the Grain*, London: Verso.

Edwards, Lee (1984) *Psyche as Hero: Female Heroism and Fictional Form*, Middletown, CT: Wesleyan University Press.

Eliot, George (1851) 'The creed of Christendom', *Leader* 3: 899.

—— (1857) 'Belles Lettres', *Westminster Review* 67: 306–26.

—— (1878–80) *The Works of George Eliot*, Cabinet edition, 20 vols, London: Blackwood.

—— (1954–78) *The George Eliot Letters*, 9 vols, Gordon S. Haight, ed., New Haven: Yale University Press.

—— (1963) *Essays of George Eliot*, Thomas Pinney, ed., London: Routledge & Kegan Paul.

—— (1979) *The Mill on the Floss*, A. S. Byatt, ed., Harmondsworth: Penguin Library.

—— (1981) *George Eliot: A Writer's Notebook 1854–1879*, Joseph Wiesenfarth, ed., Charlottesville: University Press of Virginia.

—— (1985) *Selections from George Eliot's Letters*, Gordon S. Haight, ed., New Haven: Yale University Press.

Ellis, Sarah (1843) *The Wives of England: Their Relative Duties, Domestic Influence, and Social Obligations*, London: Fisher, Son & Co.

Emery, Laura Comer (1976) *George Eliot's Creative Conflict: The Other Side of Silence*, Berkeley: University of California Press.

Ermarth, Elizabeth (1974) 'Maggie Tulliver's long suicide', *Studies in English Literature* 14: 587–601.

Fernando, Lloyd (1977) *'New Women' in the Late Victorian Novel*, University Park: Pennsylvania State University Press.

Feuerbach, Ludwig (1854) *The Essence of Christianity*, translated by Marian Evans, London: Chapman.

Fisher, Philip (1981) *Making up Society: The Novels of George Eliot*, Pittsburgh: Pittsburgh University Press.

Freud, Sigmund (1984–6) The Pelican Freud Library, 15 vols, translated by James Strachey, Harmondsworth: Penguin.

Fuller, Margaret (1844) *Woman in the Nineteenth Century, and Kindred Papers Relating to the Sphere, Condition, and Duties of Woman*, reprinted 1971, New York: W. W. Norton & Co.

Garrett, Peter (1969) *Scene and Symbolism from George Eliot to James Joyce*, New Haven: Yale University Press.

Gilbert, Sandra and Gubar, Susan (1979) *The Madwoman in the Attic: The Woman Writer and the Nineteenth-Century Literary Imagination*, New Haven: Yale University Press.

Greene, Gayle and Kahn, Coppelia, eds (1985) *Making a Difference: Feminist Literary Criticism*, London: Methuen.

Greer, Germaine (1971) *The Female Eunuch*, London: Paladin.

Haight, Gordon S. (1940) *George Eliot and John Chapman; With Chapman's Diaries*, New Haven: Yale University Press.

—— (1966) *A Century of George Eliot Criticism*, London: Methuen.

—— (1968) *George Eliot: A Biography*, Oxford: Oxford University Press.

—— (1985) *Selections from George Eliot's Letters*, New Haven: Yale University Press.

Haight, Gordon S. and VanArsde, Rosemary T., eds (1982) *George Eliot: A Centenary Tribute*, London: Macmillan.

Hardy, Barbara (1959) *The Novels of George Eliot: A Study in Form*, London: Athlone Press.

Hardy, Barbara, ed. (1970) *Critical Essays on George Eliot*, London: Athlone Press.

Heilbrun, Carolyn G. (1973) *Toward a Recognition of Androgyny: Aspects of Male and Female in Literature*, London: Gollancz.

Holmstrom, John and Lerner, Laurence, eds (1966) *George Eliot and Her Readers: A Selection of Contemporary Reviews*, London: The Bodley Head.

Hyde, William J. (1957) 'George Eliot and the climate of Realism', *Publications of the Modern Languages Association* 72, March.

Irigaray, Luce (1974) *Speculum de l'autre femme; Speculum of the Other Woman*, translated by Gillian C. Gill (1985) Ithaca, NY: Cornell University Press.

—— (1977) *Ce Sexe qui n'est pas un; This Sex which is not one*, translated by Catherine Porter and Carolyn Burke (1985) Ithaca, NY: Cornell University Press.

Jacobus, Mary (1981) 'Reviews of *The Madwoman in the Attic* and *Shakespeare's Sisters*', *Signs* 7: 517–23.

Jameson, Anna (1852) *Legends of the Madonna as Represented in the Fine Arts*, London: Longman.

Kettle, Arnold, ed. (1981) *The Nineteenth Century Novel: Critical Essays and Documents*, second edition, London: Heinemann.

Knoepflmacher, U. C. (1965) *Religious Humanism and the Victorian Novel: George Eliot, Walter Pater, and Samuel Butler*, Princeton: Princeton University Press.

—— (1968) *George Eliot's Early Novels: The Limits of Realism*, London: University of California Press.

—— (1975) *Middlemarch*: an avuncular view', *Nineteenth Century Fiction* 30: 53–81.

Kristeva, Julia (1981) 'Woman time', translated by Alice Jardine and Harry Blake, *Signs* 7: 13–35.

Laski, Marghanita (1973) *George Eliot and her World*, London: Thames & Hudson.

Leavis, F. R. (1948) *The Great Tradition: George Eliot, Henry James, and Joseph Conrad*, London: Chatto & Windus.

Lerner, Laurence (1967) *The Truthtellers: Jane Austen, George Eliot, D. H. Lawrence*, London: Chatto & Windus.

Levine, George (1981) *The Realistic Imagination: English Fiction from Frankenstein to Lady Chatterly's Lover*, Chicago: Chicago University Press.

Lewes, G. H. (1874–9) *Problems of Life and Mind*, 9 vols, London: Trubner.

Linton, Eliza Lynn (1899) *My Literary Life in London* London: Hodder & Stoughton.

Lucas, John, ed. (1971) *Literature and Politics in the Nineteenth Century*, London: Methuen.

MacCabe, Colin (1978) *James Joyce and the Revolution of the Word*, London: Macmillan.

Main, Alexander (1871) *Wise, Witty, and Tender Sayings in Prose and Verse from the Works of George Eliot*, Edinburgh: Blackwood.

REFERENCES

Max Müller, Friedrich (1873) *Introduction to the Science of Religion*, London: Longman.

Mintz, Alan (1978) *George Eliot and the Novel of Vocation*, Cambridge, Mass.: Harvard University Press.

Moers, Ellen (1978) *Literary Women*, London: The Women's Press.

Moi, Toril (1985) *Sexual/Textual Politics: Feminist Literary Theory*, London: Methuen.

Myers, William (1984) *The Teaching of George Eliot*, Leicester: Leicester University Press.

Nestor, Pauline (1985) *Female Friendships and Communities: Charlotte Brontë, George Eliot, Elizabeth Gaskell*, Oxford: Oxford University Press.

Norris, Christopher (1982) *Deconstruction: Theory and Practice*, London: Methuen.

Oliphant, Margaret (1899) *The Autobiography and Letters of Mrs M. O. W. Oliphant*, Mrs Harry Coghill, ed., Edinburgh: Blackwood.

Paris, Bernard J. (1965) *Experiments in Life: George Eliot's Quest for Values*, Detroit: Wayne State University Press.

Paul, Charles Kegan (1883) *Biographical Sketches*, London: Kegan Paul.

Pinney, Thomas, ed. (1963) *Essays of George Eliot*, London: Routledge & Kegan Paul.

Plaza, Monique (1978) ' "Phallomorphic power" and the psychology of "woman" ', *Ideology and Consciousness* 4, Autumn: 4–36.

Redinger, Ruby V. (1976) *George Eliot: The Emergent Self*, London: The Bodley Head.

Roberts, Neil (1975) *George Eliot: Her Belief and Her Art*, London: Elek.

Ryan, Kiernan (1984) 'Toward a socialist criticism: reclaiming the canon', *Journal of Literature Teaching Politics* 3: 4–17.

Sadoff, Dianne F. (1982) *Monsters of Affection: Dickens, Eliot, and Bronte on Fatherhood*, Baltimore: Johns Hopkins University Press.

Smith, David (1965) 'Incest patterns in two Victorian novels', *Literature and Psychology* 15: 135–62.

Spacks, Patricia (1976) *The Female Imagination: A Literary and Psychological Investigation of Women's Writing*, London: Allen & Unwin.

Spencer, Herbert (1904) *Autobiography*, 2 vols, London: Smith Elder.

Spender, Dale (1980) *Man Made Language*, London: Routledge & Kegan Paul.

Stacey, Judith (1983) 'The new conservative feminism', *Feminist Studies* Fall: 559–83.

Steig, Michael (1971) 'Anality in *The Mill on the Floss*', *Novel* 5: 42–53.

Stephen, Leslie (1902) *George Eliot*, London: Macmillan.

Stone, Donald (1980) *The Romantic Impulse in Victorian Fiction*, Cambridge, Mass.: Harvard University Press.

Sturrock, John, ed. (1979) *Structuralism and Since: From Levi-Strauss to Derrida*, Oxford: Oxford University Press.

Sully, James (1877) *Pessimism, a History and a Criticism*, London: Kegan Paul.

Thomas, Donald (1979) *Swinburne: the Poet and his World*, London: Weidenfeld & Nicolson.

Todd, Janet, ed. (1980) *Gender and Literary Voice*, New York: Holmes & Meier.

Uglow, Jennifer (1987) *George Eliot*, London: Virago.

Welsh, Alexander (1984) *George Eliot and Blackmail*, Cambridge, Mass.: Harvard University Press.

Williams, Raymond (1958) *Culture and Society, 1780–1950*, New York: Columbia University Press.

—— (1970) *The English Novel from Dickens to Lawrence*, London: Chatto & Windus.

Witemeyer, Hugh (1979) *George Eliot and the Visual Arts*, New Haven: Yale University Press.

Wittig, Monique (1981) 'One is not born a woman', *Feminist Issues* 1: 47–54.

Wollstonecraft, Mary (1792) *A Vindication of the Rights of Woman; with Strictures on Political and Moral Subjects*, 2 vols, London: J. Johnson.

Woolf, Virginia (20 November 1919) 'George Eliot', *The Times Literary Supplement* 18: 657–8.

—— (1925) *Mrs Dalloway*, London: Hogarth Press.

—— (1929) *A Room of One's Own*, London: Hogarth Press.

Young, G. M. (1963) *Victorian England: Portrait of an Age*, Oxford: Oxford University Press.

INDEX